THE CREATIVE SELF

BEYOND INDIVIDUALISM

MARI RUTI AND
GAIL M. NEWMAN

Columbia University Press   *New York*

Columbia University Press
Publishers Since 1893
New York   Chichester, West Sussex
cup.columbia.edu

Library of Congress Cataloging-in-Publication Data
Names: Ruti, Mari, author. | Newman, Gail M., author.
Title: The creative self : beyond individualism / Mari Ruti and
Gail M. Newman.
Description: New York : Columbia University Press, [2024] |
Includes bibliographical references and index.
Identifiers: LCCN 2024033245 (print) | LCCN 2024033246 (ebook) |
ISBN 9780231218931 (hardback) | ISBN 9780231218948 (trade paperback) |
ISBN 9780231562508 (ebook)
Subjects: LCSH: Self. | Creativity. | Individualism.
Classification: LCC BF697 .R87 2024 (print) | LCC BF697 (ebook) |
DDC 153.3/5—dc23/eng/20240906
LC record available at https://lccn.loc.gov/2024033245
LC ebook record available at https://lccn.loc.gov/2024033246

Printed and bound by CPI Group (UK) Ltd, Croydon, CR0 4YY

Cover design: Julia Kushnirsky
Cover images: Shutterstock

THE CREATIVE SELF

CONTENTS

PREFACE

This book has crystallized out of years of conversation. We have shared thoughts on our experiences as teachers and scholars, the various theories and practices of psychoanalysis, and our fears and hopes about life in our time. It thus seemed natural to write together on a topic of burning interest to both of us: how to counter the insidious undermining of people's creative potential that results from neoliberalism's narrow and excessive focus on success, performance, and self-improvement. We thought about a couple of different formats before landing on this one, which allows both the overlaps and the differences between our respective ways of thinking to come through. Our chapters have slightly different tones in the sense that, as is Mari's tendency, she paints with broad strokes, whereas Gail, steeped in literary research and teaching, focuses on close readings that open out to broader insights. Our hope is that our distinctive ways of reading enrich this book by offering two different, yet conceptually related, lenses through which to understand the centrality of Milner and Winnicott to theorizing creative living and thereby to providing an alternative to neoliberal self-optimization. When it comes to Winnicott, there may be a bit of conceptual overlap—especially regarding Winnicott's famous discussion of true and false selves—between our chapters. This is due to the fact that we wrote our chapters independently of each other even though we discussed them repeatedly while we drafted them. Our hope, again, is that any overlap that may exist deepens the text by providing two different perspectives on the same topic.

We are grateful for the time that we have been able to spend together that has culminated in this book. Gail is particularly grateful; what follows is a personal note following Mari's tragic death in June 2023. When we began the project's more intensive phase in the spring of 2022, Mari was still able to pursue multiple writing endeavors with her characteristic zeal, despite her illness's significant debilitating effects. Throughout her life, Mari embodied a quiet resistance to neoliberalism in her very way of living. What in our usual language would be called her "productivity" was fueled, not by ambition, but by her overflowing love of ideas, experiences, and people. Ideas were like precious, tangible things for her to mold, combine, and play with, like the "beads" that Marion Milner collected as bits of joy in her world. Indeed, Marion Milner herself became such a bead for Mari, serving as a "sublimatory antidote to lack that [brought] her enough enjoyment (jouissance) to render her life meaningful." In her life, Mari moved from bead to bead, finding and creating them in the spirit of Winnicott's playing in the intermediate area. For as crucial as solitude was to Mari, she was always in close contact with the world. Sharing ideas and experiences with friends, colleagues, and students was the very stuff of her life and her books. Those books became, in turn, a sort of transitional object for her readers who could, through them, find and create ideas that would play a central role in the shaping of their own lives.

Milner's beads align with one of Mari's most important contributions to intellectual discourse: her explication of the way in which we are able to experience transcendence—even a kind of immortality—in the immanent. This insight is derived, not just from her deep knowledge of the philosophical and theoretical literature, but also from her lived experience. Mari was firmly committed to life itself—*this* life—as the only source necessary for moments of transcendence. Indeed, she showed us that we do not have to turn to "high" culture to find the sublime; she was as much a fan of popular television as she was a lover of the most magnificent features of the natural world. Mari's kind of transcendence cannot be fixed in time or space; it depends on the serendipity that emerges in conversation with dear friends or in solitary wanders. In this respect, such transcendence could never harden into dogma nor be reduced to a commodity. It is necessarily transient, but as Mari says, this "in no way diminishes the value of transcendent episodes, for they are what, arguably, ensures that we are not completely overtaken by the hegemonic structures of the social establishment."[1]

Mari Ruti was a unique figure in the intellectual world. Her element was the ether of high theory, but she always remained thoroughly grounded in a quiet love for nature and deep care for others. Her lifelong study of Lacan yielded insights that subtly, but powerfully, changed the usual orientation, especially toward his late work. Key to these insights is the recognition that the lack at the center of all human psychic life is different from the structural lacks associated with phenomena such as racism, homophobia, and misogyny. The remediation of structural inequities is a desideratum for any humane society or individual, while the Lacanian lack must be acknowledged as constitutive of our very being. In fact, as Mari describes in this book as well as elsewhere, it can paradoxically be the source of joy and creativity. The capaciousness of thought that can imagine negative and positive as necessarily informing each other shows up in

Mari's generosity toward other thinkers as well, even those whose ideas are at odds with her own. Her mode of engagement with her interlocutors subverted the adversarial approach that is all too familiar in the academic world. Mari had an uncanny ability to embrace, but also to critique, the other's point of view, allowing it to become the ground upon and against which new figures play.

Collaborating with Mari on this book has been more than the highlight of my professional career; it has enacted for me a kind of being with another that counters the toxic relationality that I, like many people, have experienced in my life, whether it is academic competitiveness, rigid familial obligation, or false intimacy based on nothing but neediness and narcissism. Mari's generosity and honesty combine to create a space where you can try out new things, confident both that she will tell you—gently—if it is nonsense and that she will be there while you try again. She never intrudes ("impinges," in Winnicott's terminology) but is always available, and she learns from you while you learn from her. While writing this book together was, for Mari, one in a series of increasingly innovative collaborative projects that she undertook in the last years of her all-too-short life, for me it was a new experience, both in content and in form. Through our discussions—mostly in Vienna's storied *Kaffeehäuser*—I got to know Mari's writing process, which I had, up until that point, only encountered in its finished form. I gradually realized that her signature tightly textured weave of ideas from theorists of all critical stripes, rendered in gloriously lucid prose that sacrificed none of its conceptual rigor for the sake of clarity, is born of a "freeing of the imagination from the shackles of the ego," in Mari's words. In Marion Milner's, it is a "plunge into the abyss."[2] Mari was intimately and urgently familiar with the abyss in the form of a viciously progressing cancer, and the more familiar I became with her writing process the more I realized how courageous it was to let go of control, trusting herself to be able to pull shape from the depths of sometimes terrifying shapelessness. My writing and my life were profoundly affected by the exchanges with Mari over our manuscript. Mari's achievement of my own goal of depth and complexity plus precision had drawn me to her in the first place, but it was a revelation to understand the role of the unformed in her crystalline form. My process will never duplicate Mari's, but I like to think that I became a little braver because of her.

INTRODUCTION

The Creative Self and Neoliberalism

This book is about creative living. More specifically, it is about creative living as an antidote to neoliberal self-optimization. By *neoliberalism* we refer to the transactional orientation of contemporary Western societies, which are primarily organized around economic imperatives. Although neoliberalism as a concept, technically speaking, refers to the reign of free market economics that became institutionalized during the Reagan and Thatcher era of the 1980s, in contemporary progressive theory the concept is often used more broadly to characterize the instrumentalist, individualistic, opportunistic, and narcissistic ethos that has permeated social life in the West at least since the Second World War, and especially since the 1980s. Indeed, this version of neoliberalism arguably constitutes one of the ingredients of the general modernization of life that has gradually taken place since the Industrial Revolution. We use the term in this looser sense to indicate the fact that life in the Western world—and increasingly across the globe—has become predominantly governed by economic motivations which, in turn, trigger the kind of utilitarian mentality that leaves little space for creativity and the imagination.

For the individual, neoliberalism almost automatically translates into what we have chosen to call *self-optimization*: the
attempt that many people make to constantly improve their
performance and efficiency, especially in the context of their
working lives, but increasingly in their personal lives as well.
Self-optimization includes the idea that the self is perfectible,
that through effort and a positive attitude, we can augment our
performance, productivity, and efficiency, thereby becoming
happier and more successful. From making "rational" choices
about our education—for instance by choosing law school or
business school over a graduate degree in the humanities—to
making sure that we eat well, exercise regularly, and marry the
right kind of partner, we are optimizing our lives without even
necessarily realizing that this is what we are doing.

People in contemporary society are taught to optimize their
lives from an early age, in some cases as early as kindergarten.
Moreover, as professors, we work in one of the hotbeds of neoliberal anxiety. Our students have been pushed, and have pushed
themselves, to be accepted into our institutions and continue to
experience intense demands to set themselves up for the perfect
adult life. We are aware that the pressure toward self-optimization
has increased steadily during the last few decades. Today's young
people are urged to make "smart," rational choices regarding
their futures in ways that were not the case even just twenty years
ago. Sadly, it is not only the nonacademic world that views literature, philosophy, theory, history, art, and related fields as
worthless but, increasingly, universities themselves are shutting
down or decreasing the size of their humanities departments.
This could be considered the epitome of neoliberal optimization:
given that education lies at the foundation of our society, guiding the entire tone of this society, the marginalization of fields
that have historically been associated with creativity rather than

with quantifiable "knowledge" says a great deal about our current social priorities.

This book's two chapters—the first on Marion Milner by Mari and the second on D. W. Winnicott by Gail—delve deeper into the nitty-gritty of neoliberal self-optimization. However, the main goal of *The Creative Self* is to present an alternative to this mentality. We do so with the aid of psychoanalysis, which almost by definition encourages the flourishing of the creative self. When people enter into analysis, it is often because they feel that their lives lack purpose or meaning. They are frequently explicitly seeking to cultivate their creative capacities. Other times, they do not realize that this is what they are after: they are merely aware of a gnawing malaise that makes them feel like something essential is missing from their lives. We argue that (usually) what is missing is their capacity to mobilize their creative potential which has, for one reason or another, become stuck or thwarted. One of the aims of psychoanalysis as a clinical practice is to free this potential, thereby allowing the analysand to lead a more fulfilling and multidimensional life. In this manner, psychoanalysis more or less inevitably works against neoliberal self-optimization.

It is true that there have historically been efforts to turn even psychoanalysis into a tool of self-optimization, as happened in the United States during the 1950s, when some analytic schools sought to produce better-adjusted citizens. However, for the most part, psychoanalysis has always been intrinsically a matter of fostering the creative self. That is especially the case with the two psychoanalysts whom we have chosen to foreground in this book: Milner and Winnicott. As our respective chapters illustrate, nothing mattered more to Milner and Winnicott than the liberation of the individual's creative potentialities. Both thinkers—who were friends and deeply influenced by each other's work—began to publish during the early 1930s and both generated an impressive array of theoretical work. Much of this work, as our book shows, focuses on the ways in which individuals may augment their creative and imaginative capacities, including their ability to play.

It would be difficult to find better advocates for the ideal of leading a creative life, and therefore implicitly at least, for resisting neoliberal self-optimization, than Milner and Winnicott. Neither uses the terminology of neoliberalism, but we trust that it will quickly become clear why we believe that both can be considered as its opponents, for their way of conceptualizing human life as a matter of creative self-fashioning—what Mari, drawing on Nietzsche, portrays as living one's life as poetry—is absolutely antithetical to everything that falls under the goal-oriented, zero-sum approach to the self that dominates today's society. Both Milner's attempt to extract from each day the item, object, moment, or experience that made her happy or most piqued her interest, and Winnicott's theorization of the parameters of a true self—the kind of self that is capable of exercising the full range of its creative potentialities in the context of playing with the boundaries of self and other—provide us with a blueprint for creative living, at least as an ideal. Both recognize that, most of the time, most of us fall short of this ideal. Yet both believe in the unquestionable value of the ideal itself and foster every effort to approximate it.

Milner and Winnicott both define creativity broadly, as any activity that brings meaning, substance, or pleasure to the individual's life: not limited to intellectual, artistic, or spiritual achievements, creativity entails the capacity to build a life that feels worth living. For our part, we recognize that creativity, even in this capacious sense, is a topic that can only be decently raised once the basics of survival have been attended to: people need sufficient access to the concrete necessities of life, such as housing, food, clean water, physical safety, community, and so on, before they have the mental space to worry about the place of creativity in their lives. In this sense, creativity—or creative living—is a luxury even as it (at least in our assessment) remains essential for the psychic, affective, and physical well-being of human beings.

This paradox hovers in the background of our thinking even as we focus on largely ontological, even existential, questions about the contours of human life, such as what the so-called "good life" might entail and what might bring vitality and meaningfulness to individual lives. As Gail's chapter illustrates, learning to live with paradoxes without striving to resolve them is one of the most challenging yet most necessary components of human life: it may even reside at the very core of creative living. We therefore admit that we cannot unscramble the paradox that creativity is at once secondary to survival and indispensable to thriving. All we can do is to propose that creativity is worth protecting, developing, and striving for, even under circumstances that are (consciously or not) designed to stifle it.

One of the primary paradoxes embedded in psychoanalysis is its recognition that the quest for a rewarding life cannot be separated from the psychic and affective realities of loss, lack, negativity, and nothingness. Psychoanalysis is, of course, not the only intellectual orientation that begins from this premise. Many philosophers, perhaps most famously Jean-Paul Sartre, have recognized the connection between negativity and creativity: the idea that a sense of inner nothingness motivates the human quest for meaning, invention, and beauty, among other valuable things. However, there are certain psychoanalytic thinkers—including Milner and Winnicott—who have theorized the relationship between lack and loss, including self-loss, on the one hand and creative living, self-fashioning and self-actualization, on the other in ways that we find particularly generative for countering the falsely optimistic tenor of neoliberal self-optimization.

In this context, it is worth noting that in recent years, and particularly since the COVID-19 pandemic that gripped the world for over three years, dissatisfaction with the seemingly universal and eternal dictates of neoliberalism has surfaced in various forms. Even while Anglo-American-style ruthlessness is undermining Western European social systems and destroying Indigenous economies in the name of efficiency, profit, and individual self-realization for the wealthy, ordinary people have begun to resist. The resistance has mostly taken place on the individual and small group level; neoliberalism's tentacle-like pervasiveness makes forming large-scale resistance movements extremely difficult. Nonetheless, the pandemic managed to expose some of its most egregious effects and generate some groping attempts at remediation.

The most system-wide impact of the pandemic has been the change in work patterns and attitudes. From so-called "quiet quitting" to the "great resignation," many individuals have begun to reject their employers' co-optation of their time and energy into a system that ostensibly brings the employee "success," but in reality, only benefits the employer and its stockholders. Reckoning with questions of what work should look like will be one of the biggest challenges that we face in the coming years. The remote and hybrid work mode that emerged during COVID might seem to be a simple solution to the problem of overly controlled, rigidly structured workplace environments, but it brings with it further atomization in a society that is already excessively oriented toward the individual, at the expense of the societal. Nonetheless, when individuals are unable or unwilling to participate in it, the system's flaws and weaknesses become more evident, and the possibility of change is opened up.

A thoroughly positive change that has already begun to take place is the destigmatization of mental health problems. The isolation and anxiety generated by the pandemic plunged many, especially young people, into mental health crises. Indeed, a vicious cycle developed in which the suffering associated with living alone in an exclusively virtual world—and/or being trapped in toxic home environments—can only be mitigated virtually and individually via the valuable resource of telehealth services that sprang up out of necessity. Nonetheless, despite the fact that these young people have gone through what boils down to several lost years during the time when they most urgently needed social contact and guidance from adults who are not their family, they are not accepting their lot as inevitable. Instead, they are telling their stories of psychic and emotional pain and asking that resources be allotted to deal with it. Mental health providers, including college counseling services, have been overwhelmed by the hugely increased demand for their work, but the ripple effect of that demand is that society is now better able to tolerate the idea that everyone is not ok, and many institutions and organizations are starting to read their members' malaise as a signal to reflect on structural changes that will improve the health of all.

Perhaps most encouraging is the subtle, but powerful, shift that we have witnessed among our most recent students toward seeking a holistic, sustainable life rather than perpetuating the ethos of achievement and acquisition that has been dogging them since birth. For the most part, these shifts in life goals are visible on the individual level, but increasingly, young people are gravitating toward cooperative groupings where nurturing each other goes along with a kind of engagement with the social and natural environment that represents an alternative to capitalistic gain. These developments, born of widespread disaster, allow for a hesitant hope that the human urge toward creative living will prevail. It is in this spirit that we lay out, here, the ideas of Marion Milner and Donald Winnicott. Both of these thinkers were acutely aware of the ways in which the deeply negative often shadows, or even conditions, the most profoundly creative processes. Each of our chapters details different, but closely intertwined, dimensions of creative living.

Mari's chapter focuses on Milner's efforts to connect self-loss, especially the surrender of the ego, to the subject's creative, sublimatory capacities and its potential for what Mari calls *worldly transcendence*: the kind of transcendence that does not require the subject to exit the world but, rather, takes place within the weave of everyday life. Mari is especially interested in how Milner employs the mundane details of her life to generate extraordinary, even sublime, experiences. She demonstrates how Milner's poetics of being provides an effective remedy for neoliberal self-optimization. However, in order to offer a backdrop for her analysis of Milner, Mari begins her chapter with a general discussion of neoliberalism and self-optimization, along with some of the most famous critiques that twentieth-century thinkers launched against these mentalities. The opening sections of her chapter are therefore designed to provide the necessary background for both her analysis of Milner and Gail's analysis of Winnicott. Throughout her chapter, she also supplements her arguments regarding Milner with insights from Nietzsche, Jacques Lacan, Julia Kristeva, and—most importantly—Winnicott. Her hope is that her references to Winnicott generate a degree of continuity between her chapter and Gail's. However, she intentionally leaves the details of Winnicott for Gail to fill in.

Gail's chapter is a close reading of Winnicott's theory that highlights both its developmental and its (more broadly) cultural dimensions. After an introductory discussion of the rise of the individual from the eighteenth-century Enlightenment

through to the optimizable neoliberal *I*, she details the Winnicottian self, which is structured like a Russian doll with a
singularly special but ultimately incommunicado core and a
surrounding layer of caregiving that is attentive without being
intrusive. Winnicott is probably best known for discovering
the crucial role of the "transitional object" in children's development. Most closely associated with the familiar teddy bear
or baby blanket, the transitional object occupies a figurative
space that Winnicott called the "intermediate area" between
internal and external reality. Here, the nascent self can experiment with the boundaries of self and other, dependence and
independence, safety and risk in a playful way that fosters a
creative approach to life. Gail elaborates on the implications of
the arts and humanities as a site of sublime experience and
creative potential, linking Winnicott's theories to her own
experience through analyses of German literature and observations on contemporary academic and political life. Throughout, Gail attempts to get at, and preserve, the paradoxes at the
core of Winnicott's work: the infant proto-self that is both
everything and nothing, the true self that must be and cannot
be expressed, and the authentic relationship with an other person that is conditioned on their fantasmatic destruction.

A final note on vocabulary: we use the terms *self, individual,*
and *subject* more or less interchangeably depending on what
makes most sense in a given context. For instance, *the subject* is
a technical philosophical term deriving from late eighteenth-
century Idealism in Europe, so that when Gail discusses the
origin of modern Western individualism in Kant's theories or
the Romanticism that follows Kant, she uses *subject* and *object*
instead of *self* and *other.* Similarly, *the subject* is a key term in Lacanian theory, so that whenever Mari discusses Lacan, she uses
this term as a synonym for the self. Indeed, because of Mari's

background in Lacanian theory, her tendency is to talk about the subject more than the self or individual. We ask the reader for leniency in relation to this tendency, which is by now deeply ingrained. We also ask for the reader's indulgence in relation to our preference for the gender-neutral pronoun *it* as a way of referring to the subject and the self, for this is common practice in our respective fields of critical theory (Mari) and literary studies (Gail). When it comes to the individual, *it* does not seem appropriate, so we try to find other gender-neutral rhetorical strategies. The point is that we avoid *he* or *she* as much as possible because even reversing the common practice of using *he* by using *she* merely reinforces the very gender binary that we have spent our entire careers opposing.

1

MARION MILNER'S
POETICS OF BEING

MARI RUTI

In the Western world, we live in a society where the ethos of neoliberal self-optimization has, to a large extent, replaced any genuine interest in creative living as an essential component of human flourishing: concerns about how successful we are; how well we perform our jobs; how much money we make; how seamlessly we project an image of confidence and self-sufficiency; how easily we brush off disappointments; how quickly we recover from painful experiences; and how many *likes* we get on social media have arguably eclipsed concerns about how meaningful our life feels, how deeply we experience things, how well we are able to tolerate the inevitable complexities, contradictions, and paradoxes of human experience, and how well we recognize, let alone dare pursue, what truly inspires us.

Or at least, so it seems. One of the aims of this chapter is to propose that even though the creative impulse can be damaged, it is possible—as D. W. Winnicott suggests—that it may never be definitively extinguished, so that beneath our attempts to lead a levelheaded life governed by neoliberal principles of pragmatism, performance, productivity, efficiency, and cheerfulness, one can detect a desire for "something more," for the kind of life that would leave more space for creativity, the imagination, and fulfilling relationships, along with time to adequately process both hurtful and joyful experiences. One detects a yearning for alternatives to self-optimization—for modes of life that, viscerally and affectively, feel worth living.

I want to illustrate that this is what the theories of the twentieth-century psychoanalyst and experimental writer, Marion Milner, also suggest. Like Winnicott, Milner gestures toward the possibility that no matter how deeply buried our desire for creative living may be, it is never fully destroyed, so that in some shadowy corner of our being persists a yearning for a more rewarding life and that this is the case even when we do not have a good sense of what such a life might consist of. Moreover, Milner offers a concrete account of the imaginative processes that, for her at least, satisfy the requirements of creative living. Milner is single-minded in her quest for a wholly unique "poetics of being," for sublimatory practices that feed her body, mind, and soul alike. Incorporating key insights from Winnicott, Jacques Lacan, and Julia Kristeva, this chapter outlines the details of Milner's poetics of being to illustrate that there is a viable antidote to neoliberal self-optimization. Milner may not have been consciously looking for such an antidote, but it is precisely what she manages to present—and indeed, quite convincingly.

LACANIAN LACK-IN-BEING

On a basic level, of course, the desire for something more is simply the human condition in the sense that, regardless of how satisfying our lives may be, we are programmed to want more. From this viewpoint, the desire for more is an ontological and existential feature of human life. This is one of Lacan's main lessons. He notoriously proposes that our subjectivity is founded on the kind of constitutive lack—negativity or emptiness—that nothing can fill. This lack is the inescapable result of the fact that, as children, we are inducted into a preexisting world of collective rules, regulations, and linguistic structures—what Lacan calls *the symbolic order* or *the big Other*—over which we have no control and which consequently makes us feel deficient and dispossessed of something unfathomably precious (yet unnameable). We feel deprived of a reassuring unity of being—of a blissful union with the world, including our caretakers—that we imagine having once possessed. Lacan even names the entity that we envision having lost: *the Thing*, the primordial (non)object that promises unmitigated satisfaction—jouissance—that we are forced to circle from a distance for the simple reason that unmediated jouissance would instantly destroy us as socially intelligible beings. This means that we arrive to the world of collective life as beings of lack, forever driven to heal a wound that we believe has been unfairly inflicted on us.

In reality, we have lost nothing. Lacan postulates that there never was any unity of being or any union with the universe to begin with. There was not even the kind of seamless intimacy with our primary caretakers that some psychoanalytic thinkers attribute to the opening weeks of infancy.[1] Lacan claims that the unity, union, or intimacy that we imagine having lost is a mere retroactive fantasy with no foundation in infantile experience, which is in actuality governed by chaotic and unruly drive energies that are far from comforting. There may be moments of symbiotic unity, union, or intimacy, but these are inevitably disrupted by either internal drives or external distractions. The infant may feel physically uncomfortable, or the caretaker may not be feeling well. Alternatively, the caretaker may take a phone call, attend to the demands of their professional life, or do their taxes while taking care of their child because, after all, their life cannot be reduced to their child. However, this does not prevent the adult subject from concocting a fantasy of primordial deprivation—the loss of the Thing—that motivates it to pursue a remedy for the wrongs that it believes it has experienced.

On the one hand, this pursuit of a remedy is an existential blessing in the sense that it turns us into creatures of desire: although we experience our lack as a deprivation, it is also what motivates us to look for, and sometimes even invent, the kinds of ideals, objects, experiences, aspirations, and relationships that enrich our lives. That is, our lack causes us to turn toward the outside world in search of things that might compensate for it. As I demonstrate shortly, it is unfortunate that our attempts to fill our lack frequently fall prey to the seductions of consumer capitalism. At the same time, it is nevertheless the case that creativity in its various forms represents one of the most reliable and rewarding antidotes to this lack. In this sense, although our lack causes us to feel incomplete and constitutionally dislocated— never entirely at home in our bodies and psyches—it is simultaneously the origin of everything that is worthwhile about human life. In short, the lack within our being generates the desire to fill it and desire, in turn, gives rise to all of our creative endeavors, including our efforts to craft a singular art of living.

On the other hand, even though desire as the foundation of creativity is a positive characteristic of the human condition, the quest for ontological wholeness that it also gives rise to is entirely pointless, as Lacan never tires of telling us: the Thing is not an entity that we can ever obtain in any concrete sense, with the result that the ideal of curing our lack is a misguided fantasy. This is why Lacan suggests that the only "cure" for our lack is to recognize that there is no cure for it. He believes that it is only when we accept this simple—yet difficult to tolerate—reality that we can begin to direct our efforts to endeavors that actually have some chance of satisfying us. Instead of squandering our energies on the hopeless task of mending the void within our being, we may begin to spend these energies on undertakings that offer us an always partial yet nevertheless rewarding sublimatory satisfaction.

The fact that we are forever barred from the ultimate object of our desire, the Thing, does not mean that all is lost, for it is possible for us to approach the Thing's sublimity through little morsels, crumbs, or slivers of jouissance—what Lacan calls *objets a*—that have become detached from it. Such little morsels of jouissance may find their way into entirely ordinary objects, lighting them up with a special glow. In this sense, being forced to circle the Thing at a distance is not the tragedy that it may appear to be: even though the promise of healing or self-completion offered by objects that are infused by the Thing's sublimity is deceiving, there is nonetheless something special about such objects. They beckon us with their radiance, bringing us a satisfaction that is not a matter of filling the void within our being but, instead, of bathing us in the sublimatory satisfaction of brushing against the Thing's aura.

We can be guided to the Thing's glow by people—artists, creators, and inventors of various kinds—who possess a stronger than average capacity to either extract it from an already existing object or to install it in an object that they create from scratch. Lacan's example of the latter phenomenon is the manner in which Cézanne paints apples.[2] Lacan claims that an apple painted by Cézanne is never merely a simple depiction of an apple but, rather, contains an aura of a mysteriousness that viewers respond to. While Cézanne's apples do not give us the "Thing-in-itself," they grant us a little taste of the Thing's sublimity.

Lacan's broader point is that more or less any object, however commonplace, can come to contain the Thing's luminosity. Artists such as Cézanne are able to generate this luminosity for the rest of us to admire. However, we ourselves—regular people with regular creative abilities— are also able to bestow such luminosity upon objects that we either discover or invent. Lacan depicts this process as one through which we render ordinary objects extraordinary. Sublimation, he posits, is a matter of raising "a mundane object to the dignity of the Thing."³ In other words, Lacan suggests that, through sublimation, we confer upon a commonplace object the kind of radiance that makes it glisten like the most precious of treasures. Although it may be easier to find already existing objects that contain the Thing's glow, many forms of creativity are a matter of generating this glow. Lacan thus suggests that both the discovery and invention of treasured objects can be considered to be sublimatory activities.

As my discussion of Milner reveals, the reason that she was unusually successful in generating her unique poetics of being is that she was extraordinarily adept at raising mundane objects to the dignity of the Thing. She saw the potential for sublimity in the most commonplace of items, objects, moments, and experiences so consistently that she managed to fill her private universe with what I call *worldly transcendence*: the kind of transcendence that does not ask the individual to leave the world behind but that, instead, takes place in the weave of everyday life.⁴ Milner explicitly cultivated her capacity to capture the morsels of sublimity around her, with the consequence that she was able to imbue her life with jouissance. She never shied away from the recognition—the very recognition that Lacan believes is essential for the subject's capacity to lead a fulfilling life—that her subjectivity was founded on a void. Instead of lamenting this fact, she chose to devote her time to populating her life with (frequently small but highly meaningful) items, objects, moments, and experiences that gave her access to the same kind of sublime glow that Lacan discovers in Cézanne's apples. She dedicated herself to finding the *objet a*—the lustrous, iridescent shard of the Thing's sublimity—in as many places as she possibly could.

Lacan specifies that the *objet a* functions as the *cause* of our desire, as the enigmatic entity that renders the object that we fixate on desirable for us. Although there may be something about the object itself that makes it a good candidate for serving as a vessel for the *objet a*, it is we, ourselves, who unconsciously place the *objet a* within this object. Yet the fact that we are the architects of our own desire does not decrease the relevant object's ability to draw us in with an inexplicable, irresistible force. We may even come to value it so highly that our desire for it feels nonnegotiable. In other words, due to the hidden link between the Thing and the *objet a*—the fact that the *objet a* contains a smidgeon of the Thing's aura and therefore always in the final analysis refers back to the Thing—our desire for an object that seems to contain the *objet a* can become so strong that we are willing to sacrifice a great deal for it.

Lacan proposes that when we chance upon an object that engages us in this profound manner—that grants us a higher than usual degree of jouissance—the object in question arrests our desire. If our desire usually slides from one object to the next in a manner that suits the objectives of consumer capitalism, discovering an object that carries an unusually compelling trace of the Thing can stop our desire in its tracks, thereby, as Lacan puts it, salvaging our "dignity" as human beings: instead of remaining mere playthings of the Other's desire, we choose to invest our desire in one object above all others;[5] we remain true to our own desire, willing to resist the Other's desire even if doing so costs us part of our social intelligibility. One could liken this experience to falling head over heels in love with someone in ways that render all other potential objects of desire—however attractive or otherwise enticing—powerless to compete with our beloved.

Milner deliberately cultivated this mode of meeting the world: she honored the Thing's aura as a means of arresting her desire as well as making the world come alive, even sparkle. The world then rewarded her with a steady stream of items, objects, moments, and experiences of special significance. Milner did not use Lacan's vocabulary—she did not talk about raising a mundane object to the dignity of the Thing—but her attitude toward life arguably embodied his theory of sublimation. She in fact turned the ordinary into the extraordinary so reliably that it is possible to characterize her life as a constant quest for the sublime within the mundane.

I have offered a synopsis of Lacan's theory of sublimation precisely because it helps us to make sense of Milner's skill in finding the otherworldly within worldly items, objects, moments, and experiences. However, my more general point is that Lacan enables us to understand why the lack of a definitive cure for our inner malaise prompts us to undertake various sublimatory activities in order to improve the quality of our lives. His analysis of the Thing's power to guide our desire explains how we have ended up with a world full of novels, poems, philosophical treatises, paintings, music, sculptures, handicrafts, skyscrapers, architecture, highway networks, bridges, museums, flower beds, gorgeous pottery, fine china, coffee cups, silver forks, sheets with lace trimmings, beautiful blue plates, furniture, cars, tractors, machines, windmills, computers, the internet, newspapers, phones, televisions, critical theory, literary criticism, complex medical procedures, physics, mathematical algorithms, theories about the birth of the universe, theories about the birth of more or less everything, universities, and everything else under the sun that humans have invented. Moreover, as I argue in this chapter, we should consider self-fashioning or self-reinvention as important components of creativity, as well. This creativity is what Milner seeks to safeguard through her theoretical reflections and her concrete poetics of being.

Much of what humankind has created holds incredible beauty and grandeur. Strolling through the historic core of Vienna—where I drafted this chapter and discussed its progression with Gail on a weekly basis—reminds us of the riches that the generations before ours left behind. From opulent architecture, gorgeous artwork, intricate artistry, and delicious chocolate cake, a one-square-mile area of the city's center contains an astonishing array of some of the most remarkable things ever invented. Other major cities across the globe house similar wonders: their offerings point toward limitless human creative capacity. At the same time, the impulse to fill the world with our creations has also, unfortunately, produced much that is not beneficial, as is evident from nuclear weapons, machine guns, bioweapons, sweatshops that exploit cheap labor, polluting factories, global warming, and the huge amount of plastic and other garbage floating in our oceans.

Human inventiveness has sometimes exacted a high price, often in the context of colonial exploitation. This may be easy to forget when admiring picturesque architecture; elaborate sculptures and statues; stunning window displays; shops brimming with silver dishes and other luxuries; magnificent cafés with high, vaulted ceilings; exquisite medieval castles; gleaming art galleries; or vineyards with endless rows of evenly spaced grapevines. The fact is that much of the manufactured magnificence of the world rests on various forms of violence, oppression, and injustice. Some of the world's brutality predates neoliberal consumer capitalism, in some cases by hundreds or even thousands of years. There have been efforts to eradicate some of its most obvious genres, such as slavery and the overt subjugation of women. Yet these efforts have not reached far enough, in the sense that our society still relies on the propagation of racism, sexism, and other social inequalities; on the prison industrial complex; on precarious, outsourced labor across the globe; on African children mining materials for our laptops; on cheap immigrant labor; and on skyrocketing amounts of pollution, to which nature responds with increasing vengeance.

In this context, it is essential to distinguish between two different levels of lack, injury, or dispossession. Throughout this chapter, I focus on the kind of ontological (existential) *lack-in-being* that Lacan discusses, and that appears to facilitate the emergence of the kinds of creative and sublimatory activities that are worth safeguarding. As I have observed, this type of lack is constitutive of the human condition. Simply put, if we removed this lack from our conception of what it means to be human, we would have to entirely reconfigure our entire understanding of the coordinates of human psychic and affective life. However, this unavoidable, foundational lack must be dissociated in the strongest possible terms from the kinds of more structural (context-specific or circumstantial) forms of lack and dispossession that arise from social inequalities such as poverty, racism, homophobia, transphobia, and other collective injustices.

If the former—ontological—type of lack does not have a cure, the latter—structural—type of deprivation could, in principle, be cured by more egalitarian socioeconomic and cultural arrangements. I want to keep this distinction firmly in mind throughout my discussion, lest there be any misunderstanding about the intent of my arguments. For instance, when I say that the subject has no choice but to accept its constitutive lack, I am referring to its ontological lack; I am definitely not implying that those who suffer from social marginalization should reconcile themselves to their lot without complaint. It is also worth adding that Milner, like Lacan, focuses almost exclusively on ontological forms of lack, which may be a weakness in her theories, although it is by no means uncommon among European thinkers whose careers began in the 1930s.

THE LURES OF
NEOLIBERAL SELF-OPTIMIZATION

I take it for granted that human beings are haunted by the kind of lack that Lacan outlines and that it is therefore true that it is part of the human condition to be a creature of desire—to want more than we have. One reason for the persistence of this predicament is that most of us have failed to internalize Lacan's claim that it is only when we abandon our quest for a cure to our lack that we may begin to live rewarding lives—lives that offer items, objects, moments, and experiences that bring partial satisfaction without being able to definitively conjure away the feeling that some fundamental component of our lives is missing. This is a difficult lesson to learn because most of us do not want to accept that there is no remedy for our ontological malaise. Instead, we tend to look for ways to distract ourselves from this malaise. Indeed, it is possible that neoliberal consumer culture has been so successful—has become the socioeconomic system that everyone seems to want to gain access to, despite its obvious inequalities and injustices—in large part because it provides plenty of appealing distractions.

Accepting our constitutive lack is just about the last thing that neoliberal consumer culture—which is keen to enhance our productivity and efficiency, and thus our purchasing power, even at the cost of our well-being—wishes us to do. Even though the centrality of lack—of foundational deprivation, suffering, and anguish—to human life is more or less self-evident to anyone who pauses to give the matter any thought, neoliberal society strives to deny or at least obscure this fact by focusing on enjoyment, entertainment, and the power of positive thinking. In addition, and perhaps even more adamantly, it refuses to acknowledge the existence of the kinds of injuries that arise from unequal socioeconomic and political arrangements. Alternatively, if it concedes that structural forms of suffering exist, it expects the individuals who are affected by such suffering to figure out how to conquer it on their own—to prove that they are worthy of a membership in neoliberal society. Unfortunately, many structural forms of suffering are more severe and cut deeper than ontological negativity. As I just emphasized, they are, in principle, curable. Yet our society makes no serious effort to address them.

The strongly materialistic inflection of neoliberal consumer culture takes advantage of our ontological tendency to want more. It feeds our desire by implying that the massive array of items that it makes available to us can heal our lack. It promises that the more we purchase the less we lack, when in reality, owning more items merely pushes our lack into new manifestations, with the result that our desire slides from one object to the next: it constantly finds new directions, new items to pursue. In fact, the more we have the more we appear to want, which is exactly what consumer culture counts on. Because no item we buy is ever *it*—the item that heals us once and for all—we keep going back to the stores for more.[6]

Neoliberal capitalism therefore profits from our desire by promoting the false impression that the commodities that it makes available can plug the void within our being. Indeed, even though it appears to offer a palliative to our lack, in reality it augments it, first by offering such an abundance of commodities that even a person with a relatively good income can never amass all of them, and second by skillfully hinting that we have not yet chanced upon the *right* commodity—the item that will finally put an end to our yearning—but that this commodity resides within our reach (perhaps even in the store around the corner). Even the fact that we are repeatedly disappointed in our quest for the perfect item does not seem to shake our faith in the system's ability to eventually, at some future point, fulfill our desire; that is, even repeated disillusionments with consumer capitalism's capacity to seal the gaping hole within our being do not succeed in toppling our conviction that as long as we stay patient and keep trying, in due course our desires will be met in a definitive manner. This results in a regrettable dynamic where we seek a remedy for our lack from the very entity in whose interest it is to intensify this lack. The contemporary big Other does not want us to feel satiated because if we did, we would automatically stop buying things, thereby destroying the very foundations of consumer capitalism.[7]

Even those who do not have the financial means to participate in the frenzy of consumption frequently hope that one day they might be able to join the ranks of those who do, which is one reason that television shows in affluent settings are so seductive. Who would not want a beachfront mansion, an infinity pool, a villa in the South of France, a penthouse apartment in Manhattan, a Vera Wang wedding gown, an Aston Martin, or a Harry Winston necklace (the one that Julia Roberts wears in *Pretty Woman* will do nicely, thank you)? My point is that, even if lack is an incurable ontological characteristic of human life, consumer society has found ways to convince us that there is a solution to it: it has managed to persuade large numbers of people that wealth is the most effective way to end their yearning for self-completion, thereby closing off alternative avenues of self-fulfillment. In addition, it assures us that self-optimization is the surest means to obtain wealth, which is why so many of us have turned into disciples of the neoliberal mindset: it is easy to believe that if neoliberal self-optimization results in wealth, and if wealth in turn results in self-fulfillment, self-optimization is the correct strategy to follow if one wishes to extinguish one's lack. It is no wonder, then, that self-optimization has become the reigning ideology of present-day Western societies.

The contours of the neoliberal narrative of what the good life entails are intuitively familiar to many of us: a prestigious, lucrative job coupled with a harmonious family life; a couple of kids in private schools; enough leisure time to travel to exotic locations; the means to dine in expensive restaurants; the ability to socialize with friends in hip bars; art galleries, theater tickets, or—for those more athletically inclined—prime seats at sporting events; country clubs, spas, yoga, and organic food; expensive cars and first-class plane tickets; and generally speaking, living life to the fullest in the sense that consumer capitalism defines the concept. Being able to purchase the coolest gadgets, keeping up with the latest version of the iPhone, and maintaining an active social media presence are essential components of this version of the American dream, as is being able to shop for new clothes, cosmetics, and jewelry even when one does not need them. Ironclad health is taken for granted to the extent that falling seriously ill can be seen as a personal failure, as if the individual in question caused their illness by not adhering to the right regimen of healthy living. Aging is also frowned upon: old people who walk slowly on sidewalks and down supermarket aisles are regarded as a nuisance. Looking young for one's age is valorized for anyone over thirty-five. And our television and computer screens advertise one anti-aging cream after another, as if getting older were a crime.

One could say that within neoliberal society, creativity has been replaced by productivity: how effectively and profitably we produce is more important than the fulfillment that we might feel from creating something new. Of course, innovation is still valued, but usually merely as a stepping stone to increased market value. Innovation for the sake of innovation remains an ideal for a small number of people—such as writers, painters, sculptors, songwriters, and academics, among other producers of beauty, culture, and erudition—whose reasons for wanting to create things usually go deeper than wanting to make money. For instance, many writers keep writing even when their work proves to be completely unprofitable, which implies that they are driven by inner forces that elude the grasp of neoliberal capitalism. In other domains of life, innovation only matters if it can be translated into profit. Amazon, Apple, Twitter/X, and Pfizer are respected precisely because of their extraordinary ability to turn innovation into billions. Even in the realm of individual self-fashioning, the goal no longer appears to be to arrive at a creative, multilayered self that is capable of ethically—with attention to its responsibility toward others—carving a singular path through the world. Rather, the goal appears to be to hone one's ability to generate as much profit as possible.

I do not mean that we have stopped inventing things. I merely mean that, with the exception of the work of writers, artists, and other explicitly creative individuals, our emphasis appears to have shifted toward the pragmatic: we tend to measure the worth of the objects, concepts, or designs that we produce by their utility or monetary value, which means that our society rewards those who manufacture cars, coats, computers, and cost-efficient machinery more than those who write poetry or restore old buildings. And an overly simplistic self-help book on a topic that is guaranteed to sell, such as how to catch a man or climb the corporate ladder, is given a bigger advance by publishers than a literary novel of much greater aesthetic intricacy. The one exception to the denigration of artistic creativity is the entertainment industry, where successful actors and singers are amply remunerated. The fact that many of us believe, as if by default, that it would be insane to expect poets, restorers of old buildings, or writers of literary fiction to be compensated on the same level as scientists, engineers, manufacturers, or self-help authors illustrates just how deeply neoliberal values have infused our mentality regarding what we should appreciate.

In addition, neoliberal self-optimization privileges not only wealth but also individualistic self-help notions that market the idea that if we prioritize our well-being—if we learn to truly appreciate ourselves by practicing deeper forms of self-love and self-care—we will be able to achieve more or less anything, including the kind of life that brings genuine satisfaction. Along related lines, many have been persuaded by quasi-spiritual assertions that promise that if we truly want something and express our desire to the universe clearly and forcefully enough, the object of our desire will miraculously materialize.[8] In sum, our society has managed to translate the desire for inner healing into a self-serving and overly optimistic image of what the good life consists of.

The lures of neoliberal self-optimization can be difficult to resist. It can be seductive to think that we are the architects of our destinies in the sense that performing well, reaching a high level of productivity, learning to be efficient, constantly improving ourselves, and—perhaps most importantly, maintaining a positive attitude—will, over time, be rewarded. The ethos of positive thinking—the relentless optimism that suggests that a cure for our inner lack is within reach, that life without loss is possible, and that everything will turn out wonderfully as long as we genuinely believe that it will—is arguably the glue that holds together the neoliberal subject of self-optimization, facilitating this subject's ability to keep performing, producing, and smiling at the same time that it undertakes various projects of physical, psychic, emotional, and spiritual self-improvement, often in settings that require considerable financial resources.

Positive thinking is these days marketed as the solution to more or less any problem, from poverty and unemployment to cancer. It may be reassuring to trust that simply by staying optimistic we can solve our problems and improve the quality of our lives. However, the insidious flip side of this mentality is that whenever we fail to achieve what we desire, we *alone* are to blame. As I have noted, even structural inequalities such as racism, sexism, or homophobia are portrayed as obstacles that we are supposed to overcome on our own, for according to the mentality of neoliberal positive thinking, it is ultimately our personal responsibility to make something of ourselves by rising above such obstacles. In other words, the onus for surviving the various trials of life rests squarely on our own shoulders.

Consider the predicament of a person diagnosed with a terminal illness who is expected to defeat their illness through the sheer power of positive thinking. Among the many problems of this inhumane attitude is that it expects those who have received a death sentence to push aside their feelings of fear, anxiety, anger, depression, and despair; it expects them not to grieve what they have lost even though they have, essentially, lost *everything*. A person receiving a diagnosis of a terminal illness loses their health, their peace of mind, and—in many instances—many of the physical abilities that they have taken for granted; their future and all the possible directions that this future could have taken; facets of themselves that they have not yet discovered; dreams that they have not yet fulfilled; goals that they have not yet realized; and relationships that they cherish. They lose their entire life as they have known it, henceforth living in fearful anticipation of the inevitable. And, eventually, they lose their *life*—period. What more could one lose?

Asking a terminally ill person to stay positive under these circumstances seems like the epitome of cruelty, yet this request is routinely made, not just by family and friends, but even by doctors who know full well that no amount of any kind of thinking positively is going to heal an illness such as terminal cancer. Most people—doctors included—seem to make this request without much deliberation, almost automatically. It is, of course, possible that positive thinking keeps a patient more active, thereby prolonging life, so that there is an indirect link between staying positive and living longer. But the power of *thinking* alone is not going to heal an illness. Yet many people in our society have been programmed to believe the opposite, so that the idea is comforting to them even if it is not comforting to the patient, who—quite to the contrary—is likely to feel even worse whenever they fail to stay positive. The burden of thinking positively can be crushing because it implies that if you slip and get depressed about dying prematurely, it is your own fault that you die.

Generally speaking, there is little room for negative feelings within the ethos of neoliberal self-optimization. I have just named fear, anxiety, anger, depression, and despair. To these bad feelings one could add disillusionment, disenchantment, frustration, trepidation, and sadness, among many others. Within neoliberal culture, being able to smile even when we are hurting is valued, as is our capacity to keep performing—to stay productive and efficient—even when we have been emotionally injured.

The ability to push sadness aside is a strength whereas getting stuck in sadness is a weakness. That is, bad feelings are not part of the neoliberal vocabulary, even though they arguably constitute the hidden underside of the neoliberal subject who is able to uphold its façade of optimistic efficiency only by suppressing its misgivings about potentially failing to achieve everything that it is expected to achieve. The neoliberal subject of self-optimization is a gender-neutral version of the Stepford wife whose pristine image conceals a murkier reality that must, at all costs, be kept contained so as to enable this subject to maintain a persona that ensures its seamless incorporation into dominant modes of sociality by presenting a palatable portrait of happiness and self-realization.

One could, then, propose that in the context of neoliberalism, sleek instrumentalism has defeated the kinds of concerns regarding psychic and affective complexity that remain at the core of psychoanalytic theory and practice and that also remain central to many genres of philosophy and artistic expression. This defeat, however, may not be complete. Even though psychoanalysis, philosophy, and the arts can be—and have frequently been—corrupted by neoliberalism, they may, nevertheless, be among the last bastions of resistance against its ability to infiltrate every crevice of our being. One reason for their relatively robust capacity for rebellion is that they still respect the power of creativity as a corrective to rationalist instrumentalism. This is where the theories of creative living devised by Milner (and Winnicott) become relevant: they promote the reinvention of the subject along less instrumentalist lines than those demanded by neoliberal self-optimization.

It is worth reiterating here that the neoliberal culture of self-optimization that is so obvious in today's society is usually associated with—and began its march to primacy during—the

Reagan and Thatcher era of the 1980s, which marked the triumph of free market economics and the collapse of collective social support systems. However, it was already becoming ensconced in the ethos of the 1930s, when both Milner and Winnicott launched their careers. Furthermore, it quickly gained momentum during the decades after the Second World War. The fact that the early Frankfurt School scholars Theodor Adorno and Herbert Marcuse, who theorized from the 1940s to the 1970s, were able to diagnose it with a chilling accuracy reveals that its coordinates were already well established by the 1940s. The rise of the internet, along with the drastic crumbling of American (and some western European) social support systems, are perhaps the most significant factors that are missing from the depictions of excessively instrumentalist societies offered by these thinkers, and if anything, these phenomena have accelerated the intensity and urgency of the problems that they outline.

Gail and I are certainly not the first scholars to comment on the problems of neoliberal societies. It is, therefore, worth briefly outlining some notorious earlier critiques before moving onto the psychoanalytic antidotes that Milner and Winnicott offer. The Frankfurt School—to which Adorno and Marcuse belonged—represents one important node in the history of such critiques. Michel Foucault represents another important node, as does an admittedly idiosyncratically curated cast of thinkers from contemporary critical theory, broadly understood. This loosely defined version of critical theory—which has been my specialization throughout my career—combines psychoanalysis with continental philosophy, feminist theory, queer theory, affect theory, and critical race theory.[9] It acknowledges its deep indebtedness to the early Frankfurt School—especially Adorno and Marcuse—but mostly parts ways with the incarnations of the

Frankfurt School that have followed the rationalist interventions of Jürgen Habermas.

It is noteworthy that the original members of the Frankfurt School, including Adorno and Marcuse, were steeped in psychoanalytic theory and even saw it as a central component of social emancipation, whereas post-Habermasian Frankfurt School critics, for the most part, lost touch with the psychoanalytic essentials of the intellectual and political legacies of their predecessors.[10] However, in recent years, there has been a resurgence of theoretical interest in psychoanalysis among a number of prominent critics associated with the Frankfurt School. Some versions of this renewed interest have led to innovative work—such as the attempts of Amy Allen and Noëlle McAfee to draw on psychoanalysis to analyze social problems[11]—whereas others, such as Axel Honneth's interpretation of Winnicott, have seemed unnecessarily conservative.[12] In her chapter, Gail examines Honneth's contributions with a critical eye in an attempt to rescue Winnicott from becoming a thinker who would be—as Honneth's version of Winnicott largely is—wholly incompatible with feminist theory and other genres of progressive critical theory.

CRITIQUES OF NEOLIBERALISM

Adorno was a scathing critic of instrumentalist reason—of the kind of cold, calculating "bourgeois" reason that revered science as the arbiter of truth and that infused Western societies with a strongly pragmatic slant. Instrumentalist reason arguably resides at the core of the mentality of neoliberal self-optimization that I have described. According to Adorno, it contributed to the catastrophe of the Holocaust and, generally speaking, to the excessively rationalist inflection of life that had become the norm in the overly "administered" Western societies of the twentieth century.[13] Reaching further into the past, one could draw a theoretical and political connection between the escalation of instrumentalist reason and the brutal "will to mastery" that led to slavery, colonialism, attempts to subjugate nature, two world wars, and other Western atrocities. In recent decades, instrumentalist reason has spread beyond Western societies and contributed to the global exploitation of both human and natural resources and the rise of the current environmental catastrophe.

I am not saying that non-Western societies had no problems with violence or inequality before the arrival, along with colonialism, of Western instrumentalist reason. But the adoption of this reason appears to have led to increased levels of violence and inequality, sometimes due to attempts to defeat Western oppression by recourse to nationalist and populist politics. In the same way that the rise of nationalism and populism in the West has recently resulted in disastrously anti-egalitarian, even neofascist governments, nationalism and populism, however justified they may have seemed as responses to Western oppression, have historically handed power to conservative governments in other parts of the world. Although *progressive* populist movements—movements that seek the end of inequality—are a promising alternative to repressive state power, whenever populism is combined with nationalism it appears to give rise to governments that seek to set back time by undoing egalitarian reforms. As early postcolonial scholars, such as Homi Bhabha, Edward Said, and Paul Gilroy argued, nationalism is usually an inherently conservative approach to politics.[14]

The connection between nationalism and reactionary tendencies is obvious from the populist politics of Donald Trump and Vladimir Putin. Moreover, these two figures also reveal the equally obvious connection between neoliberal instrumentalism and reactionary politics. Even though it may, on the surface, appear that *reason*—even instrumentalist reason—is the last term that can appropriately be applied to these figures, for whom a fanatical genre of nationalism has replaced science as a site of devotion, what nevertheless most clearly drives their actions is the desire for power and money, the cold intersection of which is where the "heart and soul" of neoliberalism can be found. In this sense, Adorno's critique of instrumentalist reason continues to have tangible empirical stakes: he correctly saw the calculating attitude that characterizes instrumentalist reason as a key factor in fanning violence across the globe.

Some of Adorno's critics, such as Habermas, have accused him of wanting to destroy reason altogether. However, Adorno did not wish to do away with reason *tout court* but sought instead to render it more humble about its failings and more critical about its inhumane legacies and its ongoing role in real-life disasters.[15] More specifically, he believed that reason had become too disconnected from the body, the senses, affect, pleasure, suffering, and the rest of concrete lived experience. He despised the manner in which reason asserted its superiority over other aspects of life, including creativity, in the name of scientific "objectivity." Moreover, he criticized the fact that reason had abandoned its sociopolitical responsibilities: that it had come to serve oppression rather than emancipation. In other words, he wanted to restore the connection between reason and freedom, to make reason more attentive to the complex textures of human life—to the hopes, longings, and potentialities of the human spirit.[16]

Adorno's colleague Marcuse described the subject of self-optimization as a *one-dimensional man* who had become so focused on what Marcuse labeled *the performance principle* that it had ceased to cultivate the rest of its potentialities: motivated by the ideal of ever-escalating levels of performance, especially workplace productivity, the one-dimensional man (or woman) neglected his or her creative inclinations.[17] Central to Marcuse's analysis was his realization that Western capitalist societies had found two effective strategies for countering any temptation that the subject might feel, to rebel against—or even critically evaluate—dominant collective ideals. These strategies were consumerism and mass entertainment: the subject was placated by the (frequently quite real) satisfactions of consumerism as well as by the slightly narcotic satisfactions of entertainment. These satisfactions, in turn, enabled the subject to attain higher levels of productivity: as long as the subject could release work-related stress with rejuvenating shopping sprees and the soothing rhythm of relaxing nights in front of the television, it had the necessary energy to maintain the fast pace expected of it at work. In this manner, by providing a relatively high level of creature comforts and a deluge of absorbing entertainment, consumer capitalism kept people obedient without having to resort to the more explicitly authoritarian methods of totalitarian societies.

Foucault—whose relationship with psychoanalysis was much more antagonistic than that of Adorno or Marcuse even though many of his arguments agree with contemporary psychoanalytic insights regarding social issues[18]—picked up the torch from Adorno and Marcuse by analyzing the so-called *homo economicus*: a subject whose entire existence is governed by an economic mindset that promises that those who earnestly exert themselves will eventually reap the well-deserved rewards of their sacrifices.[19] Every dimension of this subject's being obeys the dictates of economic calculus. The idea is that the more of its resources it invests—the more effort it makes—the more profit it ultimately generates. Within such a calculus, activities that do not directly contribute to the maximization of profit are seen as pointless diversions. Even the sad feelings that arise when something goes wrong in our lives—when, for instance, some-one close to us dies or when we experience a deep disappoint-ment of some kind, such as a collapse of a romantic relationship—are seen primarily as distractions. Although we are given some time to mourn our losses and disappointments, we are expected to recover as quickly as possible, to pull ourselves together, and to return to the world of daily labor and productivity. Prolonged periods of depression are considered pathological; they are an indication that we are not strong enough to withstand the demands of our performance-oriented society and therefore automatically a burden, rather than an asset to this society.

Like Marcuse, Foucault recognized that capitalist societies—and by the end of Foucault's career in the 1980s, neoliberal con-sumer capitalism had become the economic foundation of many Western societies—need ways to conceal their instrumentalist mentality in order to keep people from getting so disenchanted that they will rebel. Such societies need to counteract their detached economic ethos by generating a cluster of "warm" val-ues centered around family life, children, home-cooked meals, and ideals of romantic love that make the subject feel like the daily grind of making a living is worth the effort. Like consum-erism and entertainment, such warm values are part of what Fou-cault characterized as the *biopolitical* control of our lives.[20]

Biopolitics combines the concept of *bios*—of life—with poli-tics in order to explain how our lives are controlled in invisible ways that are hard to pinpoint because they cannot be traced back to any centralized entity that is responsible for creating the con-ditions of this control. It is as if we were entangled in a spider's web of crisscrossing lines of power without the spider being pres-ent, so that we do not know where to direct our objections. Such power is only detectable in the effects that it has on us: we may feel it in the pressure to work long hours even when we would rather devote time to other activities; we may feel it in the pressure to keep smiling even when our hearts and souls have taken a beating; or we may feel it in the pressure to stay married for the sake of appearances even when our marriage makes us miserable. Foucault in fact went as far as to hypothesize—perhaps with a degree of exaggeration—that the citizens of capitalist "democracies" are, in the final analysis, no more free than the citizens of totalitarian dictatorships: the means of subjugation are simply softer and provide enough authentic pleasure for subjects to remain pacified even as the system is designed to extract as much labor from them as humanly possible.[21]

Biopolitical control works best when we actively *want* to participate in its demands, for instance when we feel that we are making an effort for a good reason, such as the goal of supporting our family. As long as our exertions are to some extent rewarded, it makes sense to endure a degree of daily hardship and boredom. Indeed, on a basic level it may be pointless to entirely fault neoliberalism—or earlier oppressive socioeconomic systems—for this state of affairs, for it may be unrealistic to assume that we could ever arrive at a political or economic arrangement that could eradicate hardship and boredom as inevitable parts of life. As I have explained, via Lacan, ontological and existential malaise is quite simply the human condition. However, it *is* possible to claim that neoliberal capitalism exacts an unnecessarily high price in this regard: a large portion of the population has no choice but to bear their soul-slaying jobs because these jobs are their only way to feed their families.

My mother worked at a merciless pace at the conveyor belt of a chocolate factory. In addition, because the factory's workforce consisted mostly of women—except for the "bosses," of course—her pay was miniscule compared to what the men who worked at a nearby paper mill earned. As long as I can recall, my mother's body has paid the price of the repetitive movements of her job: to this day, physical discomfort remains her constant companion. Likewise, my father damaged his body as a manual laborer. No matter how much he strove to improve his performance, he kept sliding backward toward financial ruin. It was almost as if the harder he worked, the higher the hurdles got, so that in the end there was no way to keep up. He accumulated more debt than income, living his entire life like Sisyphus, persistently pushing his rock up the hill, only to watch it repeatedly roll back to the bottom. This happened so many times that it crushed his spirit. By the time he stopped, his heart was so broken that, to the astonishment of his doctor, he died of a massive heart attack on the CT scan table. In his case, it is not an exaggeration to say that he worked himself to death.

My parents, like millions of others, worked so hard at jobs that brought them no joy that they did not have any mental energy to consider what they might have wanted to do with their lives: their stark choices were laid out for them before they were even born. More precisely, they may, at times, have asked themselves questions about the kinds of lives they wanted to lead, only to immediately push these questions aside as irrelevant, given how many urgent problems, especially financial ones, were pressing on them. I have always thought that among the largely unacknowledged tragedies of poverty is that people do not get the opportunity to even consider how they might want to proceed with their lives, what their singular art of living might look like. In addition, if they manage to think about the matter, the utter unattainability of the desirable life can lead to despair, depression, and bitterness, as it did for my father.

My father wanted to be an intellectual. He wanted to read books. He also wanted to write them. And he definitely had the mental capacity to accomplish this. But the extreme poverty of his family forced him into manual labor right after elementary school, making all this impossible for him. He was a dreamer who would have been better off writing books than trying to manage our family's finances, with the result that it was my mother who put food on the table. Before she went to work, the cupboards were often entirely empty. The details are fuzzy because my parents did their best to protect me from the reality of things, but I am fairly certain that there were times when we only had something to eat because friends and neighbors came to our aid. In mourning my father's recent death, what I most grieve is that he never got the chance to live the kind of life that he would have liked. He did have a life. But ultimately, he had very little control over its basic parameters. In many ways, I am the one who got to live the life that should have been his; on some level, I have always felt that I stole his dreams. This is because he sacrificed everything so that I could. My guilt about this has been its own peculiar kind of burden.

I share these details of my parents' lot in life to illustrate that I know from firsthand experience that it would be unreasonable to fault those in dire financial situations for going along with the expectations of the neoliberal performance principle. Furthermore, this same principle also confines those who are financially better off, even tremendously successful, in the sense that professional jobs usually come with extreme pressure to keep outperforming oneself. Even those whom neoliberal capitalism deems merely moderately successful—as is the case with humanities professors—find ourselves under constant scrutiny. There are annual performance reviews in addition to the extensive reviews that take place at the various stages of being promoted on the tenure track. There are peer reviews for everything that we publish. There are teaching evaluations for every course that we teach. Whether we are the student or the professor, we are being relentlessly graded and evaluated. Personally, I feel that, since elementary school, my life has been a long string of performance reviews. It has been exhausting but by no means unusual.

In addition, the better we perform, the higher the expectations seem to get. You published a book this year? Well, next year you should publish two! Even worse, people who themselves would never be able to write a book of any kind get to criticize your book publicly, to inform the whole world about all the ways in which it flounders. The reason I never criticize Taylor Swift is that I know that I would not be able to do what she does even if someone put a gun to my head. But this does not seem to stop others—even her fellow musicians—from going after her with a hatchet. Even for the extraordinarily talented, the "tall poppy syndrome" creates a great deal of suffering. Moreover, those of us who are only moderately successful keep wondering why we are not more successful—unless, of course, we have found a way to mentally defeat the expectations of the performance principle, unless we have managed to teach ourselves not to care.

I do not think that it is possible—or useful—to compare the woes of the extraordinarily successful with the woes of those who are struggling to make a living. My point is merely that the neoliberal performance principle holds all of us in its net, albeit in vastly different ways and to vastly different degrees. Regardless of our station in life, most of us take this principle so much for granted that we cannot even imagine stepping outside of it. I certainly cannot. I have trouble doing so, even though I am fully aware of the damage it causes—has already caused by destroying my health. To be sure, I try to resist the demands that come at me at a relentless pace: there seems to be a new one—or even several—every time I check my email. But much of the time, resistance feels impossible because I feel a deep responsibility toward my field, toward my colleagues, toward the editors who have published my work, and above all, toward my students. If I have to lose sleep because I am running late in writing a lecture, I will lose that sleep rather than arrive in class imperfectly prepared. This has been my pattern since middle school when I started getting up at 2 a.m. to prepare for exams. I spent most of graduate school sleep-deprived. And I still routinely wake up at 3 a.m. to finish preparing the materials for one of my courses because other obligations—such as reviewing the work of colleagues or writing letters of recommendation—have kept me from staying on top of my teaching schedule.

I know exactly what I *want* to do: I want to write books. It is just that most of my life is spent trying to get to the point where I have the time to do so. For me, 95 percent of being able to write a book is about finding the necessary hours for the task. Writing itself is not hard for me. Finding time for it feels almost impossible—and more often than not, actually *is* impossible. Other people's desires are different from mine, but I am willing to wager that many of them also feel that instead of doing what they want to do, they are desperately trying to carve out the necessary time to actually do it.

THE DISCONTENTS
OF SELF-OPTIMIZATION

It seems that almost everyone—the poor, the middle classes, and the affluent—feels that they do not have enough time and that they are forced to run from one task to the next at an inhumane pace. As usual, the poor bear the brunt of this, often because they hold several jobs to make ends meet. But the middle classes and the affluent are not spared either: professionals such as

doctors, lawyers, professors, and those who work in finance notoriously work long hours in pressure-cooker environments. Their
financial compensation may be substantial, even excessive, but
many of them find it impossible to draw a clear line between
their work and the rest of their lives. Many feel like they are
constantly "on call," anticipating urgent text messages, phone
calls, or emails late into the night. It is not surprising that, for
many, watching television is no longer enough to take their
mind off their jobs, that they need the aid of alcohol, drugs, or
sleeping pills.

Under the neoliberal regime of self-optimization, we are so
used to filling our days with various undertakings—achieving
goals—that some of us find it challenging to take a vacation that
is not jam-packed with activities. A decade ago, for several
months I tried yoga. However, my body could not handle the
profound relaxation that the sessions generated, with the result
that shortly after each session it forced itself back into its usual
state of tension by bringing me to the verge of a panic attack. I
never had one, but I found myself hyperventilating. I consider it
tremendous progress that these days I can do yoga without experiencing this type of resurgence of tension. More generally
speaking, my sense is that it is not an exaggeration to say that
many of us accept that the price of our success—or even just of
our ability to hold onto our jobs—is being willing to push ourselves to a breaking point. Whether we work in a factory, office,
store, construction site, law firm, hospital, or university, the pace
of our lives feels merciless. We keep falling behind. In addition,
for many of us, the world is overstimulating, too full of flicker-
ing images. It is too strident and loud. So damn loud.

I sometimes feel that my life mimics the experience of going
through the security line at a busy airport where security officers are screaming at me to take out my laptop, cell phone, and

bag of toiletries and place them, along with my jewelry and shoes, in the ubiquitous gray containers. "Laptops need their own container," they scream. Why do they need their own container? Why can they not be placed next to my shoes? And why are they *screaming*? I have traveled a lot. I know what I am supposed to do. I am a fast-moving person, and I am working as fast as possible to get all the relevant items out of my bag and into those gray containers. But the officers keep screaming at me anyway. Why? Probably because they feel that if they do not, they are not doing their jobs.

What is more disturbing than tolerating officers screaming at me in airports is that I have been programmed to endure an insane amount of pressure in the rest of my life. I feel that I am working as fast as I can, sometimes even literally running from one building to another at the university, yet despite my being an organized person, the pile of work on my desk does not shrink, and it feels like at any given moment a dozen people are nudging me to get things done. My email inbox is filled with reminders to complete this or that task by this or that date. I know it is someone's job to send out these reminders. However, there are many of them and just one of me. And in any case, I usually remember all too well what I am supposed to do by when, so that I do not need the reminders, which only add clutter to my life. "Stop, just stop!" is what I want to say, but never do.

Every time I log onto my email, my shoulders tighten because I anticipate demands, problems, deadlines, and tedious forms to fill out. Within fifteen minutes of being online, I am in excruciating pain. I know that I am far from alone in feeling this type of pressure and that the vast majority of those who do have no choice but to tolerate it. This is one of the costs of neoliberal self-optimization, of constantly striving to improve our performance and productivity. Such self-optimization is supposed to streamline our lives, but instead it feels like it is destroying our capacity to focus on what truly matters to us. I do not want to optimize my life. Rather, I want to concentrate on building a life that feels worthwhile, that corresponds to my interests, passions, and talents—such as they may be—and allows me to pursue the relevant activities at a reasonable speed. I am aware that this is a big ask, even a seemingly selfish one, yet it is one that everyone *should* ideally be able to make without feeling embarrassed.

Images. Speed. Noise. Kristeva calls this the society of the spectacle.[22] I am not one to moralize about hours spent watching Netflix. Nevertheless, I can relate to the gist of Kristeva's argument: we live in a society of images where we take our behavioral cues from these images. Sometimes these images push us toward naïve optimism by suggesting that we too can have the glamorous or exciting lives depicted on the screen. Other times they induct us into unimaginative modes of life. For example, they teach large numbers of us to desire the same things, more or less, with small variations. The fact that low-rise jeans, which everyone from hip teenagers to youthful soccer moms wore in the early 2000s, now seem like the epitome of uncool is an indication of how thoroughly our desires are manipulated by consumer capitalism, trendsetters, and Instagram influencers. The images that are designed to sell us the fantasy of a specific type of life set the tone of our desire, thereby setting the tone of our entire life, for desire is arguably the component of our life that, besides structural constraints, most influences the direction that this life takes (more on this later).

The combination of images, speed, and noise is most palpable in visual advertisements. However, advertisements are merely the most obvious manifestation of what Kristeva means by the society of the spectacle, which, especially after the rise of the internet, has become the status quo of our daily lives. For our purposes, it is useful to extract from her complex analysis the idea that there is something about the blend of images, speed, and noise that destroys our capacity to even consider revolting against the performance principle that governs our lives.

Kristeva's critique of the society of the spectacle in many ways replicates the critiques that Adorno and Marcuse aimed at the entertainment industry as a tool for placating "the masses," so that they would meekly comply with the demands imposed on them at work. However, Kristeva also reconfigures these critiques by reenvisioning the meaning of "revolt," for she does not use the term in its literal sense of social uprisings or revolutions but, rather, in a more metaphorical sense that refers to the ways in which ideas rotate, reverse, revolve, rearrange, and get reinvented and reimagined. She calls this *intimate revolt* because it takes place on the level of personal psychic and affective experience rather than on the collective level, even if collective transformation may be its ultimate goal.[23]

Kristeva asserts that the society of the spectacle interferes with our capacity for self-reflection, for the kind of slow rhythm of thought that would allow us to pierce the surface of things so as to reimagine what we might want from our lives. One could also speculate that this society might impede our ability to feel deeply or to feel the types of things, such as love, that require duration. This may be merely an intuition, but this is how our world feels, as if people had lost the capacity to concentrate not only on thoughts but also on feelings for longer than a moment. Action drives our lives. And the faster we act, the more respect we appear to garner. Yet, as should be clear by now, the speeding up of life exacts a price, so that it is not surprising that when we think about what it might mean to live more creatively, many of us fixate on the idea that we want to slow down and find some breathing space outside of our jobs. Alternatively, we want to create space for those parts of our jobs that inspire us.

It is crucial to carefully distinguish our legitimate nostalgia for a slower pace of life—which, if translated into a reality, could genuinely alter our lives for the better—from a seductive, but deeply misguided, generalized nostalgia for an idyllic past, for the fact is that a past when the world was supposedly less traumatic and tarnished is a fantasy. It is true that things may have moved more slowly. This part of the past seems worth resuscitating. However, there were plenty of appalling evils, such as slavery, colonialism, the oppression of women, the persecution of sexual minorities, and a large number of other tyrannical traditions, that I would never want to see resurface. I am not saying that the current world is free of racism, imperialism, misogyny, or homophobia. But at least in some segments of our society, there has been improvement, and the creation of a more egalitarian society persists as an explicit objective. For this reason, it would be a mistake to confuse the desire for a slower pace of life with an indiscriminate yearning to revive traditional ways of life.

Capitalism has played a complicated role in the history of social hierarchies. The rise of capitalism obviously amplified financial inequalities, widening the gap between the rich and the poor. At the same time, it may have helped mitigate a number of other hierarchies because profit-generating consumerism demands a degree of equality: slaves under the control of their masters and women under the control of their husbands had little buying power, so that from the point of view of early capitalism, their liberation may have appeared economically advantageous. This does not mean that the "liberation" in question was genuine. For instance, slavery in the United States was arguably merely replaced by the prison industrial complex—a version of slavery that appears more palatable to our modern sensibilities than plantation slavery because those imprisoned can be argued to have caused their own misery.[24] The idea that prisoners are wholly to blame for their own fates works perfectly with the general ethos of neoliberalism, which as I have pointed out, holds individuals personally responsible for their destinies without paying any attention to their circumstances.

By now, people are increasingly aware of this reality, with the result that the West currently finds itself in a paradoxical situation. On the one hand, those who applaud consumer capitalism and the free market keep reassuring us that capitalism, by definition, automatically augments equality by undoing traditional systems of hierarchy. On the other hand, many people are both skeptical of this argument and disillusioned with capitalism due to the precarity of their everyday lives: when hard work does not offer financial security; when retirement means a diminished standard of living—even poverty—for people who have worked their entire lives; when those who need health care cannot obtain it; when social support systems crumble at the same time as the economy behaves erratically; when the quality of education in public schools plummets; when the environment collapses at the same time as wars and violent conflicts erupt around the world; when the number of refugees stuck at border crossings increases; when the likes of Trump and Putin manage to break the rules of ethically decent behavior without being held accountable for their crimes; and when the very foundations of democracy appear to be dissolving due to the election of neofascist leaders in several European countries, it is difficult to maintain one's faith in the economic arrangement that is supposed to sustain the system.

The paradox can be restated as follows: even as the tycoons of consumer capitalism appear entirely unfit to rescue us from our various crises, it seems more or less impossible to envision alternatives to the reigning composition of economic, political, social, and cultural life. Neoliberal self-optimization—with its deluge of images, excess of speed, and deafening noise—has become such a taken-for-granted component of Western daily life that attempting to change it appears entirely futile. That is, the possibility of a different kind of life does not appear to be conceivable for most people, even as they find their concrete circumstances increasingly untenable: it is difficult to alter things when the current mode of life appears to be the only possible mode of life. Within such a scenario, most people opt to try to make the most of their situation.

However, this is becoming more and more demanding. Even the relatively affluent in the West find the good life slipping through their fingers: many people are not able to live up to the ideals of neoliberal self-optimization even when their circumstances are relatively auspicious. This has become startlingly evident to the current generation of young middle-class people who are facing an uncertain world where, in addition to the problems that I have already named, a high level of education no longer guarantees a job, let alone financial success. Without a doubt, compared with much of the rest of the world, the West remains affluent—even criminally so when this affluence has been built upon the backs of people in other parts of the world—but even in the West, the concentration of resources in the hands of a relatively small group of people has resulted in a situation where the middle and working classes are struggling to keep up.

Even young people who are privileged enough to attend university get depressed and anxious about the pressure to perform in ways that are palpable to those who teach them, as Gail and I do. Gail will focus on this issue at greater depth in her chapter. Here, I merely want to say that although depression and anxiety arising from the demands of a university-level education have most likely always been present, they appear more acute now than they did even twenty years ago. In part, this may be due to the fact that it is now acceptable to talk about them, so that we hear more about them. However, it is partly because those getting an education realize that it may not get them very far in the rest of their lives.

It used to be that many people were caught up in what Lauren Berlant called "cruel optimism," defined as the false hope that values, ideals, goals, aspirations, relationships, and modes of life that keep hurting us will, in the end, reward us or make us happy.[25] Cruel optimism means that we place our trust in the very social happiness narratives—narratives regarding the good life that we have internalized from our culture—that impede our flourishing. At the core of cruel optimism is the expectation—and this is where cruel optimism aligns itself seamlessly with the ethos of neoliberalism—that if we just keep trying hard enough, eventually we will reap the benefits of our labor. According to this mentality, obstacles are mere stepping stones to success. Every impediment can supposedly be overcome, every hardship can be transcended. Every goal is obtainable as long as we remain persistent. Indeed, our success may not even feel entirely real unless we have first had to clear a few hurdles. Even when things do not appear to be improving, the hope is that just down the road, after we have made one final effort, lies the well-earned break that we have been waiting for.

However, as I have started to suggest, cruel optimism may be losing its traction in the sense that people are increasingly able to see through its ruses. The general state of the world is currently so grim that it has become more difficult for neoliberal society to convince people that positive thinking will make a difference, that higher levels of performance will eventually pay off, or that consumer capitalism is the answer to the catastrophes that we are witnessing across the globe. The result is a sharp rise in deep pessimism. This response is undoubtedly more realistic than cruel optimism, but it can unfortunately shut down the ability to envision that things could be different, which in turn is the first step toward being able to bring about collective transformation. In this sense, neither extreme—excessive optimism or excessive pessimism—is a particularly useful reaction to our predicament.

As José Muñoz noted, being able to recognize that the world in which we live is not "good enough"—is not the world in which we *want* to live—is a necessary precondition of being able to change it.[26] From this viewpoint, excessive pessimism can mean the extinction of the human imaginative capacity to conceptualize alternatives to present realities, which in turn makes such alternatives even harder to attain for the simple reason that we have to be able to imagine a better world before we can begin to build one; the ability to create something new begins with the capacity to visualize it as a potentiality. Although cruel optimism is clearly not the answer to the failings of neoliberal self-optimization, neither is pessimism of such proportions that it forecloses the future as a space of possibility.

NIETZSCHE'S ART OF LIVING

What, then, do we want from life when we manage to sidestep both excessive optimism and excessive pessimism? By now it should be clear that I assume, or at least hypothesize, that many of us are looking for a meaningful, imaginative, creative, and possibly slower way to live—that we want to actively participate in the fashioning of our destiny. This may not be true of everyone. But my wager is that many of us, with various degrees of explicitness, appreciate Nietzsche's suggestion that we should strive to become "the poets of our life—first of all in the smallest, most everyday matters."[27] By this notion of becoming the poets of our lives, Nietzsche refers to our capacity to steer our lives in satisfactory directions even if we can never fully predict where we will end up. He, in short, urges us to develop an art of living that accentuates the uniqueness of our being—our inimitable "style"—even when this uniqueness defies conventional social dictates.[28]

Another way to express the matter is to say that Nietzsche valorizes the notion of becoming "what one is."[29] At first glance, this may appear as an invitation to pursue one's essential self, to settle into a stable understanding of oneself as soon as one, perhaps after some detours, finds a modality of being that fits one's self-perception. However, a more accurate interpretation of Nietzsche's ideal of self-fashioning is to recognize that "what one is" in the Nietzschean sense is an ever-evolving entity, with the result that becoming "what one is" means becoming more robustly and gracefully capable of continual self-transformation. At any given moment, there may be a compilation of elements that appears to lend consistency to one's being. However, given the constant mutability of human life, such consistency is necessarily transitory: it only holds until the next compilation of elements gains ascendency. The self's development is too unpredictable to be linear: there are always events—good ones such as falling in love and bad ones such as accidents, illnesses, or losing a beloved person—that throw the self off the course that it might have set for itself.

As Alain Badiou explains, an event such as falling in love can alter the coordinates of the subject's life so thoroughly that it finds it impossible to keep living in the manner that it used to live before the event. Badiou discusses three other genres of events—political, scientific, and artistic revolutions or innovations—that have the same power to transform the subject's entire life.[30] I would add to these positive events more negative ones, such as falling terminally ill or losing someone that one loves.[31] All these events, whether positive or negative, usher the subject onto a path that it may not have expected to take. Nietzsche's vision of living one's life as poetry must be able to accommodate such unforeseeable events, which further demonstrates that it cannot be a matter of stabilizing the self into an essential incarnation but, rather, of augmenting its nimbleness in relation to life-altering events.

Nietzsche's poetics of living therefore demands our ability to incorporate a complex array of experiences into our process of becoming. As a consequence, his model of self-fashioning may, on the surface, share characteristics with that of neoliberal self-optimization. He even emphasizes the value of being able to reinterpret our past in such a way that its debilitating elements can be transmuted into valuable components of our present. That is, he appreciates the manner in which our losses, failures, disappointments, and other devastating experiences feed our singular art of living. However, Nietzsche's alchemy of retroactively reinterpreting hardship has nothing to do with the neoliberal quest to turn obstacles into tools for profitability or self-improvement. Rather, it attempts to generate a vision of human life that is capacious enough to accommodate what is damaged about us. Indeed, even his notorious celebration of joyfulness cannot be dissociated from his deep appreciation for the shadowy side of life, which means that this celebration must be distinguished from neoliberal positive thinking.

It could be said that our character serves as a repository for the losses that we have experienced over the years. This suggests that without loss—and the suffering that loss brings in its wake—our character would lack depth, breadth, and complexity. Nietzsche's account of self-fashioning reveals an understanding of this basic facet of life, which is why it invites us to incorporate our suffering into our art of living. Unlike neoliberal self-optimization, he does not ask that we transcend our suffering, but merely that we acknowledge it as one of the building blocks of our character. Although he believes that "the constraint of a single taste" should determine the parameters of our self, he does not wish to exclude what cannot be tamed—what sticks out, remains awkward, or causes pain—from this self.[32] As he puts it, even our weaknesses can come to "delight the eye."[33]

Nietzsche's ideal of becoming the poets of our lives suggests that there are more and less rewarding ways to live. Insofar as many of us would like to live as fulfilling a life as possible, there is undeniably something deeply compelling about a philosophy that tells us that we have some choice over the matter, that we possess the capacity to develop a poetics of being that gives us a measure of agency over how our lives turn out. That said, Nietzsche arguably greatly overestimates the amount of agency that we in reality possess. As psychoanalysis has taught us since its inception, we have less power over the parameters of our lives than we would prefer: the existence of the unconscious—let alone of the kinds of powerful bodily drives (jouissance) over which we have little control—makes it impossible for us to master our destiny to the extent that Nietzsche would like.[34] The same is true of the impact of external factors, including social inequalities, that we cannot single-handedly alter. Nevertheless, the advantage of Nietzsche's manner of conceptualizing the contours of subjectivity is that, like existentialist philosophy—which owes a tremendous debt to Nietzsche—it asks us to take a relatively high degree of responsibility for how we live. That is, how we respond to the unforeseeable events that derail our plans is, at least to some extent, up to us.

I would say that even though psychoanalysis stresses the impossibility of self-mastery, it nonetheless values the ideal of continual self-transformation and the possibility of changing our destiny. If it did not, there would be no point to psychoanalytic clinical practice, which seeks to enable analysands to overcome harmful patterns of behavior—repetition compulsions and other symptomatic tendencies—in order to open up more satisfying avenues of living. Regardless of their theoretical or clinical orientations, most contemporary psychoanalytic thinkers would probably agree with Jonathan Lear's observation that "whether we like it or not, we are always in the business of becoming human. We are making meanings about who we are, what things mean for us, which in fact shapes who we are."[35] In other words, psychoanalysis recognizes that questions about who we are and what things mean to us sculpt the outlines of our being at the same time as the process of becoming "who we are" by necessity remains open-ended. This seems more or less identical to Nietzsche's vision of the art of living as a matter of becoming "what one is."

Neither Nietzsche nor psychoanalysis suggests that we one day arrive at a fixed identity that expresses something essential about our being. Instead, both imply that we spend our entire lives devising new versions of ourselves. Some of us enter this process of self-fashioning with a degree of consciousness, deliberately striving to develop an art of living that allows us to forge a life that feels worth living and that, as much as possible, fulfills our potential as human beings. Others do not intentionally embrace the process of becoming, yet it nevertheless takes place: "what we are" changes over time regardless of whether or not we make a purposeful effort to guide the process of continual self-renewal.

For those who wish to actively participate in their self-renewal, psychoanalysis can facilitate the process of developing the kind of self that stays true to its singularity and creative potential. No self is perfect or devoid of damage. Nevertheless, we tend to find some versions of ourselves more compelling than others, and it is one of the tasks of psychoanalysis to enable such versions to materialize and flourish by allowing us to work through—and thereby to some extent neutralize the power of—the types of wounding personal histories, traumas, and neuroses that might hold us back or sabotage us. Although a degree of self-sabotage may be an inevitable component of human life, in many cases it is possible to diminish its intensity so as to create space for the more constructive components of our being. This, again, is not a matter of a neoliberal obfuscation of suffering but rather of knitting suffering into the fabric of human experience in ways that keep it from completely debilitating the subject who has undergone it.

Both Nietzsche's ideal of living our lives as poetry and the psychoanalytic ideal of allowing us to rewrite the parameters of our lives suggest that, despite the limitations imposed on us by the complexities of our psychic lives and despite the constraints introduced by the concrete conditions of our lives—including social injustices such as poverty, racism, and sexism—we can play a part in determining the tenor of our lives. Even though the materials that we are forced to work with are frequently beyond our control—dependent on the particulars of our background; the advantages or disadvantages that come with that background; and a whole host of unpredictable past experiences—we nevertheless remain, to some extent, accountable for what we make of these materials. As I have stressed, I believe that there are tangible limits to such accountability. For example, I would never blame anyone in my parents' situation for not being able to break the cycle of poverty. Still, beyond such concrete obstacles, there is such a thing as taking responsibility for our poetics of becoming; there is such a thing as taking at least a partial responsibility for our destiny.

I have brought Nietzsche into my discussion because I believe that the kind of psychoanalysis that interests me in this chapter advances an art of living that shares components with Nietzsche's poetics of self-fashioning, albeit with the significant modification that the psychoanalytic self has less agency than the Nietzschean self.[36] Both versions of the self are always in the process of evolving, of becoming. Both strive to define their destiny within the constraints imposed on them by their familial and social histories, contexts, and circumstances. And both recognize that a singular art of living is not always beautiful, pleasing, or comfortable. For both, such an art entails the ability to tolerate the heavier frequencies of life—its barriers, hardships, breakdowns, and disenchantments—even as it also includes the capacity to welcome life's myriad delights; it entails an appreciation for the fact that life is made of a complex interplay of light and shadow.

It is worth restating that this mentality differs from the neoliberal ideal of overcoming affliction in the sense that it does not assert that we should be able to transform impediments to advantages, let alone to profit, but merely that we should accept them as inevitable parts of life. It is true that both Nietzsche and psychoanalysis, on some level, imply that obstacles can, in the long run, contribute to a richer texture of life. However, where neoliberalism seeks to translate obstacles into stepping stones for success, both Nietzsche and psychoanalysis regard them as ingredients of a multifaceted psychic structure that allows the subject to sit with its sorrow, as it were. Instead of striving to erase its suffering either by buying into cruelly optimistic promises of the good life or by succumbing to the seductions of consumer capitalism, the psychoanalytic self, like the Nietzschean self, accepts that life, by necessity, includes adversity even if its goal is to live as creatively as possible.

In Lacanian terms, Nietzsche's perspective is akin to the idea that we need to accept the fact that there is no cure for our ontological lack. Even more significantly, both Nietzsche and Lacan believe that being able to come to terms with the realization that our lives will never be perfectly happy or fulfilled is the precondition of our ability to fashion a life that may, ideally, feel rewarding to us. As should be clear, I am referring here to ontological forms of negativity rather than to painful social inequalities. Regarding the former, as I noted at the beginning of this chapter, Lacan's argument—which in some ways is also Nietzsche's argument—is that when we fail to accept lack as constitutive of our being, we all too easily get stuck in the pursuit of the kind of healing that is intrinsically impossible; we get stuck in the notion that we cannot move forward before we feel whole and fully self-realized, which means that we will never move forward.

MILNER'S POETICS OF BEING

Milner's poetics of being—which constitutes the focus of the rest of this chapter, albeit with some contributions from Winnicott that foreshadow Gail's arguments in the next chapter—shares many commonalities with Nietzsche's ideal of becoming the poets of our lives, at the same time as it leans heavily toward a psychoanalytic appreciation for the shortcomings of agency. In fact, Milner explicitly seeks to dissolve, rather than to prop up, the subject's agency in the sense that the erosion of the ego—the seat of the subject's agency—is one of the preconditions of her poetics of being. Like Lacan, she is deeply suspicious of the ego and its narcissistic pretentions of self-mastery, viewing these as the very antithesis of her particular version of self-fashioning. The reasons for this will become clear in the course of my analysis.

It is worth prefacing my analysis by noting that Milner has long been among the most underappreciated thinkers and writers of the twentieth century. Her career was long, spanning from the early 1930s until the late 1980s and generating a large number of remarkably original texts. Yet until recently, academics and clinicians alike have almost entirely ignored her rich contributions to psychoanalytic theory. However, these contributions have fortunately, finally, become esteemed in part due to their deeply autobiographical inflection. Generally speaking, interest in "autotheoretical" writing—writing that combines an autobiographical approach with theoretical reflection—has increased sharply during the last decade. The fact that Milner's work falls under this category has undoubtedly contributed to its recent resurrection as worthy of scholarly attention.

It is important to recognize that autotheory did not begin in 2013 with Paul Preciado, in 2015 with Maggie Nelson, or even in the 1970s with Roland Barthes.[37] Now that critics are reaching back to the past in search of precursors to contemporary autotheory—among other things, resurrecting Black feminist critics such as Audre Lorde and Angela Davis, whose autobiographical style became denigrated in the context of the rise of poststructuralist theory in the American academy of the 1990s—it feels fitting to introduce Milner as a notable figure in a specifically psychoanalytic version of autotheory.[38] This also feels fitting due to the fact that Gail and I have chosen to include a number of personal anecdotes in this book. However, the main reason that I have opted to highlight Milner's work is that although Milner does not explicitly name neoliberal consumer capitalism as her adversary, I believe that her account of creative living offers a potent corrective to today's ethos of competitive and highly individualistic self-optimization.

My discussion of Milner's work draws on three of her texts: *A Life of One's Own* (1934); *An Experiment in Leisure* (1937); and *Eternity's Sunshine: A Way of Keeping A Diary* (1987). I have picked these three texts because they revolve around similar questions; use a similar stream of consciousness rhetorical style; and are genuinely autobiographical, relying heavily on Milner's personal journal entries and other personal reflections. Most relevant for our purposes, the treatises that I consider are devoted to basic questions regarding what constitutes a creative life. Each volume approaches the theme differently, but all three revolve around the ideal of fashioning a life that is fully lived, with desire, passion, interest, attention, and delight. Milner wants to make sure that life does not merely pass her by, that she is an active participant in the parameters of her poetics of being. However, as I show through my analysis, she discovers that in order to be such an active participant, she—somewhat counterintuitively—needs to find ways to push aside her rational ego, to accept a stance of self-surrender.

Milner's three volumes employ material from her journals, where she records the items, objects, moments, and experiences that bring her happiness, arouse her interest, or crystallize something meaningful about the process of fashioning her particular art of living; they provide a record of her efforts to be fully present in the folds of everyday life. In addition, she casts a wide net over Western literature, painting, sculpture, architecture, religion, and culture more generally speaking to supplement her autobiographical observations. Finally, she draws on detailed depictions of nature: trees, flowers, insects, animals, rocks found on the beach, the tenor of the sky—whatever happens to capture her eye. Her sensuous texts are also filled with detailed commentaries on her psychic, affective, and physical states. Each text presents the reader with a byzantine assemblage of materials that invites them into its sumptuous mesh. Her depictions of the items, objects, moments, experiences, events, affects, sensations, visions, observations, and flashes of special significance are often visual, tangible, and veer toward the mystical.

Milner uses writing like a fisherman might use a net to haul in the day's catch, only holding onto the items, objects, moments, or experiences that feel most precious to her. In *A Life of One's Own*—whose title is influenced by Virginia Woolf's *A Room of One's Own* (1929)—Milner poses the simple question of what makes her happy. She decides to write down, at the end of each day, the item, object, moment, experience, event, or relationship that made her happy. She does not do so consistently: there are often long gaps between her diary entries.[39] However, over seven years, a degree of consistency emerges from this experiment: what makes her happy are (usually) entirely mundane things that arrest her attention. Sometimes it is a conversation with a friend that brings her joy. However, most frequently it is a solitary encounter with an object of some kind, such as a work of art or a natural entity—a tree, a flower, or the delicate hues of the fading sun—that generates a profound feeling of contentment that provides a response to her question regarding what happiness consists of. In this text, happiness becomes associated with items and objects, moments of contemplation, or experiences of perception that allow something seemingly ordinary to take on a transcendent inflection. It should already be clear why I connect Milner's observations to Lacan's definition of sublimation as a matter of raising a mundane object to the dignity of the Thing.

In *An Experiment in Leisure*, Milner's goal is to determine what most interests her. In *Eternity's Sunshine*, in turn, she collects what she calls *beads*—small epiphanies that consist of the most engaging and memorable moments of each day. Although the object of her inquiry thus slides rhetorically from happiness to interests to "beads," the common denominator across her three texts is her attempt to determine the components of a creative life that not only feels meaningful but also offers morsels of the kind of enjoyment that Lacan calls jouissance. Milner deliberately hunts for precious items, objects, moments, or experiences that fulfill her by giving her a taste of what I have called *worldly transcendence*: the kind of transcendence that allows her to experience bits of sublimity without leaving the world behind. She courts such transcendence with a rare persistence, constantly on the lookout for the intimation of sublimity in each item, object, moment, and experience that she fixates on.

In *A Life of One's Own*, Milner depicts the process of reaching worldly transcendence, which she explicitly aligns with psychic and affective self-renewal, as a matter of employing "wide perception." By wide perception, Milner means a way of looking that allows her to focus on a specific object for a long period of time, at the same time as she softens her gaze—thereby widening her perception—and relaxes her mind and body into a meditative trance. She gives an example of sitting in a café in the Black Mountains in Germany and staring at a lush tree in the distance. She decides to fixate her gaze on this tree until the distinction between her and the tree begins to dissipate, with the consequence that she gradually becomes a part of what she is looking at.

On the one hand, Milner's wide perception is a matter of observing an object in a somewhat detached, almost absent-minded manner; on the other, it is a matter of making room for the object of her gaze by erasing her own presence. Milner's depiction of her experience of uniting with the object of her perception in fact resembles Heidegger's argument that for the object to step forth from its hiding place, it is necessary for the observer to create a "clearing" for it by taking a step back.[40] This is how even a skittish object—one that might flee the scene if somehow startled—may come into view as an object of contemplation. In this scenario, it is the subject's willingness to subtract itself from the scene that opens a space for the object to appear. Milner reports that after some time spent concentrating her attention on an object like the tree—or even an ordinary tin cup—and stopping all interfering thoughts, she experiences a harmonious oneness with the object. She begins to see it in a new register: the barrier between self and object disintegrates, her ego slides aside, and things about the object that normally remain concealed reveal themselves. Milner, in short, obtains an attitude of worldly transcendence. She reports that this practice is especially helpful in enabling her to reach a calm state of mind whenever she feels agitated or anxious.

Milner's wide perception—which she distinguishes from the "narrow perception" that dominates everyday life—allows her to fall into meditative states that open up a world of wonder for her: instead of boredom and despair, she experiences joy and pleasure; things appear vividly and in intricate detail; and the sublime mysteriously arises in the midst of mundane experience. Milner gives numerous examples of natural entities that allow her to encounter the world in this manner. There are also many man-made objects that have the same effect, such as paintings and buildings. Although on some level the object appears less important than Milner's decision to dedicate her undivided attention to it, it is also the case that there are specific objects that appear to capture her devotion more strongly than others. In other words, some objects seem to resonate on a frequency that elicits an intense response. Such objects turn into beads that she admires with passionate concentration.

Milner appears to always be looking for the *punctum* of a natural scene, a piece of art, or a cultural artifact. The *punctum* is a term used by Barthes in the context of photography to describe a tiny detail of a photograph that "pricks" the viewer, taking them by surprise and startling them, because it represents an unexpected tear in the photograph's representational surface, in its *studium*.[41] The *studium* is what the photograph is "about," whereas the *punctum* arrests the viewer's attention in the same way that Milner's special items, objects, moments, and experiences arrest hers. It throws the image slightly off-center, even wounding the viewer, yet in so doing it renders the image more intriguing and poignant. This experience of being "pierced" by items, objects, moments, and experiences is one that Milner avidly seeks.

For instance, in addition to describing the many religious items that she encounters during her trips to Greece, Milner spends a great deal of time on a painting by Seurat, *The Bathing Boys*. The deeper she descends into the world of this painting, the more pleasure she is able to obtain from its details, such as the vacant look on the face of the boy at the center of the painting which reminds her of the wide perception (absent-mindedness) that she herself practices in relation to objects. Her objective is to demonstrate that by paying intense attention to details—such as the fact that the boy's hat resembles a crescent moon—she is able to arrive at a special way of observing things that allows her to experience a bit of sublimity in relation to seemingly commonplace objects. The reward for practicing such intense attention is that the world appears as more scintillating, even extraordinary.

As I have suggested, in Lacanian terms, one could say that Milner is able to appreciate the Thing's aura within mundane objects. Even if the satisfaction offered by objects that appear to contain this aura remains enigmatically undefinable, Milner is unusually skilled at focusing on items, objects, moments, and experiences that emit its magnetic pull. As I have explained, Lacan proposes that when we encounter an object that carries a strong enough trace of the Thing, our desire gets arrested to the point that we are no longer interested in other objects. When this happens, an object that contains a convincing enough residue of the Thing defeats the cruelly optimistic notion that an even better object—perhaps even one that could definitively heal us—might reside somewhere else, with the consequence that we stop looking; instead of chasing new objects, we invest fully in the one that we have already found. To reiterate Lacan's memorable claim, at such moments we honor our own desire rather than the desire of the Other, thereby managing to reacquire some of our dignity as human beings. In other words, when we find an object that truly speaks to our desire, we thwart the cycle of consumption, bypassing the Other's lures and well-disguised traps, including its ploys to keep our desire endlessly mobile. This means that our cruel optimism comes to a halt.

I myself had an experience like this when, during my visit to Vienna, I found in a tiny shop that sold trinkets, three silver rings that I simply loved. These rings summoned me with a mesmerizing force. They were not expensive, and I bought all three without hesitation. Although I am usually careful with what I purchase, cognizant of how consumer capitalism draws us into its net, in this instance there was no question that these rings—which were definitely not mass produced—belonged to me. After I bought them, I immediately knew that they were the last rings I would ever buy for the rest of my life. Over the years leading to this moment, I had seen hundreds of rings, some of which had been fairly similar to the three that I bought. I had even purchased a few along the way. However, there was something so powerfully satisfying about these particular rings that they completely eclipsed all others that are available in the world. In this way, they arrested my desire. Essentially, in acquiring them I raised three insignificant mundane objects—one adorned with a small fake pearl—to the dignity of the Thing. My point, in relation to Milner, is that she managed to court these types of encounters on a consistent basis, rarely by purchasing items but, instead, because she possessed a well-honed capacity to find the right item to admire in the midst of the world's offerings. She was repeatedly able to obtain a slice of sublimity within the confines of her daily life. And she spent her entire life honoring this ability.

MILNER'S BEADS AND
OTHER DELIGHTS

I want to linger on *Eternity's Sunshine* because it expresses perfectly Milner's ability to raise mundane objects to the dignity of the Thing. Indeed, I am struck by how this text, written fifty years after the other two, single-mindedly pursues the same quest for worldly transcendence that the earlier volumes had begun. As I have explained, the text of *Eternity's Sunshine* is organized around metaphorical "beads": items, objects, moments, and experiences that strike Milner as especially weighty, intriguing, or singular. Rhetorically, the beads she names—often details of the natural world, a painting, a sculpture, a religious artifact, or an architectural curiosity—amalgamate the elements of her memoir; gradually, through the unfolding of her text, they form a sequence of delights that she treasures.

Each of Milner's beads provides a response to her question, "What is the most important thing that happened today?" Milner, moreover, explains that the beads act as bridges between different layers of her self, integrating her mind and her body, and knitting together "thinking and feeling, concepts and percepts, reason and imagination."[42] Reading her earlier work in light of her commentary in this text, it is not inaccurate to say that even though she does not use the term *beads* in the earlier volumes, both of them are ultimately a matter of collecting figurative beads, which her writing strings together like a pearl necklace. Each pearl—or bead—representing an item, object, moment, or experience that adds to her art of creative living.

When I think about where I find my beads, I realize that I am less likely than Milner to discover them in works of art or cultural artifacts than in natural details such as the glittering waves on a rocky beach; the ripples on the surface of a lake; the turning leaves in Vermont; a quiet forest; a foggy mountain that looks like a Japanese painting; the lush vineyards of the South of France; or the way that the moon lights up the world with its mysterious glow. The manner in which the full moon illuminates the snow-covered landscape of the Nordic *kaamos*, the darkest time of the year, when there is no (or almost no) daylight, is especially awe-inspiring. In an entirely different setting, the turquoise water and rugged mountain ranges of the Greek islands leave me breathless (whereas, unlike Milner, I do not find the ruins of ancient temples particularly compelling). I am also likely to find my beads in shop windows that display small, often old or old-fashioned items such as jewelry, dishes, vases, or used books. I rarely buy such items, but looking at them brings me a sense of harmony.

I also like wandering the streets of Paris, or another French or Italian city, at dusk and looking through the windows of people's lit apartments, imagining what the lives of those who live in them might be like. When I was younger and penniless, this was a deeply melancholy activity because I felt that the lives of the people who occupied the beautiful apartments were completely unavailable to me. They still are. But now at least I have a home of my own that contains little things that I have collected over the years. Although my style is minimalist, I own an array of meaningful decorative objects that bring charm and calm into my world. I recently even invested in a set of nice dishes, which are a daily pleasure. It may be that I appreciate Milner's attempt to collect her beads so much because I share her gratitude for small mundane things that bring a genuine and enduring satisfaction.

Milner explains that she did not choose the term *beads* randomly, that on a literal level the term refers to clay beads that she made as a child and, after baking them in the sun, painted in bright colors. During the same childish adventure, she also made a small clay pot that she buried overnight in hot ashes. In the morning, she was thrilled to find that the pot had turned from a dirty yellow to a lovely pinkish-red. She reads this as a metaphor for how "out of the ashes comes the transformation."[43]

It might be tempting to interpret this figure of speech to mean that Milner is interested in transcending difficult moments by rising from the ashes like a phoenix, which would bring her uncomfortably close to the neoliberal mentality of overcoming obstacles as quickly as possible. However, a closer look reveals that she is more invested in the idea that it is the act of staying in the ashes—of sitting with one's sorrow, as I phrased the matter in the context of Nietzsche—that may ultimately lead to a rewarding resurrection. After all, her clay pot had to stay buried in hot ashes overnight in order for its dirty yellow hue to turn into a gorgeous pinkish-red. Milner's message thus appears to be that attempting to rush a self-transformation is not the right strategy, that one must allow oneself to dwell within one's despair before one can expect to find one's way onto a less devastating terrain.[44] As she states, "When one's life seems to have gone to dust and ashes, if one can only hold it there, hold the despair and lack of hope, that raging that it ought not to have happened, then there *is* a resurrection, the belief that life could be worth living does return."[45]

In my view, this attitude aligns well with Lacan's claim that the only cure for the subject's constitutive lack is to recognize that there is no cure for it, that it is only when the subject accepts the impossibility of a definitive cure that it can begin to devote its energies to endeavors that have some chance of bringing it (an always partial) satisfaction. The subject cannot acquire the Thing, heal the void within its being, but it can attain the kinds of substitute satisfactions—items, objects, moments, and experiences—that Milner describes. Milner's beads serve as sublimatory antidotes to lack that bring her enough enjoyment (jouissance) to render her life meaningful. Furthermore, because the kinds of sublimatory satisfactions that she is able to obtain are, by definition, temporary—as they are for all of us—she feels that she has to renew her quest for them throughout her life. This is why it is not surprising that there is a seamless sense of continuity between her books from the 1930s and her book from 1987.

As I have emphasized, Milner's beads, for the most part, sidestep the lures of consumer society. In the three texts that I am discussing, the sole indication of her ever having gone in the direction of consumer items is when in *A Life of Her Own*—in which, as the book's title suggests, she is preoccupied with defining her identity—she admits that after draining social engagements she sometimes finds herself so restless, so without an identity of her own, that she feels like a chameleon who adopts the color of her surroundings. During such times, she sometimes wanders around stores looking at clothes until "in the look of some dress"—and once in a pair of red shoes—she discovers her "lost sense of identity" and regains enough of her balance to return to work.[46]

My sense is that, in such situations, Milner's experience in relation to certain dresses is akin to my experience with the three rings that I came across in Vienna: these items arrest her desire, even stabilize her identity, but they do not send her on a shopping spree. As I have established, her quest for rewarding objects is almost exclusively focused on objects that are available for observation, but not for purchase. She clearly spends more time exploring museums, galleries, churches, and Greek ruins, than department stores. Furthermore, she pointedly defies the performance principle. Instead, she embarks on "an experiment in leisure"—of deliberately slowing down her life—as the title of her 1937 book indicates.

The ideal of leisure obviously has important socioeconomic connotations: leisure is one of the things that working-class and poor people lack, and frequently covet. It is clear that Milner is only able to embark on her experiment due to her middle-class status. Yet it is also clear that her definition of leisure differs from the word's colloquial meaning: in "experimenting" with leisure, she is less interested in pursuing a life of repose and luxury than she is in finding a creative alternative to the instrumentalist mindset that measures the worth of people on the basis of what they accomplish (or how fast they work); she seeks ways to evade the performance principle that I have criticized throughout this chapter and that, unfortunately, tends to impact the most diligent, industrious, and conscientious of us the hardest.

Unusually for a woman of her generation, Milner worked for much of her life, first as a psychologist at a girls' school and, after having trained as a psychoanalyst, in private practice. Interestingly, her work gets almost no attention in her texts, nor do her husband and son, whom she only mentions in passing. It feels like her "real" life is lived largely between the written page and the items, objects, moments, and experiences that she relishes. For her, the pleasure she derives from gazing at a tree for so long that she feels united with it, or the satisfaction she obtains from discovering a bead that grants her a sense of worldly transcendence, is more important than her job performance. At least, she does not feel moved to write about her work in her diary.

Milner dynamically and consistently resists collective definitions of what the good life consists of. Like Lacan, she wishes to sidestep the Other's desire in order to determine her own, to ensure that she does not allow the Other to dictate her interests, passions, or activities. To put the matter differently, Milner is uncommonly invested in the truth of her desire. She explicitly aspires to remain loyal to her own idiosyncratic desire, not wanting to be guided by forms of desire that her social environment, including consumer capitalism, strives to impose on her. Indeed, one reason that she starts to keep the journal that eventually culminates in *A Life of One's Own* is that she realizes that she is too dependent on the opinions of others. Moreover, she judges herself to be too easily distracted, with too many goals and too little focus. As she explains, she finds herself "drifting without rudder or compass, swept in all directions by influence from custom, tradition, fashion" and "swayed by standards uncritically accepted" by her friends, family, compatriots, and ancestors.[47] This is why she begins to pay attention to what she truly wants.

In this context, it may be important to distinguish between the hegemonic Other—the dominant symbolic order—and intimate, trusted others. Milner goes quite far in rejecting even the latter, in rejecting the opinions of her friends, family,

compatriots, and ancestors, thereby making it sound like relationality as such is a problem for her. There may be a kernel of
truth to this in the sense that Milner is not merely bothered by
the Other's abstract demands but also by the demands that
those who are personally close to her make. She discloses that
sometimes the presence of even those she loves or appreciates
can derail her creative process. She admits that her forays into
solitary activities of creativity and sublimation sometimes,
after the fact, render her more open to her intimate others—
that her withdrawal to her own world in some cases feeds her
overall ability for relationality. Yet, ultimately, she goes further than any contemporary thinker that I know in valorizing
solitary activities without feeling apologetic about privileging
them over more relational undertakings. While she is not a
hermit—she is, after all, married and works in a highly social
profession—she openly appreciates the lifestyle of hermits
(more on this later) and, in many ways, reaches as far as she
can toward self-isolation within the confines of her social and
relational responsibilities. There is a welcome honesty about
her admission that the pursuit of sublimity is, for her, usually
a solitary activity.

Furthermore, it is interesting that Milner exhibits that same
burning desire to avoid social compliance at the age of eighty-
seven as she did as a young woman. In *Eternity's Sunshine*, she
confirms that she wants to limit her activities, to choose her
interests carefully, because she does not want to squander her
energies by imitating others. She wishes to reserve her vitality
for undertakings that she experiences as genuinely hers. In this
sense, Milner was a pioneering thinker who spent her entire
adult life trying to figure out how best to fend off collective
desires so as to determine the truth of her own desire and stay
faithful to that desire.

For Lacan, the truth of the subject's desire is connected to the Thing, the idea being that the type of idiosyncratic desire that fixates on objects that convey the Thing's luminous aura—and therefore generate a greater degree of jouissance than more ordinary objects—is more truthful than the type of generic desire that follows the directives of the Other. This implies that the subject's idiosyncratic, truthful desire is intrinsically disruptive to the dominant social order: inasmuch as it merges with jouissance, it automatically defies the Other's edicts. To be sure, it is not as overtly rebellious as pure jouissance—the utter unruliness of the drives—would be, but it nevertheless diverges from the Other's desire by bringing the subject within striking distance of the Thing. Indeed, if this genre of desire interests me, it is because it connects the subject to the singularity of its desire—and thus of its being—without resulting in the kind of self-annihilation that jouissance, in its unmediated form, would produce. It is closer to Kristeva's ideal of intimate revolt as a matter of a sublimatory reworking of psychic and affective material than to the complete collapse of social intelligibility that Lacanians such as Slavoj Žižek and Lee Edelman have advocated.[48] I do not think that it would be unreasonable to suggest that Milner's relationship to her desire is a matter of a continual intimate revolt.

Intimate revolt is more difficult to adhere to than following collectively established pathways of living because it asks the subject to reach beneath its socially intelligible façade to the primordial drive energies that connect it to the Thing; it asks the subject to sidestep its ego in order to mobilize a portion of the jouissance that animates its being. If, under normal conditions, the ego generates the kind of psychic and affective coherence that allows the subject to integrate itself into the rhythm of collective life, the eruption of jouissance represents a disruption of this coherence. This is why the Other and jouissance pull the subject in opposite directions. It is also why many people flee from the singularity of their desire, for accessing this singularity cannot be dissociated from the risk of falling into the vortex of jouissance. Yet, for Milner, as for Lacan, the emergence of the truth of the subject's desire—which is in many ways synonymous with the unique truthfulness of its being—requires jouissance, however temporarily, to triumph over the Other's injunctions.

Moments when the ego is neutralized in this manner have a special intensity to them. This intensity is what Milner pursues through sublimatory activities. More specifically, writing, along with wide perception and other meditative activities that allow her to experience the world in an unmediated manner, becomes an essential instrument of creative living for her. It is in fact directly aligned with what may be her most significant finding; namely, that in order to feel fully alive, she needs to learn to surrender herself, to let go of all attempts to control things. This is merely a different way of saying that she discovers that the precondition of creative living is the ability to push her ego aside so as to access the primordial energies that percolate in the chaos beneath it.

SIDESTEPPING THE EGO

One of the most consistent themes of Milner's poetics of being is her conviction that the ego interferes with our ability to lead a creative life. The ego functions as the interface between our inner world and the outside world, which means that it serves as the conduit through which the messages of the outside world reach our psyches. For this reason, the ego is among the most socially compliant parts of our being in the sense that it tethers us to collective dictates of acceptable, normative behavior. As I have demonstrated, what makes Milner so successful in her quest for creative living is that she recognizes that such living requires her to (temporarily) neutralize, or at least marginalize, her ego so as to evade the social filters that usually mediate our relationship to the world. In this manner, Milner gains a relatively unmediated access to the items, objects, moments, and experiences that bring her the meaningfulness that she values.

The psychic, affective, and physical states that Milner aligns with creative living militate against the ego's need to stay in control. Indeed, I have resorted to the Lacanian notion of raising a mundane object to the dignity of the Thing to capture the gist of Milner's sublimatory practice because I see Milner as reasoning along the same lines as Lacan does. If Lacan posits that the Thing—and the jouissance that connects the subject to the aura of the Thing—and the ego are intrinsically antithetical to each other, Milner suggests that unmediated experience—which is also ultimately a matter of jouissance—and the ego are mutually exclusive. That is, if the Lacanian Thing can only be approached through jouissance, Milner's wide perception and worldly transcendence also draw the subject close to jouissance, which carries not merely destructive but also revitalizing, replenishing energies. For both thinkers, sublimatory activities require these revitalizing and replenishing energies, which means that they also entail some of the destructive side of jouissance; the subject, in short, cannot access the enlivening side of jouissance without simultaneously risking some of its derailing aspects. From a slightly different perspective, one could say that sublimation ushers the subject into what Lacan calls the *real*: the domain of unruly bodily energies that, among other things, function as the dwelling place of the Thing. The real, in turn, eludes the Other's control, which is exactly what Milner most seeks in the context of her ethos of creative living.

The Other, as I have noted, is synonymous with the collective symbolic order within which we strive to find our bearings. Lacan suggests that creativity arises when the jouissance of the real is able to nudge the symbolic order into fresh significatory practices, such as literary, artistic, political, or scientific innovations.[49] Creativity, in short, emerges when jouissance manages to reanimate the signifying chains upon which the Other relies for the production of collective meanings. One can visualize this concretely as a matter of a specific signifying chain dipping itself into the nebulous realm of the real in order to revive its imaginative aptitude. One can also visualize it in terms of signifiers and the real commingling in ways that allow signifiers to replenish themselves. Sometimes I even picture tiny morsels of jouissance latching themselves onto the underbellies of select signifiers so as to give them the kind of boost that enables them to resuscitate the domain of signification.

My point is that without the steady input of the energies of the real, signifiers would quickly become anemic, unable to generate anything new; they would lose their vitality and capacity for creative transformation. If this were to happen, the entire symbolic order would become equally uninventive, losing its capacity to renew itself, to give birth to new versions of itself, including its reality principle. Were this to happen, the Other would become the static, ahistorical entity that some of Lacan's critics mistakenly claim it to be.[50] Fortunately, we have not yet reached a world in which the jouissance of the real is not able to rejuvenate the symbolic.

The capacity of jouissance to infiltrate every system of signification, every paradigm of meaning production, ensures that the symbolic order keeps reinventing itself. The same applies to individuals. None of us can engage in any kind of a poetics of self-fashioning without the revitalizing impact of jouissance—without the very force that distances us from our socially intelligible image. As Milner stresses, unless we are willing to let go of our preoccupation with this image, with what others think of us, "there will be no new beginning, no freeing from the old prisoning rigidities, no spring-timbre renewal."[51] More specifically, as Milner recognizes, being able to dissociate ourselves from the Other in this manner demands our willingness to surrender our ego; it demands our willingness to fall into the amorphous domain of jouissance, beyond both our ego and the symbolic order that this ego answers to.

For Milner, the ego is mostly a nuisance to be outwitted so as to create an opening for the transcendent experiences that she is after. She therefore spends a great deal of time trying to figure out how to evade it, reaching the conclusion that the best way to accomplish this goal is to surrender herself to what, in Lacanian terms, we could call the jouissance of the real, but what Milner herself calls her "private sea of being."[52] This private sea is an oceanic, watery, and at times even swampy space beneath her ego that is populated by water reeds and "the swaying weeds" of her body's "inner darkness."[53] Milner's private sea is therefore, first and foremost, a murky and mysterious place—certainly not the kind of place that first jumps to mind when we think of sublime, transcendent experiences.

Interestingly, although the unconscious is important to Milner as a psychoanalytic thinker, she tends to focus more on her ability to fall into bodily, jouissance-filled modes of experience than on the unconscious, per se. Creative living, for Milner, is strongly associated with the kinds of unmediated bodily experiences that she can only access by pushing aside her ego. She, furthermore, repeatedly claims that whenever she dives into her private sea, she finds herself guided by what she calls the *other* or *not-me* within herself. She is convinced that this other or not-me knows more about the truth of her desire than her ego does. As a result, she abandons ego-bound logical reasoning and instead waits for the raw materials for her creative activities to arise from amid the reeds and weeds of her private sea.

Milner thus builds a personal mythic universe that is directly opposed to mass-produced mythologies, asserting that in order to discover "what one really really is," one has to "stop being pre-occupied with what one is supposed to be, would like to be, is expected to be."[54] In short, creative self-fashioning only becomes possible when one abandons one's ties to collective injunctions and allows the other or not-self within oneself to direct one's actions. Somewhat counterintuitively, Milner concludes that the only way to live authentically is to allow herself to be sustained by the enigmatic force by which she "is lived."[55] While the neo-liberal subject of self-optimization strives to control the contours of its destiny, Milner's surrenders herself, including her destiny, to the impenetrable alterity within her being. She renounces her controlling ego, yielding to a state of absentmindedness—and recall that absentmindedness is also at the heart of her wide per-ception—in order to fuse the fragments of her interiority into novel patterns without having any sense, ahead of time, regard-ing what these patterns might look like.

For Milner, self-surrender to the extent of absenting herself from her consciousness therefore serves as a means of self-reinvention. This vision, which shares some characteristics with Kristeva's intimate revolt as a form of rotation, reversion, and reinvention, but which also seems more extreme than Kristeva's revisionary model, is arguably the furthest one can get from the neoliberal subject of performance, productivity, cheerfulness, and self-optimization. For Milner, self-loss rather than self-promotion facilitates creative living. She hypothesizes that it is through the admission of her utter powerlessness that she reaches the possibility of creativity.

In a Lacanian vein, the freeing of the imagination from the shackles of the ego, for Milner, entails an "acceptance of emptiness."[56] As she explains, one has to denounce the illusion of power that knowledge grants in order to accept a blankness—the futility of all effort and striving—and to think, "'I leave it to you.'"[57] According to her, "The inescapable condition of true expression" is "the plunge into the abyss," "the willingness to recognize that the moment of blankness and extinction" is "the moment of incipient fruitfulness, the moment without which the invisible forces within could not do their work."[58] More specifically, Milner's creative self must be willing "to risk letting go the solid ground" and "to leap into the unknown."[59] At the core of Milner's vision is, thus, ego-dissolution: the self's complete capitulation of its ego-bound allegiances to the world and its surrender to the other or not-me within itself.

Milner realizes that her purpose, ultimately, is to have no purpose. Not willing to be guided by the crowd, by social convention, or by questions of practicality—and increasingly wondering why she is driven to get things done or obtain things in the first place—she wants to allow her desire to "roam unfettered by purposes."[60] This, in turn, leads her to the realization that instead of grasping, striving, and allowing herself to be guided by her ambitions, by her ideals of achievement, she needs to relax all her exertions. She in fact claims that she is only able to obtain worldly transcendence if she abandons "clinging to assertive aims, purposes, wanting things" and, instead, allows herself to "sink right down inside to the bottom of things."[61] Only in this manner is she able to resurface from the experience "truly refreshed and ready for renewed, enriched contact and interchange."[62]

Speaking of writing, Milner declares that she must accept not only emptiness but also depression before she can "begin to raise the inner fires of concentration" necessary for the task, concluding as follows: "if I accept this futility, give up my purpose to write . . . just sit still and feel myself to be no good— then the crystallization begins—after the corruption, blackness, despair."[63] At first glance, this may appear like a disturbingly masochistic approach to creativity. Yet, for Milner at least, it leads to joy and the ability to write. She explains that whenever she feels her anxiety rise in relation to writing, whenever she is flooded by the fear of not being up to the task, she undertakes "a ritual sacrifice" of all her strategies and designs: instead of trying harder, she recites to herself, " 'I'm nothing; I know nothing; I want nothing,' " with the result that her anxiety dissipates, leaving her calm and happy.[64] She reports that, during such moments, her mind begins, as if entirely independently of her, to generate productive ideas. By deliberately surrendering her ego, she creates space for ideas to emerge from the other or not-me within her which lies in wait beneath her ego, looking for a chance to express itself.

Surrendering her ego therefore allows Milner to activate her creative abilities without any exertion. Like the muses of yesteryear, the other or not-me within her takes possession and mysteriously grants her the capacity to write. Gradually, Milner learns to trust the power of this other or not-me, which she sometimes calls "the answering activity," noting that "the main paradox" of her discoveries is that the price of drawing on the answering activity as a source of creativity and living wisdom is that she "must want nothing from it."[65] She must turn to this other or not-me expecting nothing and "wanting to change nothing."[66] It is only then that she receives "those illuminating flashes" that are essential in shaping her life.[67] Hence, a high degree of humility appears to be the precondition of freeing "the imagination from the dominance of the ego."[68]

Milner's rhetorical register is much more mystical than that of Lacan, but he and she appear to be working with the same basic idea, namely that out of emptiness arises creativity, even a kind of renewal or rebirth. In this sense, it is only insofar as there is lack that there is even the possibility of creativity. Milner goes as far as to suggest that those who wish to experience a metamorphosis "must periodically go through the Valley of Humiliation, must deliberately lose the sense of their own identity."[69] As she sums up her perspective, "it is only through the loss of power, the destruction of the striving, that the artist can emerge."[70] She concludes as follows: "the artist must surrender to darkness in order to elude the ego's drive to mastery."[71] Being an artist, then, demands "continual self-sacrifice, continual extinction of the personality": "it is only by demolishing the ego, by shattering what Winnicott would call the false self, that we can fathom the sources of our being and embark upon the art of life."[72]

WINNICOTT ON TRUE
AND FALSE SELVES

Given that Milner explicitly equates the "continual extinction of the personality"—the kind of demolition of the ego that for her is the precondition of creativity—with the shattering of what Winnicott calls the *false self*, it seems worth making a brief detour through some of Winnicott's main ideas, especially ones that pertain to his famous distinction between true and false selves. I touch on some of the same concepts as Gail discusses in her chapter, but I limit myself to ones that are directly related to Milner's ideas. I drafted my commentary on Winnicott before I read Gail's chapter, which means that there is no intentional attempt to align our insights with each other. Nevertheless, some overlap is unavoidable. However, I paint with the kinds of broad strokes that I hope will function as a preface to Gail's more detailed interpretations. Ideally, our discussions complement each other in productive ways.

Winnicott's distinction between true and false selves communicates the difference between a creative self—a self that actively participates in its poetics of being—and a socially compliant self that defends itself against the world's harshness by forming a façade, a carapace of sorts, around its vulnerable core. For the purposes of my argument, Winnicott's notion of the false self can be aligned with the narcissistic posturing of neoliberal self-optimization. That said, it is important to specify that even though this way of defining the false self may seem to suggest that the true self is intrinsically desirable, and the false self is intrinsically deplorable, Winnicott's theory renders the matter much more complicated. For example, although the true self is what Winnicott, like Milner, would like to see materialize, there are times when Winnicott presents the false self as being indispensable in ensuring the true self's survival: simply put, without the false self, the true self might have little chance of ever emerging. Furthermore, Winnicott maintains that no subject is ever comprised solely of true or false components. Rather, both components reside in the self simultaneously, so that what determines its overall tenor is the relative prominence of true and false elements at any particular moment in its life.

In addition, in the same way as the erasure of the ego for Milner is always a temporary state of affairs, it is possible to argue that the Winnicottian false self can never be definitively erased. At the same time, the true self is equally tenacious in the sense that Winnicott proposes that regardless of how dire the subject's circumstances may seem, the true self dwells within its being as a potentiality that is waiting for an opportunity to express itself. I will return to these complexities shortly. For now, suffice it to say that the caricature of the true self is that it is filled with vitality and creative energy and the caricature of the false self is that it is rigid and defensive; while the true self feels real and alive, the false self feels fake and numb, as if it were merely going through the motions of living.

Winnicott defines creativity as a matter of "coloring of the whole attitude toward external reality," specifying that he hopes that the "reader will accept a general reference to creativity, not letting the word get lost in the successful or acclaimed creation."[73] Creativity, in other words, is "a feature of life and total living."[74] Indeed, because creative living is not equivalent to being a successful artist, even artists who are highly acclaimed may experience a failure "in the field of general creative living," for the creative self is not necessarily always "to be found in what is made out of products of body and mind, however valuable these constructs may be in terms of beauty, skill, and impact."[75] Winnicott therefore envisions creativity in the same capacious way as Milner and I do: as an all-encompassing vitality that motivates the subject's open and curious relationship to the world. As a consequence, Winnicott notes that "a creation can be a picture or a house or a garden or a costume or a hairstyle or a symphony or a sculpture; anything from a meal cooked at home."[76] As he concludes, "The creativity that concerns me . . . is universal. It belongs to being alive."[77] This is exactly the definition of creativity that I am working with in this chapter: creativity is a matter of feeling alive, whether one is engaged in solitary activities or interacting with others. Winnicott in fact maintains that creativity encompasses the entirety of the subject's personality, so that a "link can be made, and usefully made, between creative living and living itself."[78]

Creativity is hence the antithesis of the kind of social compliance that tends to characterize the false self even if this self
cannot be reduced to such compliance. Social compliance,
Winnicott claims, generates a feeling of futility: it "is associated
with the idea that nothing matters and that life is not worth
living."[79] "In a tantalizing way," Winnicott continues, "many
individuals have experienced just enough of creative living to
recognize that for most of their time they are living uncre-
atively, as if caught up in the creativity of someone else, or of a
machine."[80] Such individuals find themselves in an especially
aggravating predicament: they have gotten a taste of creative
living, so that in principle they know what they are looking for,
but they are not able to attain their goal, which only alienates
them further from creativity and therefore from the kind of life
that they would like to lead.

If some people struggle to attain the spark of creative living,
others may lose their spark, so that the sense that their life is
real and worth living tragically disappears. I have already talked
about people whose circumstances prevent them from pursuing
the kinds of lives that they would like to live. However, there
are also those whose circumstances shift for the worse—who,
for instance, lose something precious, such as their health, job,
or a loved person. In such cases, it is hardly surprising if their
catalyst for creative living begins to wane. Moreover, this can
happen for entirely enigmatic, undefinable reasons.

There are countless reasons—some collective, others
personal—for why people may, either momentarily or for long
periods of time, find it impossible to cultivate their true self.
Some may even find it impossible to *ever* reach the kind of inner
vitality that the true self implies: maybe they live in war-torn
areas where survival is their only concern; maybe they are too
hungry, overworked, or oppressed to be able to even consider

what a creative life might entail; or maybe they grow up in abusive families that force them into defensive modalities of being. Others may be struck by a catastrophic event, such as a terminal illness or the death of a loved person, that extinguishes the liveliness that they once felt and cherished.

In the former examples, the individuals in question may, however vaguely, have yearned for a psychic and affective vitality but have never been able to attain it. In the latter examples, in contrast, the subject has lost an aliveness that it might have assumed nothing would ever quench. Both scenarios may entail deep depression: those who have never had a chance to cultivate a true self mourn what eludes them; those who have lost a vibrant self mourn what they once had but can never recover; they mourn a future that could have been, should have been, and might have been if things had turned out differently. What is more, the sad fact is that although there may occasionally be miraculous reversals of fortune that allow individuals to overcome their predicament, in many cases, their grim assessment of their situation is perfectly realistic.

This alone is sufficient cause for desolation. However, things are made even worse by the fact that the contours of what has been lost (or never gained in the first place) often remain to some extent enigmatic. As Freud hypothesized, persistent melancholia tends to arise when the individual has some sense of what they have lost but cannot fully grasp the implications or ramifications of their loss, including what their life might have been like without the loss in question.[81] This is exactly the predicament of the subject who has some sense of the fact that it has never been able to give expression to its true self or who has lost its ability to do so. Such a subject knows that it is missing something precious, but it does not know exactly what kinds of potentialities of being it has lost; it does not know the particulars of what its life might have been like if its circumstances had been more conducive to the thriving of its true self. This creates a situation where chronic melancholia, in the quintessentially Freudian sense, is virtually impossible to avoid.

There are therefore many circumstances that impede the flow of the kind of vitalizing energy that the true self thrives on. Yet Winnicott suggests that no matter how dreadful the subject's predicament may be, its desire for the true self can never be entirely extinguished. Its capacity to obtain a dynamic, spirited form of life may be blocked, but its desire for such a life cannot be wholly demolished. Although Winnicott admits that there are environmental factors—both structural and personal—that can prevent a given subject's entry into creative living, he speculates that no matter how badly the subject's life has been mutilated, "one has to allow for the possibility that there cannot be a complete destruction of a human individual's capacity for creative living and that, even in the most extreme cases of compliance and the establishment of a false personality, hidden away somewhere there exists a secret life that is satisfactory because of its being creative or original to that human being."[82] In other words, regardless of how drastically the subject's life has been damaged, and regardless of how seamlessly its false self has taken over and dominates its life, its aptitude for creative living nevertheless persists as a concealed potentiality.

Winnicott thus suggests that even though the subject may be bruised, injured, or utterly broken—and even though it may be forced to live under oppressive circumstances where it has no choice but to bend to the will of others—its potential for creative living nonetheless persists. The yearning for creative living may be eclipsed by arduous circumstances to the point that it is no longer discernible even to the subject itself, but its embers keep smoldering somewhere deep within its being. Admittedly, it is not hard to imagine scenarios where the subject's situation is so catastrophic that the true self, even as a potentiality, is lost. However, if it indeed is the case that the existence of this potentiality can become hidden even for the subject itself, there is no way to definitively prove the matter either way.

Winnicott acknowledges that in severe cases, when all that is real, creative, and original about the self remains concealed, giving no sign of existing, the subject may not care whether it is dead or alive. In such scenarios, the subject may undergo an experience of disintegration—a concept that, for reasons that will become clear shortly, needs to be carefully distinguished from unintegration. Simply put, if unintegration is the infant's original state of being—its condition of jouissance prior to the establishment of the rudiments of its ego—disintegration entails damage to this very ego. For example, disintegration (even a psychotic break) may be the final resort of subjects who have no other way to cope with extreme trauma—who have no other way out. More commonly, disintegration in much less drastic forms refers to the kind of erosion of the ego that Milner advocates.

Subjective disintegration, in the sense that Milner promotes it, can only take place after a sufficient degree of integration, a sufficient degree of ego strength, has been achieved; simply put, people who do not have an ego to begin with cannot even imagine surrendering it in the manner that Milner endorses. That said, one reason that children are capable of playing in ways that most adults are not, is precisely that their egos have not yet become fully integrated. This makes it easier to understand why Milner regards the ego as an enemy of imaginative activity: after ego-integration has taken place, it takes some effort to undo the impediments that it generates for the subject's ability to access the kinds of energies—now trapped beneath the ego—that allow children to play freely. In some ways, the creative adult must be able to regain some of the capacity for play that children automatically possess. On a basic level, this is what Milner is getting at with her rhetoric of ego-dissolution, plunging into the abyss, accessing her private sea, and allowing herself to be lived by the other or not-me within. All of this is a matter of peeling off the layers of impediments that ego-integration has created between the self and its creative energies (jouissance).

At the same time, a degree of ego-integration is necessary for the child to grow into a socially functioning adult. Milner is not interested in this part of the picture because she, like Lacan, regards the ego primarily as an obstacle to creative living. As is the case for Lacan, the ego for Milner represents everything that is false and unimaginative about the self. Winnicott, in contrast, acknowledges the importance of the ego—and even the possibility that it may, in some circumstances, be necessary for the ego to congeal into a false self—because even though he is invested in the ideal of the creative self, he is also realistic about the kinds of demands that the external world imposes on all of us. The fact is that those who have not gained sufficient ego strength, or whose egos have been brutalized by structural or personal tragedies remain, in practical terms, further from the possibility of ever gaining access to creative living than those whose egos have had a chance to crystallize. I will return to this theme shortly. For now, let me merely say that one of the main weaknesses of Milner's model, like that of Lacan, is that neither is willing to consider the fact that ego-integration—the child's ability to move from a state of unintegration to a state of relative integration—is a precondition of ego-disintegration and therefore of creative living.

For the child, the path from unintegration to integration takes place through what Winnicott famously calls *transitional objects*—intimate objects that establish a bridge between the child's inner world and the external world. Such objects connect the child to the outside world at the same time as they also separate it from this very world by offering a rudimentary point of reference for what is no longer a part of the self. In other words, transitional objects link the child's inner world with the outside world at the same time as they tentatively signal to the child that it needs to distinguish between itself and the rest of the world. Typically, transitional objects are everyday objects that infants and children like to play with, such as blankets, teddy bears, dolls, and other toys. In the treacherous path from unintegration to integration, where the possibility of sliding backward is always present, transitional objects play an important role, gradually allowing the child to "transition" from its solipsistic inner world of hallucinatory sensations to a world of tangible external objects. It is only when this transition has been successfully negotiated, when a degree of integration has been achieved, that the child can be said to have an ego in the sense that it recognizes itself as separate from its surroundings, even if it also obviously stays connected to these surroundings.

Although adult subjects possess a greater degree of ego-integration than children, this integration, as I have stressed, can get threatened by debilitating conditions or serious traumas. When this happens, the subject may, somewhat counterintuitively, resort to disintegration as a defense against utter unintegration because in a state of disintegration, the state of reintegration remains a possibility: integration hovers in the background as something that can eventually be regained. Unintegration, in contrast, would signify a fall to the utter infantile helplessness of the newborn child who has not yet experienced any degree of ego-integration. From such a state, there is no coming back without the help of a supportive environment akin to the one that sustains the infant during the first weeks of its life.

Although a degree of integration is necessary for the subject's ability to function in its quotidian life, Winnicott suggests that the false self suffers from excessive integration: its contours have congealed into unnecessarily rigid, banal, and predictable patterns, with the consequence that it is no longer capable of the kind of elasticity and flexibility that makes creative living possible. Winnicott specifies that those who operate primarily on the level of the false self may be able to successfully imagine and emulate the characteristics of the true self, which means that they may appear convincingly authentic and multidimensional to other people. However, they tend to lose their credibility in emotionally complicated situations that require the participation of the whole person, that demand a high degree of psychic and affective dexterity. In such situations, the façade of the false self begins to crack, and others are able to perceive the self's lack of psychic and affective aliveness.

In this context, I want to stress that I do not believe that being unable to appear full of life—conventionally "vivacious"—in social settings invariably renders a self "false." After all, there are plenty of introverted people with rich inner lives whom others interpret as boring or uninteresting. Yet such individuals may be full of creative energy. Indeed, for some creative individuals, withdrawal from the world—a certain "deadness" to the world—is a precondition of their ability to write books, produce works of art, compose songs, design buildings, or perform other genres of solitary creative labor. This, I would guess, is exactly what Milner is getting at with her image of plunging into her private sea. She does not valorize social gregariousness as much as the self's ability to escape the demands of such gregariousness in order to withdraw into a world of its own making where creativity has a chance to flourish. Likewise, while it may be tempting to translate some of Winnicott's statements regarding the true self into the idea that the self needs to display a high degree of aliveness to the world to qualify as true—and that a self that is incapable of doing so is inherently false—I believe that when Winnicott refers to the self's aliveness, along with its creativity, he—like Milner—means to capture something about the self's private inner experience: a person who appears effervescent to others may feel numb inside in ways that impede true self experiences. As a result, vibrancy in social settings is not an effective measure of the self's authenticity.

Conversely, Winnicott invites us to conclude that there may be individuals who manage to live their entire lives with convincing false selves without being "discovered" by the outside world but who themselves feel like they have never really begun to live. For example, it is possible for an individual to present a compelling version of the self that appears multifaceted but that in reality hides a debilitating split between the mind and the body. Such a self may never be able to achieve the kind of inner vitality that, for both Winnicott and Milner, constitutes the hallmark of the true self. Yet if Winnicott is correct in suggesting that the desire for the true self cannot ever be definitively destroyed, it may be that in the same way that the subject longs for wholeness—which is unattainable—it also longs for "truthfulness" which, while in principle attainable, remains elusive if it cannot find a way to activate it.

The Winnicottian true self integrates the psyche and the body into a unified psychosomatic entity. In contrast, in the false self of a subject who, for instance, chooses to cultivate its intellect over all other aspects of its being, the mind becomes detached not only from its body but also from the rest of its psyche—it being the case that the psyche is never merely a matter of intellectual capacity—so that the mind begins to function as a rationally elevated yet psychically and affectively impoverished entity. This may lead to uncommonly high levels of intellectual performance at the same time as the subject in question feels phony.[83] For all its achievements, it may feel that it lacks creativity and originality. This may be why Milner places such a strong emphasis on bodily and affective experience. In Western instrumentalist societies, the intellect tends to be valorized over the body and the affects, with the result that if the self is to achieve the kind of integration that both Winnicott and Milner seek, it is the body and the affects, specifically, that need to be rescued and given expression.

I want to specify that I am not interested in moralizing about people who develop their brains over other aspects of their being because there are forms of intellectual achievement—which I see as being distinct from the performance principle of neoliberal societies—that demand such a single-minded focus. The "overdevelopment" of the intellect, per se, is not a problem. It only becomes one if it leads the person who possesses such an intellect to feel despondent or devoid of purpose. Likewise, a dancer or other athlete may focus almost exclusively on training their body without this necessarily leading to any forlorn feelings about the overall shape of their lives. In such cases, I would not want to claim that the individuals in question possess a false self. It seems to me that any version of the self that *feels* true, in fact *is* true. Conversely, I can imagine a self that seems genuinely multidimensional but does not feel satisfied with itself. Such a self would be closer to the false self than the one who has wholeheartedly and contently invested in its intellect or body. In this sense, the distinction between the true and false selves may be entirely relative, contingent on how the subject itself experiences its life.

Winnicott connects the true self to the aliveness of the subject's basic bodily functions, such as its breathing.[84] Those who feel constricted in their breathing, and consequently in the movement of their bodies, may spend their entire lives feeling dissociated from their surroundings, their spontaneity, and their creativity. Some individuals may never realize that there might be more rewarding ways to live. Some may recognize that something is off but are not able to get past passively observing their lives. Others—as I have underscored—have little choice but to reconcile themselves to their situation due to debilitating circumstances, such as social inequalities. Yet others seek various ways, including therapy or analysis, to activate their true self, which they sense as a potentiality within themselves but which they have not been able to experience as a tangible entity. Even if those in the last category are not always able to articulate this explicitly, they are yearning for a more imaginative mode of living: they want to feel more connected both to themselves and to the surrounding world (by which I do not necessarily mean the social world). They are seeking the kind of depth of experience that Milner is able to obtain through her wide perception, meditative self-examination, and ultimately ego-dissolution and self-surrender.

I mentioned from the get-go that Winnicott's distinction between the true and false selves appears more clear-cut than it actually is. On the surface, while the true self grasps and respects the truth of its desire, the false self allows its desire to be dictated by the outside world, such as neoliberal culture, consumer capitalism, and even those it is intimately associated with, such as its family and friends; the false self is woefully out of touch with its own interiority and consequently complies with the expectations of the external world. However, as I have indicated, this rendering of the false self is complicated by the fact that Winnicott specifies that it is often the task of this self to protect the true self from external meddling, interference, and intrusive impingement. That is, the false self defends the potentiality for

the true self that the subject possesses but that has, for one reason or another, gotten thwarted.

Because Winnicott conceptualizes the true self as a potentiality, it is difficult to grasp it as anything but an absence.[85] As
Winnicott himself states, "There is but little point in formulat-
ing a True Self idea except for the purpose of trying to understand the False Self, because it does no more than collect together
the details of the experience of aliveness."[86] The reasons for the
true self's "experience of aliveness" being obstructed may include
external hardships such as the social inequalities that I keep calling attention to, because I believe that they play a larger role in
the subject's (psychic) life than Winnicott, Milner, or Lacan
acknowledge. Alternatively, as I have also noted, they may
include personal or interpersonal traumas that the subject experiences as damaging and that consequently send its true self into
hiding. In both of these situations, the true self exists as a concealed entity that the false self does its best to protect. The false
self itself may not possess any spontaneity, but it uses compliance with the outside world as a means of safeguarding the spontaneity of the true self—a spontaneity that might be annihilated
if it were discovered by aggressive, hostile—or impinging—
external forces.[87]

Fortunately, the more robust the true self gets, the harder its
spontaneity is to annihilate in any definitive manner. In other
words, the more strength the true self gains, the better the subject is able to tolerate temporary false self states or interruptions
to its authenticity.[88] This means that the subject is able to choose
its battles, essentially allowing the false self to play its compliant role in circumstances where the stakes are not terribly high.
It is not bothered by passing interruptions to its realness because
it knows that when it is confronted with something that really
matters, it will be resilient enough to resist the compliance that

the collective world demands. As Winnicott specifies, for the true self "compromise ceases to become allowable when the issues become crucial."[89] When asked to cooperate with the Other in situations of genuine significance, the true self pulls the emergency brake by refusing to obey; despite its willingness to endure a degree of social conformity in trivial quotidian scenarios, it is nonetheless primarily a creative self that is unwilling to sacrifice its spontaneity whenever it is confronted with a situation where loyalty to its idiosyncratic desire feels essential.

Ideally, the true self acquires enough strength to exhibit this type of courage whenever its spontaneity is threatened by external influences. When it is sufficiently supple, it interacts with the world without the kind of paranoid self-awareness and self-judgement that weighs down the false self. However, more often than not, its capacity for spontaneous self-expression remains more tenuous than this. This is why Winnicott expresses a great deal of appreciation for the protective role that the false self plays in the preservation of the true self's vitality. Although he would obviously like to see the true self gain prominence over the false self—which is not the same thing as saying that he wants the true self to obliterate the false self, for this would be impossible, given that both components of the self are intrinsic to the subject's constitution—he recognizes that compromises are inevitable. Perhaps most importantly, it is the responsibility of the false self to ensure that the true self does not get forcefully or prematurely exposed or drawn out of its hiding place.

THE RIGHT NOT TO COMMUNICATE

In this context, Winnicott connects the true self to what he describes as the noncommunicating core of the self. This core

contains what is most vulnerable yet also potentially most creative about the self. Although this core seeks expression as the
heart of the true self, it must, as Winnicott asserts, retain "the
right not to communicate"—to not be found.[90] As he observes,
"At the centre of each person is an incommunicado element, and
this is sacred and most worthy of preservation."[91] This element,
he concludes, "should never be communicated with or be influenced by external reality."[92] In other words, although the noncommunicating core communicates with the subject's internal
reality—with what Winnicott depicts as its "subjective
objects"[93]— it should never be compelled to communicate with
the outside world because, as Winnicott summarizes, such communication "easily becomes linked with some degree of false or
compliant object-relating."[94]

On the one hand, Winnicott links subjective objects to the
child's preverbal, primordial experience of bodily aliveness—an
experience that precedes the emergence of the ego—and admits
that the child's adaptation to its society's reality principle entails
a gradual shift from such objects to ones that are objectively
present. As we have seen, it is the task of transitional objects to
facilitate this process of adaptation. On the other hand, Winnicott suggests that it may be advantageous for individuals oriented
around creative activities to retain a relationship to a private
world of meaning that is reminiscent of the subjective objects of
early childhood. I have already noted that it is usually easier for
children than for adults to play, and that creative adults consequently need to find a means to replicate the way in which children relate to the preverbal energies of their being—to their jouissance, if you will. In this sense, creativity—in this case perhaps
less creative living in the broad sense than creativity in a more
narrow sense, although the issue is not irrelevant to creative living either—may necessitate a regression to rudimentary modes of

psychic life that have not yet fully cohered into the kinds of ego-centered structures that characterize much of adult psychic experience.

The subject's noncommunicating core retains a relationship to its subjective objects, to the kind of private sea that Milner describes. On the one hand, it is impossible for any subject to exist without ever communicating with the external world, nor is this Winnicott's goal, for a complete unwillingness to communicate effectively shuts down any possibility of the true self to reveal itself (and in extreme cases results in autism). On the other hand, it is clear that Winnicott believes that forcing the self to communicate with the outside world when it does not want to, or when it does not feel ready to do so, is a direct violation of its realness. A possible compromise, then, is for the subject to communicate with the world in such a manner that it does not wholly hand itself over to this world. It may communicate, but not with its entire true self; it may retain just enough space for silent (or even secret) communication with its subjective objects to safeguard its continued sense of realness. That is, it may share a bit of its realness, but not all of it, which is different from only sharing its false self.

The situation therefore requires a careful balancing act: the true self seeks expression, yet there are situations where the worst thing that could happen to it would be for it to be discovered and communicated with prematurely before it feels ready to disclose itself. As I have noted, the false self bears the responsibility for ensuring that forced communication does not take place: by building an armor around the noncommunicating core of the true self, the false self protects it from being interfered with in ways that would damage its capacity for creativity and spontaneity. In this context, Winnicott posits that it is worthwhile to consider why mystics frequently seclude themselves from the world. He speculates that it is possible that forgoing contact with "the world of shared reality," as mystics tend to do, is "counterbalanced by gain in terms of feeling real."[95]

Milner would be likely to agree. As we have seen, she shares Winnicott's insight about mystics. In addition, her personal practice of creative living entails withdrawing into a world of her own—her private sea—in ways that strongly resemble the habits of mystics. Almost none of the beads that she collects arise in collective settings. Instead, discovering them appears to demand that she temporarily extract herself from all quotidian concerns. More generally speaking, many artists undertake periods of solitude, the difference being that, unlike mystics, they are usually driven to share their creations with the world, which suggests that on some level they wish to communicate with others. Yet Winnicott specifies that if they are to retain their sense of realness they must, in the final analysis, find an equilibrium between their need to communicate—to express themselves through their work—and their equally essential need to protect a core that must neither communicate nor be communicated with.[96]

The same principle may apply to many intellectuals, for Winnicott proposes that it is isolation, silence, and quietude that "leads to the writings of those who have become recognized as the world's thinkers."[97] As a matter of fact, it makes a great deal of sense that in the case of artists, intellectuals, and others working with their minds, the self's noncommunicating core not only sustains its sense of aliveness but also facilitates its ability to bypass the distractions of the world so that it can stay focused on its task. As I revealed earlier, 95 percent of being able to write books, for me, comes down to my ability to protect myself from external demands. Although it is common for people—and perhaps especially for therapists and analysts—to

consider solitude and the refusal to communicate as pathological, these may be a decisive for intellectual and creative, let
alone mystical, endeavors.

The creative self, which is also the true self—or, if you prefer, the self that emerges from within the dynamic interchange
between the true and false selves—actively pursues the stillness
and silence of noncommunication as a means of detaching itself
from the external world, for it intuits that this world has the
power to dilute its creativity by exacting social compliance.
That is, solitude and noncommunication protect the true self
from the potentially banal or traumatic demands of the Other;
they shelter the self from being exploited by hegemonic sociality, from being "found" and "communicated with" against its
will. Such enforced sociality, Winnicott asserts, would represent a disastrous "alteration of the self's central elements by
communication seeping through the defences," and as such,
would be a "sin against the self."[98]

Winnicott observes that solitude is "part of the search for
identity, and for the establishment of a personal technique for
communicating which does not lead to violation of the central
self."[99] Solitude thus sustains our search for our unique voice by
providing a furtive space within which our inimitable singulari-
ties and idiosyncrasies are free to come to the fore. It also serves
this search by enabling us to connect to ourselves in the immediate sense that Milner advocates. Because solitude allows our
usual social defenses to disintegrate—because it permits us to
drop the various masks, personas, and façades that we uphold
for the purposes of social acceptability—it empowers us to touch
something "real" within ourselves; it gives rise to the kind of
acuteness of self-experience that allows us (for the time being)
to feel "like ourselves." This explains why we frequently need
solitude—in the same way that Milner needed to spend time

alone in stores looking at dresses and shoes—to replenish our sense of who we are after the kinds of social events that compel us into false or compliant attitudes. From this viewpoint, the exhaustion that we sometimes feel in our social interactions may arise from the fact that such interactions do not always grant us sufficient space to feel real.

Winnicott exclaims, "It is joy to be hidden but disaster not to be found."[100] I know—but did not when I drafted this chapter—that this statement is central to Gail's analysis of Winnicott. Gail's reading of it reaches deeper than mine. As far as my much more basic commentary goes, I have already explained my understanding of the first part of the sentence, namely that the true self relishes its ability to remain hidden and fears premature exposure: especially when under assault, the subject's noncommunicating core burrows deeper into its private chambers. The second part of Winnicott's sentence—that it is nevertheless "a disaster not to be found"—appears to point to the subject's fundamental need to be recognized by others.

Even if the subject's noncommunicating core fears being altered by external interference, a path of some kind needs to remain open between this private imaginative core and the world of everyday communication. It is not a contradiction to say that even though the true self does not always want to be discovered, it may not want to be entirely abandoned either, especially at moments when it wishes to communicate. The examples of artistic and intellectual labor that I have provided perhaps speak directly to this issue: as much as art and thought require solitude, ultimately it could be a psychic and affective disaster if no one responded to the artist's or thinker's exertions—if they received no recognition whatsoever. Particularly if the objective of artistic and individual labor is to reveal something about the real self, being completely ignored could lead to devastating feelings of irrelevance.

Hence, there is an intrinsic conceptual and existential impasse—an impasse that needs to be constantly negotiated rather than resolved—to Winnicott's notion of the true self. On the one hand, the true self wishes to be found and communicated with in the sense that it yearns to be appreciated for "who it genuinely is." On the other hand, being exposed by the Other, or even by an intimate other, is potentially exploitative in the sense that it can damage, or even annihilate, the true self. The self's longing for an authentic connection with others can consequently lead to the devastation of the very part of the self that esteems authenticity in the first place; although social interactions give the subject the opportunity to be reached in a meaningful way, the process of being reached is always also potentially one of being violated.

Winnicott's desire to protect the self's noncommunicating core from external interference extends to the analytic setting. Essentially, Winnicott believes that it is a mistake for the analyst to probe the deepest layers of the analysand's being before the analysand is ready to reveal these layers. When the analyst overanalyzes, she ends up knowing too much too fast and consequently becomes dangerous to the analysand because she is "too nearly in communication with the central still and silent spot of the patient's ego-organization."[101]

This may be especially dicey in situations where the analysand wants to avoid the disaster of not being found: the analysand's primary motivation for entering into analysis may be to disclose, in a relatively safe setting, a truthful version of himself that he may find difficult to disclose elsewhere. When this is the case, the analysand is unlikely to respond well to an analyst who appears uninterested in making a genuine connection. Yet an overly eager analyst who interprets prematurely, or who insists on communicating with the true self too quickly instead of waiting for the analysand to discover his own creativity and spontaneity, risks terrorizing the analysand's true self and sending this self further into exile.

The latter scenario obviously represents the very antithesis of the analytic objective. Yet the danger of falling into this trap is considerable, given that analysis by definition depends on communication. Furthermore, most analysts would probably prefer to communicate with the analysand's true rather than false self, which might tempt them to try to rush the analysand to reveal the former. Analysis may in fact be among the most difficult settings conceivable for imagining that *not* communicating may be an essential component of the subject's quest for realness. The impulse to accelerate the analytic process through various strategies that are designed to encourage communication is therefore ever-present, and the analyst may have to exercise considerable restraint in order to avoid giving in to this impulse.

Partly for this reason, Winnicott posits that the analyst must, first and foremost, establish the limitations of her interpretative powers, to make it clear to the analysand that she does not hold the solutions to his problems and dilemmas. Interestingly, despite the many divergences in the overall approaches of Winnicott and Lacan, Lacan holds a more or less identical view regarding the role of the analyst. The analyst, for Lacan, does not possess the solutions to the analysand's psychic and affective impasses but merely facilitates the analysand's ability to process these impasses. Winnicott concurs, describing his clinical practice as follows: "I interpret mainly to let the patient know the limits of my understanding. The principle is that it is the patient and only that patient who has the answers."[102]

In the context of discussing the goals of analysis, Winnicott implies that failures in the child's "holding environment"—the environment provided by the child's caretakers during the first months and years of its life—can lead to the kind of damage that it is then the task of analysis to remedy.[103] Although no holding environment is ever perfect enough to make up for the subject's primordial unintegration (its constitutive lack), Winnicott believes that acute failures in this environment give rise to a false self, characterized by "a poor capacity for using symbols, and a poverty of cultural living"—that is, a self that lacks "the essential central element of creative originality."[104] Indeed, Winnicott could not be more clear about the relationship between a strong, formative, facilitating environment and creativity: "We find either that individuals live creatively and feel that life is worth living or else that they cannot live creatively and are doubtful about the value of living. This variable in human beings is directly related to the quality and quantity of environmental provision at the beginning or in the early phases of each baby's living experience."[105]

I admit that I am not entirely prepared to accept the manner in which Winnicott seemingly deterministically connects the adult subject's capacity for creativity to the quality of its childhood facilitating environment. Perhaps because of the stark deficiencies of the holding environment within which I myself struggled to survive—deficiencies that had little to do with the failings of my caretakers but that arose from the collective struggles of my extended family to survive poverty—I cannot afford to believe that early environmental failures automatically doom the subject to a life devoid of creativity and sense of worth. I definitely did not grow up in the kind of facilitating environment that, according to Winnicott's reasoning, would lead to the flourishing of creativity. Yet even if I cannot claim to possess any unusual level of creativity, I feel that I did, to a large extent, manage to overcome my impoverished upbringing, so that my fate was not sealed during my formative years.

Admittedly, analysis played a large role in my ability to transcend the injuries of the past. For this reason, I concede that
there are obvious parallels between the child's early holding
environment and certain—perhaps mostly relational—genres
of analytic practice.

COURTING MADNESS

I find it refreshing that Milner does not dwell on the traumas of
the past. Somewhat unusually in the context of psychoanalytic
theory, the only moment that seems to matter to her is the here
and now. She does not attempt to figure out how to rectify the
damages of the subject's past. She does not even refer to such
damages. There is therefore no intimation in her theory that formative traumas in any way determine the subject's present reality. More specifically, there is no hint in her deliberations on creative living that early environmental failures play any part in the
subject's ability to cultivate its singular poetics of living later in
life. It does not appear to make a difference to Milner what the
subject's starting point in life was like, for—provided that its current circumstances allow—it is possible for the subject to learn
to live creatively at any moment. Less interested in how the subject's history might impact its present, Milner wishes to mine
the present for all that it can offer.

As we have seen, Milner pursues meditative states of mind
that allow her to experience worldly transcendence. Moreover,
even though Milner certainly displays an appreciation for the
destructive, darker elements of life, she is keenly invested in figuring out how to bring vitality, vibrancy, and effervescence into
her life. As she states, "I wonder what should be done with . . .
these little sprouts, flickers, up-rushes, [and] gulps of joy."[106]

Would kissing each joy as it flies by, she ponders, be a means of expressing gratitude for her senses, which enable her "to know the world, know people"; would it be a means of expressing gratitude "for just being"?[107] Milner is thus appreciative of her ability to experience the world in the deep, vivid manner that she does through wide perception, meditative states, and her attempts to collect as many gleaming beads as possible. For her, the world is full of little sprouts, flickers, up-rushes, and gulps of joy. It is full of little morsels of the Thing, of jouissance, that are there for the taking, if she is merely willing to exert a little effort.

I have emphasized that Milner connects her ability to access the other or not-self within her being to temporary ego-dissolution. In other words, pursuing worldly transcendence, for her, requires the willingness to plunge into the murky waters beneath the ego. In *Eternity's Sunrise*, Milner goes as far as to propose that collecting beads means being willing to get oneself muddy. She describes this experience as a matter of descending into the mud at the bottom of the ocean, close to the shore where the water reeds and wild weeds grow. She specifies that the ego would frown upon such activity, which is exactly why she needs to wipe her mind free of distracting, ego-bound thoughts whenever she chooses "to go down to the bottom, to the mud . . . and know that something is stirring in the mud—some new vista of understanding."[108] Creativity therefore arises from "being the mud itself, where there is no shaper or division, not clinging to anything comforting"—"except that the very mud . . . is in some way strangely comforting."[109] Whoever is humble enough to descend to this muddy level of self-experience is able to reemerge with a precious array of dazzling beads.

Milner acknowledges that sometimes the process of revealing and retrieving hidden treasures may take several attempts; it may require perseverance in the face of failure. For instance,

Milner describes the three trips that she makes to Greece, during which she strives to connect with the country's collection of
significant cultural and religious relics. She finds that during
her first trip, which is done as part of a tour group, she is distracted by the presence and chatter of other tourists, the excessive structure of her guidebooks, and the rigorous history
lessons that she is supposed to learn. Her intellect gets in the
way, and the milling around of other people distracts her so that
even though she can, in some instances, sense the potential for a
meaningful connection to a specific object, such as a painting,
sculpture, or architectural detail, she fails to bring about this
connection in a satisfactory manner. The moment slips by. The
object eludes her. Its mystery remains concealed.

However, when she returns to the same cultural and religious
sites alone during a later trip—when she is invited to give a lecture in Greece so that she is traveling by herself—she is suddenly able to create the sublime connection she is looking for:
the objects yield their secrets, granting her the experience of
worldly transcendence that she yearns for. In this case, she needs
to visit the same cultural and religious sites more than once before
their significance—their *punctum*, *objet a*, or aura of the Thing—
reveals itself, adding to her collection of beads.

Likewise, there are times when Milner herself tries to create
something—such as a painting—without her efforts bearing
fruit.[110] In such cases, something impedes the dissolution of her
ego, with the consequence that she is distracted, chained to her
self-consciousness, and her painting does not form. However, at
other times, she is able to slip effortlessly into a space where her
ego remains sidelined, and a painting appears as if out of thin
air. She has to find a way to neutralize her ego's critical voice, its
editorial commentary, in order to empower the other or not-me
within herself to guide her hand. The lesson is that when it comes

to our creative efforts— whether these efforts entail concrete creative labor, such as painting or writing, or whether they relate to more elusive attempts to live our lives as poetry—the ego's critical tendency can easily thwart the process.

That said, Milner has a great deal of respect for fallow periods, for times when the solution does not emerge—when the answering activity does not answer—and creativity fails. As she concedes, "It was all very well to talk of gaining strength from the feeling of becoming the mud, but I also had to face the fact that there were times when this just did not happen."[111] Milner admits that while it is easy to talk about purposeless activity and ego-annihilation, there are times when there is no other or not-self to guide her actions; there is nothing to plug herself into within her interiority. There are even times when she is mentally so paralyzed that she cannot "go down to the bottom to hold on to the water weeds," when she "can't move at all."[112] Yet Milner speculates that it is during such "pointless days" that deep inner changes take place, for it is "when all meaningful shape disappears from life that the new shapes are developing."[113]

Milner acknowledges that it can be difficult to believe that any kind of transformation is taking place when one is in the middle of a fallow period. All one can do is to wait, to allow the void of nothingness to take over until something new begins to materialize for "surely it's only a stage of what looks like empty fields, when the farmer has to wait for the first shoots to reach the daylight."[114] It can be difficult "to believe that the inner fertility cycle needs its own winter of empty resting fields if it is to have its spring."[115] Such "weather in the soul" is hard to predict, which in turn means that it is challenging "to know when to lie fallow, when to sow."[116] This can only be discovered by experimentation.

I might feel more skeptical about Milner's depiction of the creative process if it were not exactly the one that I use myself:

I find that it is only by pushing aside my ego and handing the reigns to the other or not-me within myself that I am able to write anything at all. Before learning to take the plunge into the muddy chaos of the unruly creative energies that percolate beneath my ego, I was incapacitated by a tremendous writer's block. This broke the moment that I was able to reach past my ego toward the jouissance of the real.

I had not yet read Milner when I discovered my creative "method." However, I do not think that I would have been able to do so without an understanding of Lacan's theory of jouissance, especially his commentary regarding the commingling of the signifier and jouissance—a commentary that one also finds, in a slightly different form, in Kristeva's early work. As I have shown, Lacan demonstrates that the jouissance of the real has the power to reinvigorate the signifier. Kristeva likewise regards the subject's drive energies as instrumental to the vitality of the creative process, especially to poetic language.[117] In this sense, Lacan and Kristeva gave me the gift—arguably a considerable one—of being able to write. Encountering Milner's work in turn felt like coming home: her depiction of her creative process is more or less identical to how I would describe mine.

I therefore feel a kinship with Lacan, Kristeva, and Milner because they manage to express all the essential components of the creative process that allow me to draft a text: the dissolution of the ego, self-surrender, jouissance, the experience of emerging from a state of having been absent to myself, and the mysterious sense of self-renewal that ensues from this experience. I cannot say that this process is easy. Its intensity is such that I cannot exactly call it pleasurable. The sheer volume of sentences pouring out, and the rapidity with which they form, can feel overwhelming. This is an experience of jouissance in as pure a form as I am able to experience it, which is why it is the kind of pleasure that borders on pain. I know that others experience it differently, sometimes even as an erotic event.[118] But for me it is mostly agonizing. Fortunately, things shift when I reach the editorial stage which, by comparison, is calm and calming. That is when the process slows down and writing becomes a more straightforward pleasure.

The ego functions as a sentry at the gates that separate our conscious life from our unconscious impulses and bodily drives. This is why psychoanalysis has attempted to hone a technique— free association—for disabling the ego's defenses so as to allow analysands to access their unconscious. Writers (and other creative individuals) have to attempt the same, for if our writing is too attached to our ego—if we allow our ego to criticize and edit every sentence as it initially emerges on the page—we are almost certain to impede the free flow of sentences. In retrospect, I recognize that the key to breaking my writer's block was the capacity to neutralize my ego during the drafting process. I had to learn to trust that I would be able to productively reactivate it during the editorial process, for there is nothing that the ego likes more than the precision of perfecting things. But if I attempted to draft a text with my ego sitting on my shoulder, I ended up staring at a blank page all day.

In earlier times, artists tended to conceptualize inspiration as a matter of being guided by a muse or by some other enigmatic entity that was responsible for generating bursts of creativity. Psychoanalysis, and Milner in particular, teaches us that what is guiding us are forces within ourselves that tend to be blocked by our ego. Being able to proceed is therefore a matter of activating the other or not-self within ourselves by temporarily neutralizing this ego. I realize that there are plenty of writers, and other types of creators, who work successfully with the aid of their egos. There is nothing wrong with this. It just seems like a more frustrating process. That said, I have revealed that, for me, drafting a text in an irrational state of ego-dissolution feels agonizing due to its intensity and urgency. As a result, I can well understand why many creative individuals may want to avoid such a state. Ultimately, I am not certain which method is more demanding. All I know is that if you want to produce the first version of a text, poem, song, or painting quickly, you need to learn to silence your ego's hypercritical voice. You need to learn to hand control to the other or not-me within your being that possesses the power to bring forth the rudimentary structure of what will eventually—usually after multiple rounds of revision—turn into the work that you aim to produce.[119]

As I have noted, one has to have an ego to begin with before one can dissolve or marginalize it. Those whose egos are weak may find the process of disabling it frightening, which is precisely why I had such a difficult time defeating my writer's block. When I was a child and teenager, my ego was ground to dust by my father, whose way of protecting me from the kinds of disappointments that he himself had experienced was to tell me, on a daily basis, that I was stupid, ugly, and would never amount to anything. As a consequence, somewhat counterintuitively, I needed analysis to build up my ego before I could even consider sidelining it, however temporarily. Because of the relative weakness of my ego, I was afraid that if I relaxed its reign, I might not be able to find my way back onto solid ground, that I might become forever stuck in the mud of unconscious forces and bodily jouissance. In Winnicottian terms, one could say that I feared that I would experience an irreversible unintegration of my being rather than merely a fleeting disintegration of my ego.

Another factor that has made unintegration, even psychosis, a specter that has haunted me my entire life, is that I grew up with a schizophrenic uncle who lived in our family home and who was consequently an immense presence in my early life. His resemblance to me was an obvious but unnamed fact in my family. My parents feared that I would "go mad" like my uncle—the other bookworm of the family—had done. I feared the same. I still sometimes do. Moreover, I do not think that this fear is completely unwarranted, for the line between temporary disintegration and permanent unintegration, between creativity and psychosis, can at times arguably be quite thin. Milner illustrates better than any thinker I have encountered that the creative process that she advocates—which happens to be my creative process—is on some level a matter of courting madness, of risking the possibility of getting permanently lost in the mud of the hazy underworld of one's being.

The process of dissolving the ego and plunging into the unknown beneath it demands the willingness to risk the self. Even Milner herself admits that her desire for self-loss cannot be dissociated from her fear of losing herself permanently. On the one hand, she stresses that her beads and transcendent experiences only become available to her when she is willing to push her ego aside. On the other hand, she concedes that she feels a strong temptation to keep pursuing objectives and purposeful action on the level of her ego due to her concern that if she allows herself to descend too deeply into the mud, she will disappear, even perish.

A facet of our fear of surrendering ourselves to the other or not-me within ourselves is the possibility that, ultimately, there may be nothing to depend on. As Milner explains, a factor that blocks our "creative surrender" to the answering activity is that we are not merely wary of the risks of depending on the other or not-me, but also paralyzed by a "wavering doubt" regarding whether there is anything within us to rely on in the first place.[120] After all, what proof do we have that the other or not-me exist?

And if they do exist, what guarantee do we have that they will support us? "The trouble," Milner concludes, is that we have to place our faith in what seems "like nothingness, emptiness, a void."[121] Ultimately, accepting our dependence on the other or not-me is a matter of defeating our infantile dread of losing all external support, of falling, falling, falling . . .

Milner therefore connects our fear of there being nothing to depend on to a primordial process that Lacan and Kristeva also consider as being foundational to subjectivity, namely the process through which the child who has hitherto regarded itself as the center of the universe realizes that it is, after all, not in control of its surroundings, including its caretakers. As Milner explains, our terror of falling into utter helplessness is connected to "the regal infant pride having to recognize the fact of no longer lording it in glory but tasting the bitter grapes of humiliating dependence."[122] As Lacan and Kristeva both propose, this collapse of infantile pride, of primary narcissism, takes place in the context of language acquisition, for it is through language that the child learns that it is merely an insignificant component of a complex system of meaning that it has had no hand in constituting and that it cannot single-handedly alter. This recognition of its relative insignificance is not conscious, yet it determines the future parameters of its—or, more precisely, the adult subject's—destiny. As Milner states, "We are all struggling to get back to the glory of our beginnings in some way or other," to "the time when we lorded it over our mothers and fathers, progressed like kings in our infant push-chair chariots, propelled by someone else's bodily effort, an effort that made possible the denial of our own weakness."[123]

This is exactly what Lacan and Kristeva posit as the heart of the human condition. It is what Lacan is getting at when he argues that most of us flee from the reality of our constitutive lack—the reality of being "cut" by the signifier, of "symbolic castration"—and spend our lives trying to recover a plenitude that we never actually possessed. Kristeva in turn describes how the child becomes melancholic in the aftermath of its recognition of its fundamental dependence and vulnerability, suggesting that after this recognition—a recognition that she, like Lacan, connects to language acquisition—melancholia remains forever woven into the subject's psychic life. In this manner, like Lacan, Kristeva acknowledges that much of the subject's psychic life consists of a struggle to fend off a melancholia that threatens to engulf its psychic constitution.

Yet, like Lacan, Kristeva also suggests that there is something generative about our acceptance of our nothingness and emptiness, emphasizing that one of the gifts of human subjectivity is our innovative ability to "remake nothingness."[124] Like Lacan, she recognizes that the sublimatory circling of the Thing gives rise to much of what we find worthwhile in our lives, so that "beauty emerges as the admirable face of loss, transforming it in order to make it live."[125] This is why, as I have repeatedly stressed, Lacan believes that it is important for us to accept the incurable nature of our lack, for it is only when we do so that we can begin to find sublimatory solutions to it, that we can begin the process of translating loss into beauty, thereby breathing life into this loss.

In many ways, what Milner does is to render concrete the sublimatory mechanisms through which it is possible for us to not merely endure our lack (and melancholia) but also, ideally at least, to thrive due to our attempts to transform this lack into beauty. For her, the rewards of her sublimatory efforts—which entail the temporary sacrifice of her ego—are enormous: her beads and morsels of worldly transcendence; a sense of peace, openness, and connectedness to her surroundings; and the ability to form ideas—and to write them down—effortlessly. When the answering activity within her is fully activated, ideas press on her with a degree of urgency. As Milner explains, during such periods, ideas—along with the seeds of creative processes—are handed to her "on a plate, silently."[126] Suddenly "there they are arriving from out of nothing."[127] Unexpectedly, she knows how she needs to proceed or what the answer to a question that has been preoccupying her is. As she puts it, "You put a penny in the slot and out pops the answer."[128]

Here, Milner claims that her ideas arrive "out of nothing." It is consequently worth reiterating one final time that, like Lacan and Kristeva, Milner connects creativity and creative living to the ability to embrace emptiness. As she puts the matter, what "brings the outer riches" is "loss—nothing there—a hole—a gap—a wound—even the aching pain of it. The ache of hunger too."[129] I have established that experiencing our inner nothingness, lack, gap, or wound is daunting. Many retreat from the edge. However, Milner believes that those who have the courage to follow this path are rewarded, as is clear from the rhetorical question that she poses: "To go down inside to become the emptiness, become even the pain? Then it's no longer emptiness—even no longer pain"?[130]

Milner therefore implies that out of the void of ego-dissolution—out of emptiness—arises a self that is able to translate its experiences of jouissance into writing, works of art, and other creative productions. As I have explained, this is not a matter of turning impediments into opportunities with the swiftness and expediency demanded by neoliberal self-optimization but, rather, of patiently dwelling within the alterity (other or not-me) of our being for long enough to become acquainted with the reeds and weeds that constitute the undergrowth of this swampy domain. It may not be terribly important what this irrational domain is called: we could call it the other, the not-me, alterity, jouissance, or even the true self. What should be clear by now is that when we allow ourselves to fall into this muddy domain, we momentarily extinguish ourselves as socially viable entities without any guarantee that we will ever find our way back. The self-annihilation that Milner refers to is, hence, "real" in the sense that it indicates the temporary death of our social self.

Milner herself admits that the terror of being "melted down in the Button Moulder's ladle" is petrifying.[131] She describes the paradox of fear and reward of worldly transcendence as follows: "Annihilation. Nobody, no body to be buried. But if one dares risk it, go down to the body's darkness, something does happen even to one's skin, it begins to burgeon."[132] Once this happens, "out of the held emptiness, there comes a movement, a gesture, reaching out to the world again, to the world in which wild flowers grow."[133] The individual who has made the journey into the shadowy underworld resurfaces, disoriented and squinting in the sunlight. For a moment, they feel dislocated, having just visited a place that cannot be described in the logical terminology of the rational world. But after a while, their eyes adjust, and they are able to admire the beads that they have hauled to the surface. The lesson is that if we want to keep our creativity alive, we need to risk the nothingness staring at us from the bottom of the abyss. We are, here, quite far from neoliberal self-optimization.

THE FEAR OF BREAKDOWN

Where Milner refers to the fear of being melted down in the Button Moulder's ladle, Winnicott analyzes the fear of the kind of breakdown that has already taken place. Both of these fears arguably refer to the terror of returning to an infantile state of unintegration, of complete dependence and helplessness. Winnicott in fact specifies that the fear of breakdown can entail "primitive agonies," such as the fear of falling forever or the loss of the sense of reality.[134] As I proposed a moment ago, the apprehension generated by Milner's strategy of accessing our creative energies by plunging into the jouissance of the real is related to the possibility that the line between creativity and psychosis may be too blurry, that in allowing ourselves to fall, we will keep falling forever, without being able to reappear as a socially intelligible being. The Winnicottian subject who suffers from a fear of an irreversible breakdown similarly fears the onset of emptiness, the loss of its ties to the social world. Winnicott posits that the subject who fears a breakdown does not realize that unintegration was its original state of being so that, in reality, it has already experienced the very thing that it most fears. In such a scenario, the ego works overtime to establish defenses against the possible breakdown in its organization, thereby strengthening the false self.

Why does the subject worry about what belongs to the past?, Winnicott asks. He answers his own question by hypothesizing that as long as the subject fails to experience the trauma of unintegration as something that has taken place in the past, it intrudes into the here and now and even appears as a concern about the future. In addition, the reason that the subject does not recall that the breakdown that it fears has already happened is that it did not yet exist as a subject when the breakdown occurred. It was too unintegrated, too infantile, too devoid of ego strength, to have had a sense of itself as a separate entity.

Winnicott claims that the fear of breakdown sometimes literally destroys the lives of his analysands. It certainly makes it harder for the subject to experience the kinds of creative states that Milner covets. According to Winnicott, the solution is for the analysand to experience—within the relatively comfortable confines of the analytic holding environment—the very feeling of utter unintegration that he most fears. Winnicott postulates that it is transference, specifically, that allows the analysand to undergo a breakdown of this magnitude. Interestingly, Winnicott adds that for this to happen, the analyst needs to make mistakes.[135]

I have emphasized that Winnicott, like Lacan, wants the analysand to understand that the analyst does not possess the solutions to his dilemmas and impasses. However, in the context of the fear of breakdown, Winnicott appears to go further in suggesting that the analyst needs to actively fail. Although he, generally speaking, praises the virtues of the good-enough holding environment, he seems to believe that failures of this environment may be productive in facilitating the analysand's ability to experience his breakdown. Perhaps there is something about the analysand witnessing the analyst's fallibility—which reminds him of the fallibility of all of us—that makes the idea of a breakdown more tolerable to him? Perhaps there is something about the analysand's recognition that the analyst cannot ultimately catch him that forces him to experience the kind of fall without a safety net that he fears, only in the end to realize that he has not, after all, fallen irrevocably?

It is entirely possible that the analyst's "failure" takes place unintentionally. However, I can imagine situations where the analyst withholds support on purpose in order to induce the analysand's breakdown, with the result that the analysand is forced to experience, and therefore come to terms with, his lack of integration. If the analyst consistently props up the analysand's ego in order to prevent a breakdown from happening, the fear of this breakdown will persist in the analysand's psychic life indefinitely. In this sense, it is only by failing to provide the support that the analysand expects—by failing to provide a good-enough holding environment—that the analyst is able to help the analysand overcome his terror of a breakdown. This, Winnicott argues, is equivalent to lifting repression—of making the unconscious conscious—in classically Freudian analysis.[136]

But why is it important for the subject to reexperience its infantile unintegration? By now it is clear that Winnicott believes that if it does not, its fear of future unintegration—its fear of falling irreversibly—can become debilitating. In addition, one may hypothesize that those who have experienced their unintegration and survived to tell the tale, so to speak, are better able to tolerate the inevitable moments of disintegration—which, you will recall, are different from unintegration in the sense that disintegration can only happen once some ego strength has been achieved—that from time to time take place in all of our lives.

Most adult subjects have achieved a relatively high level of integration. However, they are bound to experience a degree of disintegration or ego erosion during times when something goes awry in their lives. From accidents that cause bodily injury and traumas that result from physical or psychic violence, to losing a lover, a job, or a home can cause a profound sense of disintegration: one's life has been irrevocably altered and one is scrambling to adjust oneself to a new reality. It is possible that those who have undergone an experience of unintegration are better equipped for this task than those who have not. This is because they have learned that losing their footing is an event that they can recover from, with the consequence that their level of resilience is higher.

Moreover, as I have tried to convey, the release of the subject's creative capacities, in the sense that Milner describes the process, depends on its ability to tolerate states of unintegration. As Winnicott puts the matter, *"only out of non-existence can existence start."*[137] This is related to Lacan's argument that subjectivity, as such, is founded on lack and that the subject's sublimatory capacities revolve around the elusive *objets a* as enticing substitutes for the missing Thing—that sublimation, as we have seen, is a matter of raising mundane objects to the dignity of the Thing. It is also related to Kristeva's closely connected claim that what distinguishes human beings from other animals is their ability to remake nothingness—and even turn melancholia into beauty and meaning—through sublimatory endeavors. However, most pertinently for our purposes, Winnicott's statement is related to Milner's argument that the subject's capacity to activate its creative potential demands that it surrender its ego and allow itself to fall into a state of unintegration.

Those who defend their egos too strongly block access to their sublimatory energies whereas those who allow themselves to plunge into the unknown give both creative activity and creative living a chance. Winnicott's creative subject, like Milner's, is capable of temporarily reaching states of unintegration or at least disintegration—states of relaxation that lack purpose and that hence open to the kind of inner fluidity that makes creativity possible. As Winnicott proposes, "It is only here, in this unintegrated state of the personality, that that which we describe as creative can appear."[138] In this sense, the very thing that the subject most fears—unintegration—is the seat of its creative potential.

Hence, it makes perfect sense that even though analysands would (usually) prefer the relative certainty of integration to the utter uncertainty of unintegration, Winnicott encourages experiences of unintegration. If some people are ill (psychotic) because of being permanently too unintegrated, others are unnecessarily neurotic—suffer too much—due to their excessive integration, which blocks the flourishing of their creative capacities. For example, Winnicott posits that when the analysand's free association appears extremely cohesive, one can assume that his defenses against analysis, and therefore against creative living, are too seamlessly established. In contrast, free association that comes across as disorganized, even nonsensical, "belongs to the mental state of the individual at rest."[139]

Winnicott thus suggests that analysis can teach the subject to activate its creative potential. When the analyst knows how to step back so as to create space for the analysand's experimentations with unintegration, the analysand gradually discovers that he possesses the capacity to safely move back and forth between states of unintegration and integration. Against this backdrop, what is particularly interesting about Milner is that she is convinced that it is possible to reach the same outcome of teaching individuals how to allow themselves to disintegrate—or, in her vocabulary, to descend into the mud beneath their egos—*outside* the analytic setting. Milner is convinced that anyone can learn to access their creative capacities through activities such as wide perception, meditative states, keeping a journal, and even self-analysis.

The fear of losing oneself that I have explored may be more pronounced in settings outside the clinic than within the clinic, for those striving to mobilize their creative capacities alone lack the support offered by the analyst. Yet Milner is certain that most of us possess the ability to find our way into—and out of—the mud. This is important to her because she recognizes that not everyone can afford analysis or has the time for the analytic undertaking. If analysis was the only way in which we could marshal our creative capacities, only a tiny portion of the population would ever be able to do so. Yet it is clear that many people find their way on their own, sometimes by chance, other times by taking conscious steps to cultivate their poetics of living.

FROM INDIVIDUALITY TO SINGULARITY

For Milner, the ego must recede into the background of subjectivity if creative activity, and ultimately the creative self, is to emerge. This self is the very antithesis of neoliberal self-optimization, for its jouissance—Milner's private sea—neutralizes the possibility of a purely instrumentalist approach to the task of living. As a result, the creative self does not support normative, socially intelligible individuality insofar as such individuality is a matter of ego-bound, rational behavior. Instead, the creative self facilitates the flourishing of the subject's singularity as a function of its jouissance. In other words, the subjective singularity that is associated with Milner's sublimatory efforts to discover as many beads as possible—to find traces of sublimity within mundane objects—is entirely different from the ego-centered individuality that neoliberal society promotes.

Singularity in Milner's sense has to do with bodily drives, jouissance, the quirks of the unconscious, and other contortions and distortions of being. It is the part of ourselves that we usually strive to keep under control in public situations, especially when we need to perform, say, by teaching a class, delivering a lecture, or running a meeting. During such moments, it is our little physical ticks—the twitching underneath our eye, the shaking of our hands, the tremor in our voice, or the compulsive adjustment of our neck—that give away the excess of jouissance that is coursing through our bodies and psyches; they are the markers of our singularity even when they are not polished or comfortable. They give us a little taste of what it might mean to allow the socially seamless and intelligible image of ourselves to shatter. Milner has little respect for this image: what matters to her are all the muddy things that this image hides. Winnicott may have more respect for our need to cultivate such an image. As we have learned, he comprehends that we often need the protection of our false self in order to guarantee the survival of our true self. Yet, ultimately, for him as well, the objective appears to be to usher us to a place where we are able to tolerate a breakdown of our public image without thereby falling into a permanent state of unintegration.

Individuality—which forms around social expectations even if it also strives to express something about our specificity—and singularity—which arises from our bodily drives and which therefore cannot be dissociated from jouissance—arguably represent vastly different components of our being. If individuality is largely predictable, singularity is unpredictable. Sometimes the kind of jouissance that generates singularity is a sign of our over-animation, which is how we end up with the ticks that I just mentioned. But other times it is a source of vitality, even inspiration. Although both individuality and singularity constitute important facets of our being, during moments when our individuality is foregrounded, our singularity tends to fade into the background so that it is only visible in the ticks that embarrass us. Conversely, when singularity takes over—as it frequently does in the midst of intense creative processes—our ego-bound individuality tends to dissolve in the manner that Milner has depicted.

Interestingly, the embarrassing features of singularity frequently disappear when we manage to activate the vitalizing, inspiring aspects of jouissance: those who are able to dive into their private sea in search of bits of sublimity, as well as those who are able to focus on a creative process so passionately that the world seems to stand still, are not necessarily haunted by either physical ticks or mental hesitations. Likewise, those who are genuinely dynamic in public settings, such as giving a talk, tend to lose sight of their physical being to the extent that their hands no longer shake, and their voice no longer trembles. I do not mean to say that they get dissociated from their bodies but, instead, that they end up inhabiting their bodies so seamlessly that the more symptomatic side of their singularity evaporates. This may explain why the first few minutes of a public presentation are usually the hardest: it takes a moment for the body to get in sync with the rhythm of one's discourse. Once this occurs, the nervousness that one might initially feel usually vanishes.

I imagine that something akin to this also happens, for instance, to doctors dealing with an emergency: when one concentrates intensely on the task at hand, the empowering elements of one's singularity rush to one's aid while one's ticks, shakes, tremors, and compulsions dissipate. This would explain why both artists and doctors—among other creative individuals—may, after their burst of activity, feel that they have temporarily been absent from the world of quotidian life. It is as if their singularity has overridden their individuality because this was the only way to accomplish what needed to be done. In saying this, I hope to reiterate that inspiration, in the sense that Milner depicts it, is not merely the domain of artists and other obviously creative individuals, but that any person who fully invests herself in a meaningful activity—frequently one that pulls the person in question into its vortex so powerfully that the rest of the world momentarily disperses—is able to visit this domain and hence express her singularity.

Earlier, I mentioned that writers, artists, and other creative individuals may, at times, need solitude. For them, solitude may be a precondition of their ability to concentrate. For others, such as doctors, whose work is intrinsically social, solitude is not a precondition of their work, per se, but it may be a precondition of their ability to keep working; it may be a way to compensate for the hectic sociality of their profession. The same may be the case for nurses, teachers, lawyers, and a whole host of other arduous professions. One reason for this is that upholding our socially intelligible individuality takes a degree of effort. As I have mentioned, it requires us to don various masks, personas, and façades, which can get exhausting. Unfortunately, our extroverted society rarely acknowledges this, for it values sociality. Even my field— critical theory, broadly understood—exhibits a strong bias toward "relationality," at times even viewing it as the solution to all of our political and ethical dilemmas.[140] Yet some of us find constant sociality debilitating or even oppressive. Some of us may even only feel "real" when we are alone because this is when both our singularity and our creativity can thrive without any interference from the social world.

Personally, I find it impossible to write when others are present because their company sidetracks me. In this context, it may be useful to recall that while in Greece Milner found the presence of others so distracting that she was unable to forge a connection to the cultural and religious artifacts from which she was trying to extract her beads. Likewise, she found it necessary to escape to stores to look at dresses after draining social interactions. I am also among those who feel depleted by sociality to the point that I need several days of solitude to recover from it. Visiting or hosting friends is lovely. But beyond this, sociality— events, parties, meetings, and the rest of collective life—impedes the emergence of my singularity, without which I cannot reach the muddy underworld beneath my ego that is necessary for writing. For this reason, solitude is a relief. It neutralizes the need to project a socially acceptable image of any kind.

Milner, implicitly at least, celebrates singularity, for she regards creative living as an antidote to the normative demands of dominant society. As I have specified, she does not use the vocabulary of neoliberal self-optimization, but for all practical purposes, her poetics of self-fashioning amounts to an effort to find an alternative to everything that such self-optimization entails. One could, of course, legitimately ask how a person who seeks to erase her ego and even courts a breakdown is able to *oppose* normative society. Perhaps this is not the right way to characterize Milner's attitude. Perhaps resistance in her case is more a matter of bypassing the Other's dictates than of striving to defeat them. Milner does not so much resist self-optimization as she simply ignores it, thereby neutralizing any power that it might otherwise hold over her. In the same way as she looks right through the seductions of commercial culture, she pays no attention to the ideal of striving to optimize her life, seeking instead to cultivate a relaxed state of being devoid of any normative purpose. She chooses singularity over the kind of individuality that supports social conformity.

CHOOSING WHAT IS IMPORTANT

This manner of framing the issue gives us the opportunity to conceptualize resistance along less revolutionary lines than has been customary in twentieth-century theory, at least since the early Frankfurt School which owed an intellectual debt to Marx, in addition to Freud. It aligns us with Kristeva's intimate revolt, which is a matter of reassessing what we thought we knew about the world and ourselves and of repeatedly reinventing both. This framing also allows us to think of resistance in terms of a gradual erosion of the status quo rather than in terms of an outright rebellion. I am not saying that the fact that revolution seems improbable in the Western world is necessarily a good thing. Yet realistically it is very difficult to envision. The fact is that many of us cannot afford—or do not know how—to undertake revolutionary acts that would completely disengage us from the collective systems that provide us with a modicum of social, psychic, and affective continuity.

As Roland Barthes notes in his autobiography, revolution in the usual sense of the term requires us to abandon the entire system that we criticize, whereas there are ways to dissolve the system from within that do not require us to do so.[141] In Barthes's case, although he (generally speaking) opposes the normativity of bourgeois culture, he appreciates many of its aesthetic legacies, wanting to hold onto these while dissociating himself from the rest of this culture. Similarly, one could think of the kind of surrender of the self that Milner advocates—the deliberate disabling of the ego that she associates with creative living—as a means of rejecting neoliberal society's ethos of self-optimization without thereby denouncing every aspect of contemporary culture.

It may be that many of us are already resisting our society's ethos of self-optimization in various—perhaps small yet personally significant—ways. Perhaps we refuse to check our email over the weekend. Perhaps, instead of working a full day, we go for a walk in the crisp autumn air in order to admire the kaleidoscopic burst of colors offered by our surroundings. Perhaps we pause to contemplate a particularly captivating vista, practicing a gentle form of surrender in the face of beauty. Perhaps we allow ourselves to be enchanted by a muffled winter landscape of snow-covered mountains, fields, and trees. These are activities that do not augment our productivity, and that do not fall under the performance principle, yet we may find them more rewarding than the activities that we undertake on behalf of our jobs. Alternatively, perhaps we find ways to focus on components of our jobs that feel meaningful by paying less attention to components that feel deadening. Here, it is necessary to be somewhat careful in the sense that we need to keep in mind that whenever we do not do our part, someone else is going to have to step up and handle things on our behalf. The distinction between working less and making others work harder can consequently be difficult to determine. But it would probably benefit many of us to consider if there are ways to reduce our workload, or at least shift our efforts toward the more rewarding elements of our jobs, without inflicting harm on others.

If enough people focused less on performance and productivity, we would change the parameters of our society in fundamental ways. Earlier in my analysis, I was careful to acknowledge that many people are forced to work more than one job in order to stay afloat financially. Even most middle-class people would find it entirely impossible to stop working, for they need a roof over their heads, heat in their dwellings, and food on their tables. It is therefore hard to find an individual solution to what is clearly a structural, collective problem, namely that our society expects its workers to work unnecessarily hard. A shorter workday or work week would go a long way to fixing the problem, while at the same time providing employment for more people. But this would require lowering wages, which some people cannot afford, and others do not want to accept. I am therefore not saying that there is an easy solution to the problem. However, the first step toward being able to improve things would be to admit that there is a problem to begin with. This requires an increased level of awareness among a greater number of people. Somehow, too many of us have gotten so used to working harder than is good for us that we do not even consider offering resistance or—when possible—reconfiguring our lives in order to decrease the pressure. For many, the basic problem is that too many people rely on them to keep up, regardless of how exhausted they are and regardless of what else might be going on in their lives. On a theoretical level, it is easy to point out the dilemma, but concretely it is hard to know how to resolve it.

Refusing to be enticed by the shiny lures of consumer capitalism may be an easier form of intimate revolt—one that would furthermore counter the necessity of working to the point of exhaustion because it would decrease the level of consumption and therefore the need for a high income. It seems that one of the most effective ways to counter the consumerist tenor of neo-liberal society would be to make resolute decisions about what matters most to us and to organize our lives, to the extent that this is possible, around such things—as Milner does around her beads, delights, and moments of worldly transcendence. In Lacanian terms, this would mean staying faithful to the truth of our desire—to the kind of desire that connects us to the jouissance of the Thing—in ways that would limit the number of objects we desire; it would mean defeating the ability of consumer capitalism to beguile us with things that we do not need.

We are all constrained by the Other's dictates. Nonetheless, we possess a degree of freedom within such dictates: in principle, we should be able to take a close look at our lives and decide which of its components we find satisfying and which we should discard. The lives of many of us are overcrowded, too full of things and activities. In this sense, creative living may entail the simple act of limiting the array of things and activities that we allow into our daily realities. The mindful self-awareness that Milner promotes may assist us in making the types of choices that we experience as enlivening, regardless of whether or not they meet the dominant expectations of our social environment. What might it mean, for example, to choose personal satisfaction over the narratives of success, achievement, performance, productivity, and self-optimization that we have been fed all our lives?

One of the main lessons of Milner's work is that being selective about how we spend our time and about the quality of the items, objects, moments, and experiences that we accumulate makes a difference in the overall tone of our lives. In other words, the sublimatory practice of raising mundane objects to the dignity of the Thing should be highly selective. Not all objects should qualify; the objects in question should have something genuinely special about them. If they do not, we quickly drown ourselves in waste. When we lack discrimination about the objects and activities that we pursue, we overwhelm our ability to determine what matters and what does not. This in turn diminishes rather than augments the quality of our lives.

Limiting what we purchase to items that reflect the truth of our desire is a skill that can be learned. Like Milner, we can aspire to haul in at the end of the day, or the week, month, or year, only the items, objects, moments, and experiences—the beads—that contribute to a life where sublimation as an existential strategy is an explicit goal. Getting rid of excess is not demanding—all it requires is a degree of discernment and, at times, an inclination toward minimalism (which is not the same thing as austerity). Although our lives tend to include elements that we would rather be without—elements which we have not selected and over which we have no choice—we do (usually) have a choice about the things that we actively bring into our everyday world. Regarding these, being selective can alter the general tenor of our lives.

Milner reveals that our commitment to the items, objects, moments, and experiences that matter most to us informs our identities and distinctive existential approach. In other words, on a basic level, our singularity is a function of the idiosyncratic and frequently quite stubborn ways in which we care about certain things; it only emerges in relation to external entities that we deem precious enough to be worthy of our investment. It would consequently be a mistake to suggest that the external world and its offerings, per se, are a hindrance to fashioning a life that feels meaningful to us. Instead, what is problematic is the manner in which this world has been infiltrated and colonized by commercially generated enticements that are calculated to guide and often deliberately confuse our desire.

Milner teaches us that it is important for our poetics of being to hone our skill in selecting the kinds of items, objects, moments, and experiences that enrich our lives rather than draw us into the folds of a commercially engendered world that deliberately distances us from the truth of our desire. The sad fact is that many of us do not know what this truth consists of. What is more, if we have trouble limiting our desire, it is frequently because neoliberal society has trained us to believe that we deserve *everything*. For instance, the ethos of positive thinking suggests that with a bit of perseverance and the right—optimistic—attitude, we can attain absolutely anything we want. This is a completely unrealistic mindset that in the end leads to a great deal of unnecessary misery.

Those who have been told all their lives that they deserve everything that their hearts desire may find it extremely difficult to admit that they have to make choices—that everything is, after all, not available to them. More specifically, they have trouble recognizing that, as human beings, they are not meant to have everything and that if their desire feels out of control, darting in multiple directions at once, it is because they have not learned to accurately identify what actually matters. As I keep emphasizing, there are certainly many people who learn early that their options are limited—frequently far too limited. However, many others learn to think that anything should be possible. There are positive components to this attitude, for it can make you adventurous, ready to test various opportunities. But much of the time, it seems to translate into the idea that you have somehow been cheated of your birthright if you do not get everything you want. This is a recipe for disaster in terms of being able to lead a rewarding life, for those who are incapable of drawing boundaries around their desire will never feel satisfied. Such people are arguably entirely out of touch with the truth of their desire, which in turn implies that they are out of touch with their true selves.

What I have outlined suggests that sometimes finding satisfaction in our lives is simply a matter of shifting our perspective. If we start from the assumption that we deserve and should be able to obtain everything imaginable, we are unlikely to ever be gratified. In the same way that those who cannot accept lack as intrinsic to human subjectivity squander their lives in futile attempts to heal it instead of pursuing goals that are actually attainable, those who believe that all of their wishes should be fulfilled are setting themselves up for disillusionment. In contrast, learning to be content with what we already have is likely to enhance the quality of our lives, provided that we possess the basic components of a livable life (poverty being a whole different matter). In this sense, a shift in attitude can go a long way in adding joy and pleasure to our lives.

This is the last thing that consumer capitalism wants. If enough of us decided that we do not need possessions beyond what we already have, the economy would come to a screeching halt. It is the goal of consumer capitalism to create new desires, to introduce alluring items into our lives that we may not have known existed before we chanced upon a specific advertisement or catalog. This happens to me every time I flip through an airline magazine: I discover items that I have never seen before. Fortunately, they hold no power over me because I realize that if I have never before needed the item in question, I am unlikely to need it in the future. To be sure, I do sometimes buy curios that catch my eye, like the rings in Vienna. I buy such items because they emit an aura of the Thing, resonating on the precise frequency of my desire. I find them in the most random places imaginable, but an airline magazine is an unlikely source of inspiration.

An obvious problem with consumer capitalism is that we, both on the individual and collective level, consume more than we need. In this sense, what may seem like a relatively frivolous part of Milner's art of living, namely her selectiveness about the beads that she acquires, may have significant political and ethical implications: if everyone in our society learned to curtail their consumption, there would be a lot more left for the rest of the world. This would not even entail any real sacrifices in the sense of our having to give up what we actually need or genuinely want but would merely ask for a little more discrimination in what we buy. We all know that there are countless people in the world who would be thrilled to put to use the items that sit idly in our closets, cupboards, and drawers. Why, then, do we hold onto such items?

A trivial example that illustrates how simple it might be to alter our course is the following: if somewhere along the way I have learned that a slice of chocolate cake will not satisfy me as much as a scoop of chocolate ice cream, it would be stupid of me to choose chocolate cake over chocolate ice cream when both are available. In so doing, I would merely create a situation where I would be hankering for chocolate ice cream even after I had already had an enormous slice of chocolate cake, whereas if I choose the ice cream from the get-go, I am unlikely to want cake on top of it. In the first scenario I overconsume, whereas in the latter I am still eating something that most people in the world would consider a luxury, but at least I am not doubling the damage. I feel more comfortable moralizing about this issue than about most others because it is evident that sheer gluttony helps to maintain the structures of inequality that corrupt the world, at the same time as it contributes to the environmental crisis that is increasingly wreaking havoc across the globe.

In this context, I am reminded of Nietzsche's commentary on the manner in which the inability to forget past slights, injuries, and disappointments can lead to a situation where the mind is so overcrowded with spiteful thoughts that the individual becomes incapable of undertaking any meaningful activity, at the same time as they are unable to rest; they are both overexcited and enervated at once, like an insomniac running on an excess of caffeine.[142] This seems to be the lot of many people in today's world, except that instead of being burdened by disquieting memories, they are besieged by so many objects, activities, and stimuli that they are completely overloaded. It is possible that the best thing that such people could do for themselves would be to become more selective about the opportunities that they pursue. Learning to ignore 90 percent of the world's lures, offerings, and temptations seems like the key to maintaining one's sanity.

CREATIVE SELF-FASHIONING

The advantages of becoming more selective about what we pursue is thus one of the main lessons of Milner's work: instead of indiscriminately amassing items, objects, moments, and experiences, she chooses them carefully, according to what genuinely satisfies her desire. In this manner, she curtails how she responds to her desire. The point of bringing in the day's catch is to pick the most bewitching beads from among the many possible ones. In addition, as I have stressed, more often than not, Milner's beads have nothing to do with commercial offerings but, instead, revolve around the appreciation of nature or the kinds of cultural, religious, and everyday items that can be admired without being purchased. That is, Milner's beads are not linked to ownership. They reside beyond the economy of exchange.

In the same way that reproductions of Cézanne's apples—and therefore the aura of the Thing that Lacan locates in these apples—are easily available in art books that can be found in public libraries, the beads that Milner fixates on are available in the details of her surroundings, regardless of where she happens to be. Although it is true that a trip to the Black Mountains in Germany or a visit to ancient temples in Greece may enhance her ability to discover beads that merit her attention, Milner also finds them in a variety of mundane settings. For her, creative self-fashioning—which, as I have proposed throughout this chapter, is antithetical to neoliberal self-optimization—is a matter of losing herself in items, objects, moments, and experiences of special significance that are nevertheless easily obtainable in the midst of daily life. Furthermore, as we have learned, it is a matter of eroding, dissolving, sidelining, or temporarily marginalizing the ego so as to create space for the irrational layers of the self, including its jouissance. Finally, Milner offers a distinctively psychoanalytic approach to creative living in that she does not seek to activate a preexisting essence, or kernel, of the self but rather to enter into a continuous process of self-constitution in relation to both internal and external stimuli.

Throughout my discussion, I have emphasized the importance of honoring the singularity of our being, of staying faithful to our desire, and of creating space for our true self in the sense that Winnicott defines the concept. It would be easy to misinterpret these objectives as suggesting that in some remote corner of our psyche, we possess a predetermined and immutable blueprint of personal authenticity and that it is the task of our distinctive art of living to honor the details of this blueprint. However, such a reading would overlook the fundamentally psychoanalytic foundations of the arguments that I have presented, especially the fact that at the heart of psychoanalysis resides the idea that the self is open to continual revision and refashioning. As I have pointed out, if this were not the case, there would be no purpose to psychoanalysis as a clinical practice that seeks to enable the subject to rewrite its destiny, for instance by dissolving its symptomatic behavior, breaking its debilitating repetition compulsions, or unlocking potentialities of its being that may have remained buried and therefore underutilized. For psychoanalytic practice to make any sense, the self must, by definition, remain an always incomplete work in progress.

From a psychoanalytic perspective, the self is a conglomerate of potentialities—a fluid, ever-evolving entity—that can crystallize into different versions at different points in its life. What Milner's texts reveal, in particular, is a rigorous attempt to sustain her inner vitality against the flattening and deadening aspects of her culture so as to protect her capacity for self-renewal and transformation. She understands that the process of self-fashioning does not ever come to a conclusion but must be repeatedly reinitiated. I do not mean that we must be so vigilantly aware of the task of self-fashioning that we begin to confuse it with self-improvement. Self-fashioning in the service of the creative self is not a matter of constant exertion. Rather, it is a matter of the kind of existential self-awareness that enables us to recognize when we have outgrown certain elements of our being so that we can discard them in order to create room for new elements. The self does not always need to be improving itself. But it is always changing, and we need to be able to adapt to the changes that take place.

Furthermore, there is no guarantee that the self will over time improve. When something goes awry, the self may even undergo considerable backsliding. For example, new traumatic experiences may introduce severe complications that make it impossible to consider human life as a progress narrative where the transition from point A to point B invariably represents growth. This may be one of the hardest components of mortality. If we know that we will only die once our purpose in life has been fulfilled, death might seem easier to confront. However, in almost every case, death comes too early, before we have had a chance to complete whatever "mission" it is that we might have set for ourselves. We may have a clear image of the kind of person we want to be or the kinds of things we want to do before we die. Sadly, death rarely waits for us to be finished with our plans. This being the case, all we can do is live every day to the best of our ability, trusting that even the days when we feel like we are sliding backward have the capacity to contribute something meaningful to our process of living. Indeed, if we never experienced difficulties, if our hearts never broke and our health never wavered, we might not be able to appreciate the times when things are going well.

Our lives do not, then, rest on secure ontological foundations. Nevertheless, there is a distinctive "something," a *je ne sais quoi*—a spirit or idiosyncratic attitude—that makes us who we are. It is this something, this spirit, this attitude, that creative living is meant to safeguard and cultivate. What it means to become a singular person is far from self-evident. Just about the only thing that one can say about it is what I have just stressed, namely that it does not entail attaining the kind of completion that one could tidily mark with a red bow. However, as I have also attempted to illustrate, it is precisely the fact that we are not complete—that we are lacking, damaged, injured, and derailed— that not only gives rise to desire but also provides the materials for the singularity of our being. In other words, the fact that we can rarely meet our aspirations in any decisive sense contributes to our art of living by ensuring that there is always something to strive for. On this view, having aspirations sustains our continual search for the singularity of our being, which is precisely what it means to be a creative self.

A large part of creative living is the ability to handle the unanticipated. On the one hand, there is a historical consistency to our being in the sense that we recall what our self was like in the past and know how this self compares with the one that we currently have. On the other hand, there are disjunctures and ruptures that tear apart any consistency that we may have developed over time. This, too, is a part of life: the ingredients of our self change constantly, one sliding to the foreground as another slips into the background. Indeed, while there are ways in which we recognize our lives as "ours," there are sometimes events—such as accidents, illnesses, or the loss of beloved people—that derail us so drastically that we end up feeling like we are living someone else's life. There may be times when we wish that we could have our old life back. Other times, we may be glad that we have transcended it. Either way, the self's viability comes down to its ability to effectively cope with the ever-present specter of falling apart—the fact that there is no stable core holding together all the revolving components that comprise the self. It may not be a conceptual or existential stretch to claim that such viability is synonymous with creative living.

Psychoanalysis allows us to conceptualize a self that does not possess mastery or full agency over itself but that is nevertheless capable of having a great deal of influence over the parameters of its life. By forging space for the irrational components of its being; by making conscious decisions about how it wants to live (within the limitations imposed on it by external circumstances); and by striving to eradicate damaging symptoms and repetition compulsions, the psychoanalyzed self aspires to a multidimensional life without assuming that it possesses a transparent understanding of its motivations and certainly without assuming that it possesses full agency over the parameters of its life. However, the self's lack of full understanding or agency does not mean that it has no understanding or agency to speak of.

We have seen that understanding and agency are less a priority for Milner than being able to plunge into the jouissance of the real—the mud of the ocean floor. She suggests that our best chance for living a rewarding life is to adopt an attitude of radical self-surrender. At the same time, the psychoanalytic context within which Milner develops her ideas compels her to value the notion of becoming an active participant in the task of fashioning the kind of life that feels meaningful. That is, Milner's ideal of self-surrender cannot be dissociated from the fact that becoming a creative self—the creator of one's destiny—means that one needs to embrace the fact that human life consists of a continual process of subjective reinvention, renewal, revival, and rebirth. Like a snake that sheds its skin when it becomes too confining, the creative self regenerates when its life becomes too restricting or when parts of this life no longer serve the purpose that they might once have had. As Milner elaborates, when the self needs a new way of looking at things, it experiences "a kind of uneasiness that's like the feeling of a coat that has grown too tight . . . an awareness that some current way of seeing the world is getting worn out, has served its usefulness and become a constricting cliché."[143]

The creative self knows that some of its elements will inevitably become outmoded and need to be rethought and sometimes even discarded. The ideal of creative living demands that we cultivate a distinctive art of living, a conscious poetics of being, that refashions our subjectivity on a regular basis, getting rid of components that no longer work and adding others that bring fresh vitality. Even though the basic ingredients of our lives are originally given to us without our input—even though we are born into circumstances over which we have no say—we possess the capacity to fashion a life that is centered on what is most important to us. Milner's greatest legacy, her greatest gift to us, is her ability to portray such a life so vividly, with such inspiring intensity, that reading her work is like tasting a slice of life.

2

"ASKING FOR PARADOX TO BE RESPECTED"

Winnicott's Creative Self

GAIL M. NEWMAN

I t is a joy to be hidden, and a disaster not to be found." This sentence enacts perfectly the paradoxes associated with Donald W. Winnicott's notion of the self. It also carries a great deal of meaning for me personally. I still remember vividly when I discovered Winnicott's work. I was a young assistant professor tackling the project of transforming my dissertation into a book, as is generally required of humanities scholars preparing for the tenure process. The problem was, I did not like my dissertation at all. It is common for dissertations to reflect the influence of their advisors, but in my case, whatever ideas of my own I might have had had either been replaced by those of my advisor, a very prominent scholar, or had not even had the opportunity to enter my consciousness because of my tendency to mold myself according to others' reality. In my new life as a teacher surrounded by congenial, supportive colleagues, however, I had just begun to get a glimpse of what it might be like to tap into a previously unknown creative wellspring. Just at that moment, I read Winnicott's compilation of essays, *Playing and Reality*—I cannot even remember how I came upon the book—and I instantly resonated with both its tone and its ideas. Exposure to Lacan in graduate school had piqued my interest in psychoanalytic theory, which aligned with a preexisting curiosity about the workings of my own and others' minds and emotions. But the aura among the Lacanians at my university made me feel inadequate; it was not until much later that I realized the true value of Lacan's work for my own—with Mari's readings playing a large role in that process. In the meantime, though, Winnicott was the first theorist that I had encountered who described how the self could be threatened not just by neglect, but also by "impingement" from others with their own agendas. He also showed me how writing with theoretical heft could be rigorous but clear and how it could accommodate within itself the process of coming to its conclusions, even including the wrong turns made along the way. I ended up writing a new book instead of revising my dissertation, a study of imagination in the work of the early German Romantic author Novalis, with Winnicott as its theoretical framework.

Over the years, Winnicott's ideas have accompanied me in my personal life as a teacher, a partner, and a parent as well as in my literary scholarship. It is a privilege to be able to turn now to a close reading of his work in its own right. In a series of scientific papers and informal talks for groups of parents, social workers, and even reform-house guards, the British pediatrician-turned-psychoanalyst presents a vision of a self whose creativity depends on both the reliable presence of an other person who can know it on a deep level, and—paradoxically—on its absolutely inviolable right not to be known. Winnicott's work matters, I claim, for several reasons and in several contexts. First, he details a notion of the authentic self that deviates in complex and important ways from the version propagated by the self-optimization industry, notably because its contradictions remain intact. Second, he elucidates a relationship between self and other that points toward a much-needed ethos of curiosity and care. Finally, and most crucially, Winnicott's work actively and persistently resists the binarism that increasingly characterizes our way of thinking and our lived experience.

Looking back on his life toward its end, Winnicott finds paradox at its core:

> My contribution is to ask for a paradox to be accepted and toler-
> ated and respected, and for it not to be resolved. By flight to split-
> off intellectual functioning it is possible to resolve the paradox,
> but the price of this is the loss of the value of the paradox itself.
> This paradox, once accepted and tolerated, has value for every
> human individual who is not only alive and living in this world
> but who is also capable of being infinitely enriched by exploita-
> tion of the cultural link with the past and with the future.[1]

Winnicott is here making a radical statement that could not be more important at this moment in history: we must resist the temptation to choose one side of a binary—to polarize—and instead allow ourselves to live in the exquisitely uncomfortable space of paradox, of contradiction, of dilemma, before we can move forward in action.

THE RISE OF THE INDIVIDUAL

In many ways, we are currently experiencing the triumph of the individual—a phenomenon to be distinguished from the singular self, as Mari details in her chapter. The rise of the individual was a process that began in the European Enlightenment of the late eighteenth century. At that time, Immanuel Kant (1724–1804) performed what he called a Copernican turn in philosophy: he proposed that the source of our knowledge of the world lies not in the phenomena it contains but, instead, in the mechanisms of our own minds that allow us to know and understand those phenomena. In philosophical terms, there was a shift toward the *subject*, that is, the observer or knower, and hence away from the *object*, the thing being observed or known. This move in the realm of philosophy coincided with a move away from a notion of political and cultural value based on a given individual's position in a traditional religious or hereditary hierarchy and toward the idea that this value is determined by qualities intrinsic to the individual. The French and American revolutions represented both the culmination of these ideas and the beginning of their rapid propagation throughout the Western world. At the same time, industrial capitalism was beginning to replace agrarianism in Europe and would soon dominate the economic landscape. Since then, capitalism has gained almost exclusive preeminence across the world.

We can see the results of these developments in the principles and practices that govern our daily lives today. The American ethos that places both possibility and responsibility squarely on the shoulders of the individual has increasingly been exported to other nations. More and more, entrepreneurship as an economic driver, but also as a worldview, has come to be celebrated; simultaneously, in many nations regulations are being lifted and taxes lowered in the spirit of removing constraints from individuals who want to maximize their personal gain and, the logic goes, thereby enrich the society as well. One of the most telling developments in the march toward the primacy of the individual was the U.S. Supreme Court's so-called Citizens United decision in 2010, which extended to corporations the right of free expression granted to individual citizens in the First Amendment to the Constitution and allowed financial donations to political candidates to be categorized as "expression." With this decision, the

Supreme Court made visible the close connection between economic capitalism and liberal political philosophy that had been present since the nation's inception, but to a cynical extent that was undoubtedly not envisioned by the founders. The primacy of the individual is at the heart of this connection: it becomes clear that the vaunted "pursuit of happiness" is closely intertwined with the pursuit of profit and "liberty" within open markets.

The idea of the individual human subject that was born in the Enlightenment contains within it some hidden contradictions, some losses as well as gains. On the one hand, the Kantian revolution brought with it a tremendous empowerment of the subject by locating its knowledge of the world inside its mind. In other words, the mind was no longer primarily conceived of as a passive receptor that records impressions of the world, but as an active processor of that which it encounters. The powerful subject that derived from this revolutionary shift tends toward a relationship to the world that involves serving the needs of the self; we see this in Western colonialism, Christian evangelism, and patriarchal structures, all bolstered by the Enlightenment philosophy that allows the masterful subject to dominate what it deems to be merely an object in the more conventional sense of the term. On the other hand, what the Kantian subject gains in agency and independence, it loses in the potential for authentic relationships to the object. While Kant himself did not go so far as to dispute the existence of things in themselves (others who followed him did), his philosophy places a filter, so to speak, between us and the world; we are not able to experience it directly, but only via the mental capacities that structure our knowledge. This implies a lack of access to the world that can lead to a sense of alienation or confusion.

Despite the potential for alienation from the world, the Western Enlightenment subject has played out its mastery of the world with abandon. The self gains some of its power from another important dimension of the Kantian project, namely the universalizing of the mind's capacities. We might expect a philosophy that locates the source of knowledge in the subject to imply relativism, but in fact, Kant's philosophy is as far from relativism as it could possibly be. The Kantian "categories," a somewhat misleading term that refers to the structuring principles dwelling innately in the mind, like our temporal and spatial senses, that allow us to grasp the things in the world before we have any experience of them—*a priori*, as Kant says—do not belong to one individual mind, but to Mind in general; they are shared across all of humankind. Thus, the self that takes epistemological dominance over the world is not a particular one, but a universal human subjectivity that has both the capacity and the right to do so. In this respect, Kantian idealism is an affirmation of abstraction: our knowledge of the world is based on an unchanging and impersonal set of epistemological laws and functions.

This dimension of Enlightenment rationalism underlies a particularly compelling and extreme form of market and financial capitalism that came to be called neoliberalism. Its conceptual founder was Friedrich August von Hayek, an Austrian-British economist whose work, virtually ignored at the time of its publication in the early twentieth century, was revived in the 1980s by the economists who advised Margaret Thatcher, Ronald Reagan, and their followers. According to its proponents, the neoliberal market is a purely abstract— and hence morally and politically neutral—structure that governs all aspects of human interaction.[2]

Here, too, we encounter a contradiction. On the one hand, it is comforting and affirming to believe that our experiences and decisions are undergirded by a set of principles that applies to all human beings, principles that are so much of a given that they resemble the laws that govern nature itself. For at least the last 250 years, universal human rights have been the touchstone for the rational adjudication of conflicts between nations or between groups. On the other hand, our commitment to the notion of a neutral realm of universal, eternal values has obscured the fact that these values are actually grounded in a specific historical time and geographical place. This commitment has frequently served as a justification for regarding values that deviate from ours as inferior, or even as not deserving of being called human values at all. Neoliberalism taps into the idea of a transcendent, neutral realm: the market is said to exist beyond all individual political, cultural, or personal agendas; it is supposedly governed by a price structure that is akin to mathematics in the abstract givenness of its validity. Hayek and his followers discarded the Keynesian belief that economics was a tool—one tool—that humans use to achieve societal goals that are based on values determined by political, moral, and cultural discussion. Before the rise of neoliberalism, the urge toward consumerism and profit-optimization had long been at odds with the Protestant ethos of strict frugality and self-denial that has tracked along with the rise of capitalism in the United States. But since the 1980s, we have been taught to embrace wholeheartedly the idea that we are all, at base, *homo economicus*, a species guided by the perfectly rational laws of the market, where self-interest is defined entirely in terms of maximizing personal gain and relationships are entirely transactional.[3] There is no longer any shame associated with being thoroughly focused on profit; on the contrary, profit-seeking has come to be the goal that is most highly valued in our society. Indeed, such an orientation is now considered to be at the very foundation of human nature.

We see the effects of this shift in every sphere of life. On the largest level, it has driven the ever-increasing income and power gap across the world. Under the supposedly absolute and eternal laws of the market, individuals who manage to use those laws to their best advantage are lionized as winners and all others are losers. In this way, a new kind of essentialistic "morality" is crafted from the amoral structure of the market. You didn't get into college? You must be less intelligent. Your neighborhood is suffering from poverty? Its people must be lazy. You can't afford your apartment because a family member got sick? You'd better hustle up a few more benefit-less jobs to prove you deserve to have the apartment in the first place. Accompanying the rise of neoliberalism has been an exacerbation of the distortion, per-version, and emptying out of language described in George Orwell's dystopian novel *1984*. We still use the language of morality incessantly, even compulsively, but the words are hol-low. There is no longer consensus based on rational discussion among individuals about the meaning of the words. If the fruits of Kantian philosophy—the moral subject of the categorical imperative, the scientific subject holding to universal natural laws—had for two centuries thrived despite the contradictions that inhere in it, those contradictions have now become glaringly obvious.

From the perspective of the devoted advocate of neoliberal-ism, societies and individuals have been freed from the con-straints of governmental interference and have entered a world of limitless opportunity to shape their own lives—self-reliance writ large. But the reality looks different. "Self-reliance" actually equals being left to fend for yourself in a dog-eat-dog world. Working multiple jobs to make ends meet, GoFundMe appeals to meet medical expenses, gigging as an Uber driver or on a delivery bike—these are the stark realities of life in America, and increasingly in the rest of the world as well. In the wake of neo-liberalism's triumph, anxiety has risen to epidemic proportions.

It is on this more personal level that my own experience—and hence this project—is focused. I have watched with dismay as the stone-cold dictates of neoliberalism have gradually become naturalized. As a college professor for nearly forty years, I have witnessed generation after generation of young people engaged in imagining their lives, joyfully anticipating or fearfully dreading what is to come. While it is always challenging to figure out where one wants to go next, to face the barriers to one's desires, and to balance one's own needs with those of others, I know I am not alone in my perception that young people today are tackling these tasks in an atmosphere of anxiety that exceeds that of previous generations. The quintessentially American ideal of freedom has under neoliberalism become a kind of constraint, even tyranny, for individuals told that they alone are responsible for every aspect of their lives. At my "selective," "elite" private college, some have had every imaginable opportunity from birth to optimize themselves: the most competitive private schools, expensive extracurricular activities, mentoring—i.e., scrutiny—from the best coaches and teachers. Others, often the first in their family to attend college, are expected to change their family's circumstances single-handedly through their education. While it might appear that only the latter group is constrained in its ability to find its own way and follow its own desire, in fact for all of these young people the pressure to "win" acceptance to top colleges and later to med school or law school or the fancy consulting firm—in short, to become the "best"—is agonizing.

The path toward success is an exercise in double binds. Young people are exhorted simultaneously to demonstrate "excellence" according to quantified, standardized measures, from the SAT to the grading system, and to set themselves apart as completely unique individuals. Crafting an aura of uniqueness is itself an impossible Catch-22: How can I show you my singular self when certain narratives of the self—the hurdle overcome, the failure endured, the loss grieved—are privileged, even codified as necessary for success? My colleagues and I, too, find ourselves increasingly bound up in the neoliberal contradiction of hyperindividualism combined with hyperstandardization. Like their students, and nearly everyone else, teachers are required to demonstrate, over and over again, that they are worthy of their role. This takes place, unsurprisingly, via standardized evaluations that—however often improvements are made based on research demonstrating significant problems with bias—ultimately position them as commodities to be rated. In one case with which I am familiar, this takes place in a manner identical to that used to rate purchases on Amazon: students anonymously give their teachers stars on an app designed, as its website states, to "democratize" education by providing "anonymized" feedback to teachers. In the process, teachers and students alike are reduced to faceless, nameless, ultimately interchangeable units, and any possibility for meaningful intellectual engagement is erased.

Ironically, then, the drive for self-optimization greatly impedes our search for authenticity and creativity. At first glance, it would seem that hindrances to being one's self have been lifted. Earlier eras demanded much more obvious conformity with norms in order to be accepted in society; ideals of beauty, love, and success were aligned unquestioningly with whiteness, heterosexuality, maleness, and financial wealth. Those who deviated from these implicit standards were forced either to comply as best they could or to be ostracized. Now, the increasing presence in the media of Blackness, body positivity, neurodiversity, queerness, and differences in ability gives the illusion that the demand to be a particular kind of self has abated. In fact, though, the traps for authenticity today are more insidious than ever, on at least two levels. First, the celebration of "difference" gives the illusion to the mainstream that white supremacy, homophobia, misogyny, and other structural inequities have been overcome, which dilutes and disarms attempts to make actual changes in the bedrock of an inequitable society. Second, the categories of otherness that are publicly celebrated can themselves feel coercive to individual selves. What if I don't experience myself as a representative of fat positivity or neurodiversity? I have known first-generation college students and others from groups underrepresented in higher education who experience a profound ambivalence at being welcomed upon their arrival at college by an array of options to join affinity groups associated with their own identities. Although they feel, to some extent, bolstered by a community that aligns with at least a part of their own sense of themselves, they are often disappointed to realize that even the people who supposedly have so much in common with them do not "get" them in important ways. These students end up doubly isolated.

Mental health represents another realm stamped with the imprint of neoliberalism. The approach toward what we are being forced to acknowledge as a mental health crisis in nearly all corners of society is heavily weighted toward what has come to be known as "psychohygiene": our own efforts, often supported by groups of similarly suffering individuals, to take care of our selves. At the same time, individual pain is often understood as a symptom that can be aligned with a particular illness, such as obsessive-compulsive disorder, body dysmorphic disorder, or attention deficit disorder, which along with depression and anxiety, are the diseases that characterize our time, as hysteria did Freud's. Especially young people find themselves defining their identities and demanding recognition in terms of their illnesses. On the one hand, the reduction of stigma associated with mental illness is a welcome change from previous eras; people feel less shame about seeking help for mental health problems. On the other hand, the emphasis on diagnosis tends to dull our curiosity about the specificities of individuals' suffering, which is often as idiosyncratic as any other aspect of a singular personality.

More fundamental than any particular example of its negative effects, though, is neoliberalism's fostering of a thoroughgoing binarism of thinking in our society, a reductionistic version of the law of noncontradiction familiar to readers of Western rationalist philosophers from Aristotle to Kant. These philosophies differ from one another in their nuances, but all have in common the principle that two opposite things cannot logically be true at the same time. Underlying this idea is in turn the unquestioned assumption that logic itself is ethically, as well as epistemologically, the principle guiding our thinking and actions. "You're contradicting yourself!" is the worst accusation that can be leveled at an interlocutor, and the gleeful search for contradictions in arguments is a satisfying pastime for academics and nonacademics alike. Logic's quasi-mathematical abstraction is what makes it attractive; after all, we are overwhelmed daily by contingency and arbitrariness on every level, so the thought of a system completely stripped of randomness and idiosyncrasy is very compelling. The premise, until recently equally unquestioned, that objectivity is both possible and necessary, permeates all aspects of our society, from journalism to law to medicine.

Neoliberalism's insistence on a market that is all and knows all is the economic manifestation of our stubborn belief in neutrality, universality, and noncontradiction. Because it bases itself on supposedly natural, eternal, universal laws, it can claim that it reaches beyond the merely economic to human behavior in general. As a result, the mentality behind practices that have always been the object of study of economics as a discipline—commercial transactions, the maximization of wealth, the evaluation of market viability—is extended to every area of our lives. Zero-sum thinking rules: my gain necessarily means your loss, and vice versa. Discussion becomes debate, point-counterpoint, where one side wins and the other loses. Negotiation is privileged above all other modes of engagement with others, with advice abounding on how to negotiate with your parents, your boss, your spouse, your children, and even your pets. If curiosity about what we do not know about ourselves and others is cast as vulnerability, and humility as weakness, then we have lost something precious.

The tendency to accept as inescapable the mutually exclusive terms in which any issue is presented to us is, to my mind, one of the biggest obstacles to creativity that we face. When we are forced to decide between two opposite perspectives, we are not only precluding possible alternative views, we are also taking a defensive approach to our identity: in this mode, my goal is to harden myself against the other side. Instead, I might imagine that the goal of discussion could be not building a bulwark but entering, together with my interlocutor, a new territory that is not coterminous with either of the two positions that we held at the beginning of our engagement with each other. The new way of thinking that emerges is not a compromise, in which each side gives something up in order to move forward, but rather a third mode that shares some qualities of each of the two original positions but also introduces something qualitatively different.

Binary thinking tends also to be absolute thinking. Structurally, if there are only two positions in a configuration, each person has only two options: I either hold on tight to my own position or I concede to the other. Indeed, this is what we increasingly witness in public discourse, where exceedingly complex dynamics are reduced to merciless stand-offs. This is particularly tragic in situations where deep pain is involved and where there should theoretically be an opportunity for learning. I am thinking of the seemingly endless pattern of racial, sexual, gender, religious, or other harassment in higher education and elsewhere, which tends to go something like this: an individual or group of individuals is profoundly hurt by an aggressive incident perpetrated against them because of who they are. They are thoroughly destabilized by the incident, unable to concentrate, distrustful of others, depressed, and anxious. They turn to representatives of the institution for help; these representatives are shocked by the incident, but the very fact that they are surprised is experienced as a retraumatization by those whose lives are frequently interrupted by micro- and macroaggressions. The institution responds by offering the opportunity to talk the incident through, but the environment so beloved of liberal intellectuals—the discussion forum—is not a space in which systemically marginalized people find solace and an opportunity for the resolution of grievances. On the contrary, the requirement to speak in public about one's innermost reality—a reality that is not shared by the majority—is a nightmare. Pain turns to anger in the context of this misunderstanding, perceived as willful, and demands are made, often quite stark demands that are impossible to meet perfectly. The institution enters a self-defense mode, with preserving order, face, and the status quo often effacing commitments to equity and inclusion. At this point, each side feels absolutely certain that what is at stake is an equally absolute right to exist. It is impossible to break deadlocks like this so long as we remain in the binary mode that characterizes them; in the context of such absolute positions, any concession constitutes a total loss. I want to emphasize that it is not the *content* of either side's demands, assertions, or explanations that makes this situation intractable, it is their very *structure*.

In what follows, I lay out an alternative to the dichotomous thinking that derives from the exaggerated versions of Enlightenment rationalism and liberal capitalism that are at the root of our contemporary society; such thinking hinders us in our ability to be creative with both ourselves and others. In both the substance and the style of his many theoretical, clinical, and popular works, Winnicott provides us with a guide to a more grounded, open, and playful relationship to our selves and the world. Winnicott, who began his career as a pediatrician, psychiatrist, and psychoanalyst working primarily with children, produced a body of work that attempts to get at the very beginning of the self and its deepest core. For Winnicott, the self is not an essential entity—someone with an immutable essence, as we tend to think—but is, rather, constituted as a complex configuration and as a set of processes. His language, too, is dynamic and layered. Indeed, more than describing, it enacts the phenomena he analyzes by verbalizing nouns: he speaks of "playing" rather than "play" and "experiencing" rather than "experience." He also creates elaborate constructs, such as "going-on-being" or a "feeling of real," that point toward the crucial dimensions of the self without directly naming them. Winnicott's opus as a whole moves somewhat like a spiral, returning again and again to key insights that gain contour and nuance in each iteration.

My discussion follows this spiral, beginning with the configuration that constitutes and supports the proto-self in the beginning, and tracing the emergence of the creative self. Along

the way, I describe the role of an other person in the self's coming into being, and how a particular kind of presence of that
other allows the self to engage the world with curiosity and generosity. I highlight verbs that are crucial for the creative self:
playing, experiencing, destroying, surviving. I show how the
self's creative contours are formed around a core that is shadowed by the threat of annihilation and that is—indeed must
be—inaccessible if it is to remain authentic and, paradoxically,
expressible. Throughout, I bring in examples from lived experience, including my own as a teacher and a scholar of German
language, literature, and culture.

"THERE IS NO SUCH THING
AS AN INFANT"

The starting point for most psychoanalytic discussions of the self
is the *ego*, or the "I," to use the direct translation of Freud's *Ich*.
In Freud's model, the bedrock of human development is the
Oedipus complex, which famously involves a son, a father, and
a mother—the classic bourgeois nuclear family configuration.
The aspect of Freud's idea that sticks most persistently in the
popular imagination is the scenario in which the son desires his
mother and wants to kill his rival, the father, for her sexual affection; equally persistent is the disparagement of the whole scenario. But Freud is onto something—at least with regard to the
Western patriarchal context that he falsely universalized to all
of humanity. In that context, the triangular dynamic that is
driven by masculine rivalry over a contested object, often marked
as feminine, does indeed underlie a great many of our interactions. This is certainly evident in the case of political conflicts,
which usually revolve around competing claims for territory or

resources. Alternatively—or simultaneously—they might involve competition for some more abstractly defined claim, including exclusive rights to a precious master narrative. Such a narrative often has to do with establishing oneself as uniquely superior, as was the case with the Nazis, or uniquely victimized, as happened in the Balkan wars of the 1990s, where both Bosnian Serbs and Bosnian Croats cast themselves as entitled to revenge against the other as the oppressed loser of a fourteenth-century battle. I would say that Russia's invasion of Ukraine is propelled by a combination of both claims: Russia, according to Vladimir Putin, is *both* especially worthy of occupying a privileged status in the world *and* especially deprived of that status by others. The set-up behind military conflicts of this sort is mirrored in sports contests (who can claim the ball/the puck/the field position?), in business (market share), and in other analogous areas of our society. At stake in this fundamental structure is *possession* of a valued object that in turn proves the *ascendancy* of the one contestant over the other; position in a hierarchy of value defined as power is associated with ownership.

Ironically, in this model, the value of the object over which is competed is lost in the contest between the two competitors. This is particularly evident when we remember the original gendered nature of Freud's Oedipal structure. Although the original desire is for the object marked feminine, what is foregrounded are the masculine rivals for her affection. While the conflict is intense, the underlying patriarchal structure remains in place, whoever wins. Indeed, Freud noted that both father and son reap both gains and losses in the resolution of the Oedipal struggle, which involves the son stepping into the line of succession as an adult male capable of himself becoming a husband and father by renouncing his immediate claim on the father's possession. The father, in turn, wins the first round, but will eventually need to step aside in favor of his heir. In this situation, where apparent opposition masks a fundamental unity, the feminine is regarded as subversive, even dangerous. We see this in popular films that center on masculine friendship threatened by a heterosexual love interest, and much more ominously in the vicious attempts by conservatives to control women's bodies.

Returning to the structural level, it is taken as a given here that those who are competing are whole selves with distinct desires for an object, which is as self-contained as those who covet it. It is also located outside of each of them, insofar as it does not yet belong to either of them. Freud regarded the Oedipus complex as the bedrock of all ego development: the son figure comes into being as a self, and especially as a social self, through the conflict with the father. While Freud did acknowledge the masculine orientation of this ostensibly universal structure and tried to figure out its feminine equivalent, he ultimately gave up on this project, conceding that he would forever be puzzled by the question: "What does a woman want?"[4] Melanie Klein's theories complicate the picture. She shifts the focus from the oedipal father-son dynamic (with the mother as the desired object over which those two compete) to the so-called "preoedipal" situation, the relationship between the caregiver (usually the mother) and the baby; in this respect, Klein recasts the triad as a dyad. Entirely new dynamics come into view with this move. What is at stake is no longer winning or losing a competition for possession of something, but rather separation and connection: to what extent is the other a part of me, to what extent does she exist as an entity in her own right? Hence, she imagines that the baby in its earliest stages engages (unconsciously, of course) not with a whole object, in the psychoanalytic sense of another person, that it wants to possess, but with part-objects, most notably the mother's breast, that it alternately wants to reject, consume, or even destroy.

This is an important correction: not only did Klein introduce the mother into the psychoanalytic picture but she also posited a much earlier ego formation than Freud's oedipal arrangement, which presupposes already-intact boundaries of self and other. It is precisely those boundaries that are being negotiated in the Kleinian schema. Winnicott, in turn, explores a situation that, developmentally speaking, *precedes* even the preoedipal stage, and ontologically speaking is at the *core* of the self. Having noted that while "at first sight it would seem that a great deal of psycho-analytic theory is about early childhood and infancy," he concludes that aside from a small number of childhood observations, "Freud can be said to have neglected infancy as a state."[5] In contrast, Winnicott begins his study of the ego at the point where it only exists as a proto-self that is absolutely dependent on its environment for its very existence, as I explain in more detail below. If Freud's is a three-figure model based in conflict, and Klein's a two-figure model organized around the establishment and destruction of boundaries, Winnicott focuses on a situation in which one figure is in the process of coming into being but cannot do so without the presence of another.

For Winnicott, the fact that "at the earliest stages the infant and the maternal care belong to each other and cannot be disentangled" must be acknowledged fully if one is to understand the workings of the deepest layers of the psyche.[6] More than an entity, the nascent self is a complex system that involves what we might call a combination of nature—Winnicott's phrase is "inherited potential"[7]—and nurture—the "facilitating environment."[8] In this respect, we both do and do not start out with an individual self, and this particular paradox is merely the central one in a nested series that I will examine in due course. For now, let us take a closer look at the self-environment configuration. Seen from the outside, it consists of two components, what looks like a baby and a caregiver. But if things are going well, the baby itself is unaware of anything outside of the caregiving environment, which implies a one-figure baby-environment unit. In fact, in another sense, since the infant is also not aware of itself as a discrete entity, there is no self present at all. I sometimes think of Winnicott's hypothesized infant as Schrödinger's baby: like the cat in Erwin Schrödinger's thought experiment who is simultaneously alive and dead inside its closed box until the observer opens the box to check on it, Winnicott's infant is omnipresent and omnipotent at the same time as it does not exist at all.

As for the facilitating environment, it functions in a way that goes beyond providing what we usually think of as care. It is more like a kind of prosthetic or ersatz ego for the as yet unformed self of the infant. In other words, the caregiver performs the functions of a self for the proto-self, deciding when and how to regulate the temperature or provide food for a being that cannot yet perceive itself as cold or hungry. Hence, infant + environment = the self, and this is the case both on the temporal level, as a starting point for development, and on a figuratively spatial level, as the kernel of what the self is. Why does this matter? This notion of the self has implications on several levels.

In the history of psychoanalysis, acknowledging the role of a really existing external figure in the emergence of the internal world reintroduces an element that Freud had considered in his earliest work, but then subsequently rejected. When he first began studying and treating so-called "hysterics"—people, usually women, who developed unusual and pronounced physical symptoms without any evident organic cause—he discovered that in all cases, the physical symptoms functioned to communicate a traumatic memory that the patient was not able to access consciously. These memories were of childhood sexual abuse that had subsequently been relegated to the unconscious because they were too traumatic to remember. Freud's "seduction theory" of hysterical illness shone a spotlight on family, gender, and sexual dynamics in his time, the late nineteenth and early twentieth centuries, revealing a shocking disregard for the bodily integrity of children, especially girls, and a thoroughgoing suppression of female sexuality. Perhaps concerned—consciously or unconsciously—about the negative picture of men that his theory presented, Freud turned his attention to the issue of women's sexuality, focusing on the disallowed desires that were expressing themselves indirectly through his patients' symptoms. Eventually, he came to regard hysteria as involving the sexual *fantasies* of the patients that he treated, rather than sexual traumas that they had experienced.[9] The external world ceased to be of much interest to Freud as a driver of neurosis until at least the 1920s, when he could not ignore the traumatic effects of World War I on his patients. But even taking this effect into account, the intrapsychic dominated Freud's thinking and most of the psychoanalytic theory that followed.

Even Melanie Klein, who is considered the founder of the object relations school of psychoanalysis, thinks exclusively in terms of the *internal* objects, that is, the images of external persons, particularly the mother, that are lodged in the self's internal reality. Winnicott was one of the first to take seriously again the roles of actual other people and circumstances in his patients' world. The most important figure for him is the mother, although he takes pains, even in his earliest papers from the 1950s, to note that the facilitating other need not be the baby's actual mother, and later he acknowledges that fathers can be in the position of a primary caregiver as well. Winnicott also stands out for his close attention to the experiences of the caregiver (the mother) herself, and not just her effect on the infant. Winnicott's focus on the external world might have arisen in part because of the indelible effect that the evacuation of children to the English countryside during World War II, away from their parents in the cities, had on him as he began his career. He was acutely aware of the fact that psychic reality cannot be separated from the outside world. Winnicott was in this respect a forerunner of psychoanalysis today. Sociological considerations are playing an increasingly important role in contemporary psychoanalytic theory; it is impossible to account for the effects of race, class, gender, and other key factors in individuals' psychic experience without looking closely at the surrounding environment.

There are ethical implications for psychotherapists associated with conceptualizing the self as fundamentally intertwined with others, as well. Winnicott reminded his colleagues that "if the dependability of the internal figures does not derive from actual experience in early infantile life then one can say also that it does not matter whether the analyst is dependable or lacks dependability, and I feel that we cannot hold this view."[10] Beyond highlighting the crucial importance of the analyst's dependability, Winnicott reflects again and again in his writings on the damage that therapists can do to the people who entrust themselves to their care. He took Freud's notion of "countertransference"—the fact that analysts refind in or project onto their patients their own psychological issues (just as patients do with their therapists via "transference")—much further, urgently reminding himself and other analysts that providing an interpretation, however brilliant it might be, can function for the patient as a traumatic imposition of another's reality onto their inner life. Hence, not only the analysand's but also the analyst's psychic worlds are profoundly affected by external features, including and perhaps most strongly each other.

More broadly, Winnicott's model renders more complex the usual juxtapositions of internal and external, self and other that

can easily devolve into opposition. If my self is thoroughly intertwined with an other, then that self is both expanded beyond its
own boundaries and humbled by its dependence on something
outside itself. It is a paradoxical relationship: in the beginning is
a nothing that can be something, and an irreplaceable something
that cannot be itself—or even be at all—without an other.
Another paradox: in order to achieve what Winnicott calls "unit
status," in which "the infant becomes a person, an individual in
his own right,"[11] there must be a state of "primary unintegration."[12] In other words, the fullness of our selves derives from a
kind of emptiness that must be preserved if we are to come into
existence. Indeed, the only activity in this earliest state is what
Winnicott calls "going-on-being." There is no will to become
anything in particular, only the urge to continue to be as a *potential* unique self.

Here we can already see an alternative to the focus on outcomes that characterizes our usual notion of what the self should
be doing. The push for productivity is driven by fear of what is
cast as its opposite, stagnation. It even becomes moralized: laziness might very well be the cardinal sin of our modern secular
society. Going-on-being would be characterized in this model
as stagnation, or passivity. In contrast, for Winnicott, it is precisely the state of allowing being to be that forms the foundation for becoming oneself as maturation proceeds. There is not
no movement in this state, but rather subtly different kinds of
movement than the goal-oriented linearity we are accustomed
to thinking of as desirable. In one sense, this movement is indeed
linear: as growth, in the form of maturation, and as development,
that is, forward motion toward integration of a self-contained
ego and toward the possibility of a relationship to equally self-
contained objects. But in another sense, the movement in this
primal space/time is thoroughly unlike the familiar imperatives

of growth and progress; Winnicott likens it in one paper to the "music of the spheres."[13] At stake is sheer existence as a potential self, whose forward motion is fueled by its own intrinsic constitution and its caregiver's curiosity about who it is and will become.

The relationship to caregivers reveals another paradox in Winnicott's model: the self can only go on being and become its self in a state of "undisturbed isolation," but that is only possible because of its absolute dependence on another.[14] What matters is the positionality of infant and caregiver. I picture the situation as a set of concentric circles, the first circle indicating the caregiver, who functions as a kind of temporary ego-membrane, shaping and containing the proto-self at the center of the figure; this caregiver is in turn embedded in the outer circle of the larger social environment.

As I have noted, the nascent self has, under favorable conditions, no knowledge of either itself or its environment; in this epistemological respect, no relationship is present at this point, because there is no subject and no object.

It is tempting to regard this set-up as a kind of merger. Indeed, Axel Honneth, one of the most prominent social philosophers of our time, enlists Winnicott in his theory of the individual as guided by a search for recognition. The development of the subject, which Honneth claims to have derived from Winnicott's model, begins with a "symbiosis."[15] The terms "merger/merged," "undifferentiated," and "symbiosis" appear repeatedly in the discussion, designating a state in which, as Honneth emphasizes, both parties must "learn how to differentiate themselves as independent entities."[16] But accompanying the process of differentiation is an ever-present longing back to the undifferentiated symbiosis that supposedly characterized the earliest stage of life, according to Honneth. He claims that all love relationships are driven by a desire to refind this originary situation, although a successful love relationship involves also accepting the impossibility of return.

Why take issue with Honneth's model from a Winnicottian perspective? Quite simply, it is based on a misunderstanding of Winnicott.[17] While we can acknowledge that a paradisiacal, but sadly lost, state of fusion is appealing in the context of the exaggerated autonomy associated with the Enlightenment—and especially the neoliberal—self, the erasure of all difference is ultimately merely the obverse of an absolute individuality. There are several problems with Honneth's thoroughly gendered model, which pits "being able to be alone and the experience of being merged" against each other.[18] First, the two states—rigidly bounded aloneness and completely unbounded fusion—do not actually represent qualitatively different alternatives, since one is simply the absence of the other. The fundamental terms of the argument are retained: boundaries, yes or no? There is no room here for a truly new mode of being with oneself and others. In addition, Honneth's notion of merger with the mother as a lost state invokes a kind of nostalgia that can quickly become reactionary. Regarding the woman as a safe haven for the man has been at the root of a tendency to idealize that obscures women's individuality and a dangerous, sometimes-deadly rage when that absolute safety is not forthcoming. One can also see the danger of nostalgia in political movements that idealize—and in the case, for example, of Putin's Russia, weaponize—a longing for a supposedly originary unity and omnipotence that has been unfairly destroyed by outside forces.[19]

In Winnicott's model, the originary situation differs from a merger; it is not, as Winnicott directly says, a "direct union." Instead, there is the "illusion of a relationship" that involves "absolute dependence and absolute independence" at once.[20] This simultaneity exists within the infant itself, as I have detailed, and in the "total set-up" of infant + facilitating environment that constitutes the "center of gravity" at this stage.[21] Unlike Honneth, who claims a symmetry between infant and mother, with both "entirely dependent on each other for the satisfaction of their needs and incapable of individually demarcating themselves from each other,"[22] Winnicott recognizes that the situation is, as Joel Whitebook calls it, "radical[ly] asymmetrical."[23] The infant is indeed "entirely dependent" on its caregiver, but the caregiver is already an independent entity who enters into a state of identification with the infant temporarily and partially. Let us take a closer look at that state.

"PRIMARY MATERNAL PREOCCUPATION"

As I note above, idealizing an ostensible early state of fusion with the mother is a highly problematic tendency. It underlies stereotypical notions of the woman as the port in the storm for the masculine adventurer, as the keeper of the home to which the exhausted executive returns for emotional resuscitation, and ultimately as the womblike space in which the man can lose himself in sex, letting go of the need to keep himself together in order to be able to compete in the outside world. In this context, Winnicott's emphasis on the importance for the infant of the facilitating environment—and especially his famous and repeated phrase "good-enough mother"—makes it all too easy to write him off as just another male psychoanalyst who idealizes the mother as providing everything a child could ever need or blames the mother for all ills. If we wanted to rescue Winnicott's theories for today, we could try to give him a pass simply by pointing to the fact that he was writing in the 1950s and 1960s, when ideas of gender roles were different. But this historical relativism is ultimately unsatisfying. Instead, I hope to provide a balanced analysis that takes account of Winnicott's idiosyncratic approach, which was necessarily embedded in his historical context, but also points to the value of his ideas for our own.

It is important here to remember that in the 1940s, Winnicott was pressed into service as the consultant psychiatrist to the Government Evacuation Scheme in a so-called "reception area" in England.[24] Having worked with children for his whole career, first as a pediatrician and later as a child psychoanalyst, Winnicott was well-placed to provide this service, and the experience of working with children who had been evacuated from cities at danger from German bombs to homes in the countryside affected his thinking profoundly. His involvement in the evacuation helped shape his notion of psychic life at all stages and all levels as a configuration, rather than a fixed entity. In his academic papers, his analytic work, and his public lectures, Winnicott focuses on the structural arrangement that facilitates coming-into and going-on being. Within this arrangement, it is certainly the child who most obviously engages in these processes, but the parent's (mostly mother's) experience is not neglected.

This parallels Winnicott's thinking on the analytic setting itself. He turns his attention increasingly over the course of his career to the role of the analyst, concentrating particularly on the analyst's failures and even providing brief, poignant glimpses into his own feelings in the face of difficult cases. The overlap between the analytic and the family situation is clearly evident in his piece on "Hate in the Counter-Transference," which includes a section on the mother's love and hate of her child, a radical acknowledgment of what every parent knows: we have all kinds of strong feelings for our children, not all of which are positive.[25] What is more, Winnicott sees an important effect on

the child—analogous to the patient who has regressed to a pre-
or noncohesive state—in the parent's ability to hate, going so far
as to say that the patient/child cannot learn to tolerate their own
hate of the analyst/parent unless the analyst/parent can hate
them. The parent is aided in their ability to hate without acting
on it by the symbolic realm of poetry and play. I think, for example, of those games where a parent throws the child into the air
and catches it; the child can experience real danger—and the
parent can fantasmatically enact disposing of the child—for a
brief moment in the certainty of being safe. Winnicott gives the
even better example of the beloved nursery rhyme:

> Rockabye Baby, on the tree top,
> When the wind blows, the cradle will rock,
> When the bough breaks the cradle will fall,
> And down will come baby, cradle and all.

The combination of the brutal content and the sweet melody of
the song perfectly illustrates the exquisite tension between hate
and love that allows parent and child alike to experience, unconsciously of course, the ambivalence that necessarily inheres in
all relationships.

The relationship of mother to infant is perhaps the most paradoxical of all, as Winnicott outlines in his "Primary Maternal
Preoccupation." At once "ordinary devotion"[26] and also a "very
special state,"[27] the brief period that stretches from some unde-
termined time during pregnancy to an equally indistinct end
point during the baby's first months involves a fascinating alteration in the mother's sense of where she and the baby begin and
end. Winnicott calls the situation a kind of "normal illness" that
can range from withdrawal into a baby-mama bubble to a quasi-
schizoid dissociation, even a sort of "fugue" state.[28] Far from

idealizing or objectifying the pregnant and postpartum mother, Winnicott might be one of the first theorists, and perhaps the only man, to take seriously a kind of pregnant subjectivity that would later be thoroughly elaborated by the Israeli artist and psychoanalyst Bracha Ettinger. Her notion of the "matrixial space" sees pregnancy as introducing a "psychic and mental transgression of the boundaries of unicity of being."[29] This is no simple ideal state of fusion, but rather a complex subversion of our usual binary of autonomy vs. dependence.

Through the experience of a late-term pregnancy loss and a subsequent (joyfully successful) bed-rest pregnancy, I myself became very interested in the possibility that pregnancy represents an alternative kind of subjectivity, one that involves not a loss of the boundary between self and other, as some might think, but a complication of that boundary. The pregnant subject—or the primarily preoccupied mother—is both a single self, like the nonpregnant subject, and also a self + other. Its self is centered in and on the other within it, but it is simultaneously alienated, through the presence of that other, from the self that it had heretofore taken for granted. In this respect, the pregnant and postpartum subject mirrors the pre-ego "set-up" associated with infancy. Indeed, Winnicott asserts that in the grip of primary maternal preoccupation, the caregiver can "feel herself into the infant's place."[30] From one perspective, this can be interpreted as a productive regression of the sort that Winnicott considers essential for the treatment of the kind of psychic disturbance that does not respond to Freudian or Kleinian psychoanalysis. But we could also speak of a transgenerational transsubjectivity, a kind of positive counterpart to the transgenerational transmission of trauma about which we read so much today. In this model, both child and mother experience a peculiar coincidence of being everything and nothing. I have detailed this experience already with regard to the infant, but for the mother, it involves feeling like you are responsible for literally everything in another human being's world at the same time as you are completely at the mercy of that being. Like the infant, you feel infinitely vulnerable, but also empowered to be infinitely creative.

There are important differences between the infant and its caregiver, though. While the infant, as I have described, has absolutely no knowledge of its world or its self as entities, the parents possess both self-consciousness and awareness of their surroundings as separate. Their immediately pre- and postbirth status is, we will remember, a "very special state," a psychological "condition," according to Winnicott, that is temporally limited as well as being self-contained in other ways.[31] Hence, we are dealing not, as Axel Honneth would have it, with a symmetrical situation in which "symbiotic oneness" in which "both partners are entirely dependent on each other for the satisfaction of their needs and are incapable of individually demarcating themselves from each other."[32] Far from having to learn (like the infant) how to differentiate herself, as in Honneth's model,[33] the Winnicottian mother dwells only temporarily in the state that allows her to identify with the as yet unformed infant self and will return to her preexisting differentiated state. Hence "transsubjectivity," coined by Wendy Holloway following Ettinger, works better as a description of the subjective condition of the primarily preoccupied mother + proto-infant than Honneth's "undifferentiated intersubjectivity."[34] Rather than stagnantly fused, the transubjective disposition of Winnicott's early set-up is dynamic, craving movement across boundaries between self and world, familiar and unfamiliar. In fact, I will claim that the development of the infant-caregiver configuration constitutes the ideal analogy for generating a creative self.

"ASKING FOR A PARADOX TO BE ACCEPTED AND TOLERATED AND RESPECTED, AND FOR IT NOT TO BE RESOLVED"

The process proceeds, developmentally speaking, in three stages, and these developmental states in turn constitute the various layers of the creative self. Initially, we are dealing with the nested two-figure phenomenon I have already described; this first stage paradoxically both presupposes and, in a sense, brings about a dyadic configuration. A third dimension gradually appears, which Winnicott calls the intermediate area of playing with the boundaries of self and other. As I detail below, this figurative time and space where one practices a productive relationship to the world, involving both connection and privacy, is a genuine alternative to the opposites of me vs. not-me, alone vs. merged. Intermediate-area experiencing, in turn, widens out into the realm of cultural life—arts, religion, intellectual engagement—where fully-formed subjects can briefly let go of the need to keep themselves together that accompanies most of their day-to-day experience.

I have already outlined the Schrödinger-like coincidence of all and nothing that characterizes the very earliest experience of the pre-self self. Not surprisingly, this state does not, cannot, and should not last very long. Very soon, a gap opens up between the nascent subject and its facilitating environment, brought about both by the caregiver's emergence from primary preoccupation and recentering around their own interests and by the baby's maturation toward the ability to wait for its needs to be met. Just as it had been essential in the earliest stage for the caregiver as prosthetic ego to anticipate those needs, allowing the baby the illusion that a seamless continuity exists between itself and its world, it is equally essential that the caregiver now wait until a signal is given before turning attention to the baby. Without this shift, neither the self nor the other can (experientially) come into being for the baby. In Winnicott's own idiosyncratic words, "If now [the mother] knows too well what the infant needs, this is magic and forms no basis for an object relationship."[35]

It seems clear that Winnicott discovered this dangerous phenomenon through introspection about his own clinical practice, where he noticed that an interpretation, however accurate it might be, did no good—and could even be traumatic for the patient—if it was uttered without the patient having indicated (usually unconsciously) a receptivity for the interpretation. We can distill from these two scenarios—the parent-infant and the analyst-analysand relationships—a structural dynamic that is critical for the emergence of a self, and specifically a creative self: we see movement emanating outward from the subject that must meet a limit—albeit an elastic limit—in the external world in order to be able to begin to gain a consciousness of its self that in turn provides it with contours of its own. If, instead, the movement is initiated from the outside in, two kinds of problems can arise: either the self develops an all too porous boundary vis a vis its environment or it is forced to erect an impervious shell around itself to prevent erasure. I will examine the positive scenario first before looking more closely at the pitfalls.

The very earliest source of creativity for Winnicott is what he calls the "spontaneous gesture," the random movements of the infant.[36] Picture the flailing arms and legs of the very young baby, the fingers and toes grasping at seemingly nothing; the lack of what we might call a goal to the motions is irrelevant—what matters is that the impulse originates in the self. Indeed, the fact that it is incomprehensible from an adult perspective attests to its proprietary, private, idiosyncratic nature. It comes from the "centre," the core of the individual, and is inhibited neither by needing to have an intention nor by the agenda of the external world.[37] The ability to move in this way is an expression of the going-on-being that constitutes the self before it can experience itself as such. The very impulse to live, and to live as oneself, manifests itself at first as a sheer reaching out into the world, and the world must allow the reaching without expecting that the reaching have a goal.

Even hunger can be aligned with this impulse. According to Winnicott, the child seeks not merely food but also contact with the world. The infant needs "an external object, and not merely a satisfying object."[38] In fact, a too-satisfying, or rather a too-immediately satisfying object, is ultimately *not* satisfying, and even harmful, as I have described above. Paradoxes abound in this situation: not only does coming upon something genuinely other than itself facilitate the coming into being of the self as self but bumping up against the limit of the world fuels the self's potentially limitless capacity to create the world. How does this work? I picture the operation as analogous to the process of forming a pot out of a lump of clay. We might usually think of the potter as actively forming the clay into something, but from another perspective, especially when it is on the wheel, the clay becomes something on its own, so to speak, as it comes up against the hands.

A spontaneous gesture bounces off another entity, and the self that initiated the gesture begins to form in the context of another self. If, as I hope to have shown in the introduction to the chapter, the modern Western subject in general—and the neoliberal subject, in particular—has its roots in Kantian rationalism, I see here a connection between Winnicott's notion of the birth of the creative self and the musings of a follower, but also a critic, of

Kantian philosophy, the early German Romantic author Novalis (the pseudonym of Friedrich von Hardenberg, 1772–1801), who
highlights the role of what he called "productive imagination"
in the birth of subjectivity. Just as Winnicott regarded himself
as both carrying on, and importantly revising, the Freudian tradition, Novalis and his collaborators based their work in Kant's
"transcendental idealism," but found the need to provide an antidote to the "petrifying and petrified reason" to which it was
susceptible.[39] Novalis was fascinated by the theories of Johann
Gottlieb Fichte (1762–1814), who radicalized Kant's relocation of
the source of knowledge from external to internal. Fichte's theory focuses on an "absolute I" that consists entirely in the act of
positing itself. More even than being the locus of knowledge
about the world, this *I* in effect either contains the world within
itself or renders the world irrelevant, depending on the interpreter's perspective. Novalis sees in the sheer activity of self- and
world-generation an analogy to *Poesie*, a term that for him goes
far beyond what we call "poetry" to encompass a creative cast of
mind that has the capacity to transform our lives. For him and
the other thinkers in the Romantic circle that congregated in the
northeastern German town of Jena at the very end of the eighteenth century, a kind of revolution of the imagination would
have an even more profound effect than the political revolutions
in France and America.

But Novalis recognizes a disturbing tendency toward solip-
sism, even imperialism, in Fichte's philosophy, specifically in
his description of how the absolute *I* comes to consciousness of
itself. The absolute *I* as nothing but a constant, limitless emana-
tion of itself can paradoxically only achieve a higher freedom if
it becomes self-conscious through limiting itself. Hence it posits a *NotI* which functions as a kind of reflective surface against
which it can define itself, leading to a spiraling recursivity of

self-generation and self-reflection. But Novalis was troubled by the hall-of-mirrors quality of Fichte's theory, where the *I* makes and sees, effectively, only itself, even if the *NotI* is theorized as the opposite of itself. He proposes a slight but profound change in Fichte's model, retaining the dynamic energy of the self, but redefining that which facilitates self-consciousness. "We can and should only understand everything as we understand ourselves and our lovers, as we understand us and *you* [plural]," he writes in one of the thousands of fragments that constitute the bulk of his work. "Now the so-called Transcendental philosophy—the reference back to the subject . . . the relationship between object and perception—appears in a whole new light . . . (You.) (Instead of NotI—You)."[40] Here, I am enhanced—or rather, I come into being as a self-conscious entity—by the encounter, not with a self-produced theoretical limit, but with another self whom I love. That self reflects me, yes, but also adds something of its own singularity to the subjective mix. Novalis's shift from *NotI* to *You* in his conceptualization of the feature that is necessary for the *I*'s formation finds its psychoanalytic equivalent in Winnicott's shift from the internal objects of the Kleinian model to the actual others surrounding the infant in his theory of ego development.

Like Winnicott's nascent self, which experiences the entire world as itself—but is paradoxically also completely dependent on the world outside itself—Novalis's poetic self consists in the process of experimenting with creating, but also finding, the world that surrounds it. Process is everything here, more specifically, a reciprocal process of reaching across boundaries between self and other. Here are some tantalizing bits from Novalis: "Poesy dissolves foreign being into our own."[41] "The artist makes himself into everything that he sees and wants to be."[42] As we can see, Novalis, like Winnicott, does not shy away from contradiction. Indeed, he writes, "Might the highest principle contain within its task the highest paradox? To be a statement that would allow absolutely no peace—that would constantly attract and constantly repel—that would always become incomprehensible again however often one had already comprehended it?"[43] The effect of this immersion in paradox is a dynamic energy that both moves us forward, toward ever-elusive meaning, and oscillates, in the process creating something other than either of the poles between which it alternates. One final Novalis fragment in this connection:

> All being, being itself is nothing more than being free—*hovering* between extremes that must necessarily be united and necessarily be separated. From this focal point of hovering all reality flows—everything is contained in it—object and subject exist through it, not it through them. I-ness or productive imagination, the *hovering*—determines, produces the extremes, that between which is hovered.[44]

"AN INTERMEDIATE AREA OF EXPERIENCING"

This space of paradox is the very element of Winnicott's theory and practice, too. There is no evidence that he ever read Novalis, but he was a voracious reader of the English Romantics Coleridge, Shelley, and Wordsworth, who were in turn deeply influenced by the early German Romantics. Indeed, Winnicott's most recent biographer calls the English Romantics Winnicott's "cultural ancestors."[45] Nowhere is the Romantic connection more evident than in Winnicott's notion of the "intermediate area," where the incipient self plays with what became probably his most famous contribution to the psychoanalytic and developmental literature, the "transitional object."[46] One of my favorite moments, every time I've taught my comparative literature course "Literature and Psychoanalysis," is the unit on transitional objects. Even the students who had been quiet while we tackled Freud and Lacan invariably volunteer stories of their own or their siblings' rabbits, blankets, or bedtime rituals, recounting a time when their precious possession was left behind or chewed by the dog; some shyly admit that they brought theirs with them to college. What makes these objects so important? And how do they relate to the creative self?

I begin my discussion of intermediate-area experiencing on the developmental level, where it constitutes a shift in focus from the bipartite to the tripartite. As we remember, the initial situation involves a potential self that is thoroughly dependent on—and completely unaware of—its caregiving environment, which provides it with the semblance of a membrane that defines it. When this environment functions well enough to protect the incipient self from the interruption of its going-on-being through impingements external or internal, an awareness begins to dawn of the temporal gap between its needs and the response to them, and of the distinction between itself and its environment. In this opening, the child discovers, accidentally at first, and later more intentionally, phenomena that dwell on the border between itself and that which is not itself. While we might think immediately of an activity like thumb-sucking, Winnicott is at pains to distinguish what he is talking about from autoerotic behaviors, although there is a fluid boundary between such behaviors and the engagement with transitional phenomena. More concretely, Winnicott gives the example of the baby who, while sucking its thumb or fingers, simultaneously caresses its upper lip with another finger, or takes a bit of blanket into its mouth along with the fingers, or mumbles sounds.[47] If thumb-sucking can be aligned with the bipartite configuration of child + breast/bottle, these actions introduce a third feature into the mix, something that is undeniably both connected to and separate from the original pairing.

In a sense, we could say that the intermediate area that arises, or is revealed, through this activity gives form to the gap that had emerged between infant and caregiver over the course of the maturation of their relationship. Returning to Novalis's metaphor, the intermediate area is the "hovering" between subject and object that effectively gives rise to them. Gradually, in this space, the transitional phenomenon takes shape as the child, in its seemingly random grasping at all the various objects that surround it, chooses one that will become uniquely important in its life. For that is the signal attribute of a transitional object: it is simultaneously *found* and *created* by the child.[48] In a manner continuous with the early self's illusion that it must have created the source that responds to its hunger or thirst or discomfort, on one level the special object—stuffed animal, blanket, etc.—is experienced as part of the self's inner world. But it is not a hallucination, Winnicott insists. The object must at the same time be experienced as existing in its own right: "It must seem to the infant to give warmth, or to move, or to have texture, or to do something that seems to show it has vitality or reality of its own."[49]

An anecdote from my own daughter's life might help elucidate the paradoxical status of the transitional object. Hers was a stuffed zebra called (what else?) "Z"; associating a name with the object is often part of the adoption process. To my horror, being the student of Winnicott that I am, we managed once to leave Z in our lodging during a trip abroad. Our daughter was very difficult to put to bed and generally inconsolable for the several days that it took for our heroic landlady to Express Mail Z to us. I had expected a happy reunion when the zebra arrived home, so I was initially surprised when our daughter proceeded to "reprimand" Z in her toddler babble, little finger wagging, clearly chastising the treasured friend for having gone away. This is actually no surprise at all: as much as she had created Z to be the comforting, soothing presence that she needed, she also experienced the zebra as capable of defying her, a transgression that, of course, had to be set to rights.

Existing in the borderland between subjective and objective reality allows the transitional object to function both regressively and progressively. It unquestionably links back to the earlier state of continuity with the caregiver, but it also points forward toward greater autonomy of both self and other. It is empowering and humbling at the same time, too. "I made you," the child is saying by choosing this particular thing to exist in the world as singularly itself. But in its singularity, the thing demonstrates its separateness by seeming to answer back, "Thank you for choosing me." Here is one aspect of the three-dimensionality that characterizes the intermediate area: we are not dealing with merely the binary of internal and external reality, but we see in addition "an intermediate area of *experiencing*, to which inner reality and external life both contribute." The other dimension of thirdness appears implicitly in Winnicott's next sentence: "It is an area that is not challenged."[50] What makes the relationship with the transitional object possible is an outsider, usually the caregiver, who watches benignly and never asks if the special friend is real or imagined, but instead simply lets things be as paradoxical as they are.

Playing in the intermediate area is on one level a completely ordinary part of growing up, easy to overlook as we go through our daily lives. On another level, though, it is

absolutely extraordinary. Watching a child talking and lis-
tening to its transitional object, we are gripped by a stark
recognition. We feel again what it is like to believe, even for
a moment, in the aliveness of an interlocutor who seems to
understand us perfectly, but who is also capable of gently
expanding the boundaries of our understanding. There is no
better illustration of the phenomenon than Bill Watterson's
comic strip *Calvin and Hobbes*. While it is impossible to
know if Watterson ever read Winnicott, the stuffed/real
tiger Hobbes is a perfect transitional object for Calvin, whose
parents embody the active, but noninterfering involvement
that Winnicott imagines as ideal for facilitating intermediate-
area experiencing. In what follows, I read closely one of the
most poignant *Calvin and Hobbes* strips, where Calvin learns
about death.

Looking at the first page of the heart-wrenching "Raccoon
Story," we can identify immediately some of the key features of
intermediate-area experiencing (figure 2.1). The first strip shows
Calvin engaging with his friend, the tiger Hobbes; the impetus
for action certainly originates in Calvin, but Hobbes, showing
"vitality and reality of [his] own," makes a suggestion that Calvin
then agrees with. Calvin's ability to have the kind of interaction
he has with Hobbes at all is, of course, conditioned on the good-
enough reliability of the parents from an earlier stage, or perhaps as the ongoing space in which their interaction can take
place: "You don't get to be mom if you can't fix everything just
right," Calvin states confidently. Of course, he is not actually
absolutely confident, as evidenced by Hobbes's mere "hopeful-
ness" that the mother can help—the character Calvin and the
character Hobbes enact together a subjectivity on the threshold
between the child's absolute confidence in, and budding doubt
about, the reliability of its environment. Disillusionment is both
a prerequisite for and a result of the intermediate-area playing

FIGURE 2.1 Bill Watterson, "The Baby Raccoon Story," Part I, *Calvin and Hobbes*, published between March 9 and March 18, 1987. Courtesy of Andrews McMeel Syndication.

that takes place on and as this threshold. Even though the subject "assumes rights over" the transitional object, "some abrogation of omnipotence is a feature from the start."[51] Although the self's original state involves unawareness of the environment that, if circumstances are good enough, morphs into the subject's illusion that it has created the object that is responding to its signal, disillusionment must follow if the subject is not to be forever stuck in a state of undifferentiation. Part of that disillusionment is about the self's own power to create its world, but part of it involves the realization that the parents cannot in fact "fix everything just right."

The second section gives us a glimpse into the inner life of the "good-enough mother," whose doubt about her ability to save the baby raccoon is based on her knowledge of the built-in limits that structure the world.[52] Far from the perfect fixer that Calvin must believe her to be (for a while and to an extent), the mother needs to take a moment with Hobbes as a reminder of her own transitional object; after all, Winnicott says, "a need for a specific object or behaviour pattern that started at a very early date may reappear at a later age when deprivation threatens."[53] In this sequence of strips we readers, too, get an intermediate-area-style respite from what we, like Calvin's parents, know to be the impending tragedy: the third panel provides us with a playful take on typical family life, allowing us to identify either with Calvin's or the mother's perspective, or both.

This second set of strips shows both the capabilities and the limits of the transitional object (figure 2.2). Hobbes mirrors Calvin's affect as he endures the limbo between tenuous life and probable death for the baby raccoon. A comforting interlocutor while Calvin is experiencing the disillusionment of his assumption that his parents can "fix everything just right," Hobbes's stance and expressions in each frame are nearly identical to Calvin's. He is absent, however, for the decisive moment when Calvin learns that the raccoon has died. But we see the effects of Calvin's relationship to the transitional object in his ability to articulate his complex feelings to his father; indeed, the feelings he expresses involve precisely the interplay of internal and external reality that the transitional object mediates: the raccoon is simultaneously gone (outside) and not gone (inside). From one perspective, Calvin is repeating in his own words the father's wisdom: "We did all we could, but now he's gone." That is, human agency can have some effect on the world, but ultimately, we have to accept stark limits.

FIGURE 2.2 Bill Watterson, "The Baby Raccoon Story," Part II, *Calvin and Hobbes*, published between March 9 and March 18, 1987. Courtesy of Andrews McMeel Syndication.

But, in another sense, Calvin's version opens up a new possibility, where limit and limitlessness can coexist.

The exquisite tension between subjective and objective reality that characterizes intermediate-area experiencing is difficult, probably impossible, to maintain; we cannot live all the time in the intermediate area. Most of the time, we are forced to decide whether something exists in the external world or whether we have imagined it. It is in this more ordinary mode that the third and last set of strips operates (figure 2.3). The

FIGURE 2.3 Bill Watterson, "The Baby Raccoon Story," Part III, *Calvin and Hobbes*, published between March 9 and March 18, 1987. Courtesy of Andrews McMeel Syndication.

language is primarily conceptual as Calvin works through the meaning—or meaninglessness—of death, and Hobbes is present, but almost entirely silent. Perhaps sensing the end, or the edges, of his intermediate area, Calvin turns suddenly back toward Hobbes in the final frame, concerned that he might lose his precious friend. "Don't worry," Hobbes says ambiguously. On the one hand, Hobbes will always be with Calvin as an effect of the intermediate-area experience, just as he is still alive, on some level, for Calvin's mother. On the other hand, there can be no promises that the transitional object will remain as it is. Indeed, it cannot and must not do so. The intermediate area widens out into the broader cultural sphere, including this comic strip. As a text, the strip moves seamlessly between the paradoxical space of intermediate-area experiencing and the "split-off intellectual functioning" that dominates our everyday life.[54]

"THE THIRD PART OF THE LIFE OF A HUMAN BEING"

As I have noted, Winnicott's notion of playing involves shifting from a two-dimensional to a three-dimensional mode of engagement, a shift that has ramifications far beyond the developmental. Our everyday life tends to be structured two-dimensionally, that is, along the lines of two mutually exclusive alternative realities. Politics is cast in terms of a debate in which we must choose one or the other of two sides, and in which one of those sides must definitively win. In our daily lives, too, we are often asked to decide between ideas and even feelings without room for nuance. "Mixed feelings" get reinterpreted as "doubt," which in turn implies that perhaps you should not—fill in the blank—remain in that relationship, take that job, or buy that house. Ambivalence is not a state that we are supposed to live with or in. Psychoanalysis contributed a great deal to our notion of human nature by foregrounding the fact that there exists a robust inner reality in addition to the external reality that we share. Ironically, however, one of the more common results of this discovery has been an intense interest in determining which of the two realities is at work in any given situation. The recognition that there is such a thing as psychosomatic illness, for example, has led most frequently to attempts to determine whether a particular symptom is physical or "merely" psychological. It is encouraging that recent research has begun to show the complex interplay between psyche and soma that shows up in the gut, the skin, and other areas of the body. These developments point in the direction of the thirdness that Winnicott regarded as one of his most important contributions.

The child playing with the transitional object is the locus and the starting point for all of Winnicott's musings on the salutary effect of what I am calling three-dimensionality. It takes place in a space that is both an overlap of two presences—the child's and the world's—and a lack of congruence. As my discussion of *Calvin and Hobbes* demonstrates, the objects and activities that dwell in this third space, the intermediate area, are not locked in to one particular meaning, but they do possess a reality of their own. This paradoxical simultaneity of flexibility and solidity, openness and limitation, is reproduced or continued in the cultural realm, as Winnicott himself notes. Specifically, he calls the intermediate area in its extended form a "resting place for the individual engaged in the perpetual human task of keeping inner and outer reality *separate yet interrelated*."[55] Here once again, Winnicott is resisting the binary thinking that permeates our society. In the educational realm, for example, we tend to regard the humanities as opposite from mathematics and the sciences. The latter, it is assumed, is all about what Winnicott would call "outer reality"—objectivity—whereas the former is all about our subjective experience, our "inner reality." This assumption in turn dictates different approaches: a scientific approach involves discovering a truth that ostensibly resides within the phenomena that we are studying themselves, while literary or other artistic interpretation supposedly calls for finding connections between a text and our own feelings or ideas. But a Winnicottian model disallows this rigid dichotomy. In both cases, both realms are at play. On the one side, the legitimate role of the observer or researcher has been increasingly acknowledged in scientific scholarship, from the discovery of quantum physics to the rise of so-called qualitative research. I will focus on the other side, the humanities, and specifically the literary arts, where my own approach to teaching and writing draws heavily on the Winnicottian paradox.

One of the first things I feel the need to do each time I teach our introductory comparative literature course, "The Nature of Narrative," is to provide an alternative to what many of the students learned in high school about reading and interpreting literature. There—and in much popular discussion of literature—there is a dual focus on authorial intent and the text's "relatability" for the reader, a word that has gained prominence in the last several years. Here we see traces of the binarism that I discussed in the last paragraph. On the one hand, the assumption is that it is both possible and desirable to figure out what the author means to say in and through the text; this forms a kind of "objective" touchstone for the interpreter. On the other hand, the text is valuable and meaningful to me if it resonates with my own subjective experience. I will complicate each of these assumptions in turn before outlining an alternative approach that I believe enhances both our reading and, more broadly, our creative engagement with the world.

Any writer will tell you that there is no such thing as a straight line between the author's thoughts and what he or she writes. While it is undeniable that I sit down at my desk with an idea that I would like to write about, once I start to write, something almost magical happens: the words and the sentences seem to take on a life of their own that shapes and molds my idea as it is being written. It is not that my initial idea—my intention—disappears; instead, it is revealed by the process of writing to be far more nuanced, multiple, and perhaps even contradictory than I thought it was when I started out. Hence, not only is it impossible for a reader to know what is in an author's head that leads to the work being as it is, it is also, in a sense, impossible for the author to know that, at least to know that ahead of time. In this context, looking for a "message" in a work of literature involves pinning both the text and the author down in a way that artistic creation does not allow. Indeed, reduced to a message, a work of literature loses its quality as art and becomes something like a treatise or manifesto.

So if the truth of the text does not lie outside of it—in the author's intention—then it must lie inside my own mind, right? Many a student has triumphantly declared during class discussion that the ambiguity we have discovered in the story in front of us means that any interpretation is possible, "depending on how you look at it." While it is undeniable that literary and other art gains meaning *for us* according to how it aligns with our own reality, that does not imply that our personal experience determines the meaning *in it*. As reader, I can connect what I am reading to my own personal, conceptual, and affective universe by making associations with it, but that process is limited by the fact that the semantic, syntactical, and structural dimensions of the text have reality in their own right. Just as Hobbes is *both* a real tiger *and* a stuffed animal, the story that I am reading is both mine and not mine; the text is different from, as well as similar to, my associations. As a colleague of mine once said, succinctly: just because there is no one right interpretation does not mean that there are not wrong interpretations!

As an alternative to either searching for authorial intention or reading one's own meaning into the text, I propose an approach that resembles playing in the intermediate area. This approach hinges on understanding and respecting the way in which language operates as a symbolic system. By this I mean that language both does and does not align with extralinguistic reality; interpretation takes place at the intersection of symbol and symbolized but also in the gap between the two. This applies to all language, and especially to the figurative language that often abounds in literary writing. In practice, interpretation in this mode involves focusing both on what I know and what I do not. For example, on the level of the text as a whole, I might notice that certain plot elements, character utterances, or even individual words repeat in the course of the story. These patterns are an important set of data that I need to take seriously in my interpretation. But there will inevitably be bits of the text that I do not understand at all; these very often form the starting point of my investigation. On the level of the language itself, interpreters often latch on to symbols as guideposts to meaning. Indeed, metaphors often function as a kind of nuclear reactor for the text, providing energy from a deep and volatile core of potential significance. But it is important to remember that the "root of symbolism in time" is the transitional object, which possesses a productive disunion between me and not-me, internal and external, although it is connected to both. In this context, we are warned against trying to assign the symbol too definitive a meaning. Instead, the friction generated by the symbol's own semantic multiplicities, and its interaction with other words and structures surrounding it, works to ignite a kind of interpretive combustion that fuels my search for the meaning(s) of the text.

In interpersonal relationships, interpretation also plays a crucial role. Each person is constantly trying to understand the other in an attempt to craft the best relationship. Here, too, we can fall into the trap of two-dimensionality. Even the language used to describe relationships carries the mark of binarity: we seek our perfect *match*, or our *one and only* love who understands us *perfectly*. Not only is it impossible, of course, that there be just one person out there for each other person but the expectation of perfect congruity between our desires and one who can fulfill them is itself a deterrent to creative relationships. As I have described in the realm of literary meaning, if truth—or in this case, "rightness"—is defined in such absolute terms, there is no room for the vast range of human possibilities. It is only if we are open to regarding relationships as a process of playing in a space that is intrinsically paradoxical and resistant to perfect under-standing that we can enjoy the excitement of learning new things about ourselves through the other's (mis)understand-ings, and learning to love things in the other that would never have occurred to us as desirable if we operated only in our own fantasy world.

The fantasy of perfect understanding extends beyond romantic relationships, even to the political realm. It is increasingly com-mon to characterize the current climate as *polarized*, but what does that imply? Polarization implies a binary, of course—a mag-netic binary, if you will, and as we know, magnets either attract or repel. The magnetic metaphor works well with the dynamics that I have laid out here: the bipartite structure, as for example the symbol and the symbolized in its two-dimensional form, and the earliest infant-caregiver pairing, has a tendency to collapse into fusion or repel into irreconcilable polarity. This fusion is often idealized, which renders its absence an absolute failure or an irre-trievable loss. We see this in the political realm in the overwhelm-ing hope for needs to be met perfectly and in the burning fury when they are not. Indeed, the neoliberal environment itself sets up this either-or mentality. In a society whose declared reason for being is the market, individuals are encouraged to imagine a kind of consumerist utopia in which all needs are met through their purchases. Dissatisfied with your life? Buy a new car or a new house. Feeling sad? Go on vacation or visit a spa. Even alternatives to mainstream consumerism are liable to carry the same absolute expectations for perfect healing, perfect spiritual peace, or perfect health. The inevitable disappointment when such a perfect union of need and response is not achieved urges us to keep searching—hence the deep restlessness of Western societies—or to become enraged, and we have seen how society works, or rather does not work, when it is driven by rage.

Notably absent in this scenario is a third space. In Winnicott's developmental terms, the third space emerges in the gap that forms as the originary set-up—a kind of concentric togetherness of infant and caregiver—is necessarily disrupted. If the process goes well, pain at the loss of being held by a caring other is balanced by joy at discovering the world (including that caring other) as a separate entity that has exciting things to offer in its own right. Hence, in the intermediate world, the site where that balance is established, playing takes place, paradoxically, both as an exercise of subjective agency ("I can make the world – hurrah!") and as a realization of a limit to that agency in the face of objective reality ("There is something in the world that is not me – I wonder what it is."). For this process to occur, we remember, there must be a benign presence that does not challenge the paradoxical experience of the emerging subject. This figure, usually the parent, allows the third space to develop both by virtue of having naturally contributed to the young self's disillusionment about its own powers and by allowing the child's powers to play out creatively in the space between them.

In society, the position of a benign facilitating presence can ideally be occupied by government as regulator of the zero-sum orientation that is endemic to market capitalism, and as architect of a social network that provides nonperfect but still adequate support for individuals in society. The baseline support for fundamental needs—personal and family health, a living wage, childcare, housing, utilities needed for everyday life, security in old age—creates a reliable environment within which individuals can take the risks associated with becoming whole citizens. In most of the Global North, this function has either disappeared—as in the United States and those nations that have imitated it—or is under threat by the lure of low taxes and a vague ideology of self-reliance. It is painfully clear that trust in government to provide us with a reliable frame for our creative development has eroded to the point of approaching null. Using Winnicottian terms, the lack of a reliably non-self-interested presence in our lives has caused a sharp reduction of leeway for living. In German, "leeway" is *Spielraum*, room for play in both senses of the word. In one sense, there is no "play," no elasticity in the tissue of our lives, which can strain or rupture under the stress of extraordinary, but inevitable, events such as illness or job loss. We are therefore so preoccupied with keeping our selves together that we cannot afford the other sense of the word "play": playing that gives our life meaning, fosters our creativity, and allows for fundamental relationality. In other words, there is *no* "relief from the strain of relating inner and outer reality" that Winnicott saw in intermediate playing, whose adult versions include, as I have noted, engaging in the arts, religious experiences, and other culturally meaningful activities.[56]

The COVID-19 pandemic made starkly evident what happens when we lack a third space: we are thrown back into the state of absolute dependence where what is at stake is our very existence. In the process, the potential *third* position—in developmental terms, the parent whose nonchallenging presence creates and allows for the play space—regresses to the earlier all-important *second* position, the parent who is either reliable enough, in which case we can go on being, or not reliable enough, in which case we cannot go on being. In the absence of solid, stable institutions that provide such a holding environment, we are face-to-face with the arbitrariness of the power structures that surround us and are continually in existential crisis. When the always precarious state of neoliberal "normalcy"—just-in-time shipping, just enough employees to barely get by, the gig economy; I could go on and on—is thrown off by a crisis, the essential work of continuing to exist takes over everyone's lives, and especially the lives of those who are tasked with making it possible for the rest of us to continue existing.

The alternative to being, Winnicott says, is annihilation. This is a strong word, to be sure, and it seems even more so in the context of its deceptively simple explanation: "The alternative to being is reacting, and reacting interrupts being and annihilates."[57] On the physical level, *interruption* could involve temperature changes that go on long enough that one becomes constantly aware of being too cold or too hot—a state many are facing in the context of Russia's weaponization of its gas reserves in its war of aggression against Ukraine, and even more in the face of rapidly warming temperatures—or the hunger that comes from food insecurity. Psychically, perpetual worry (about one's own life or about global threats like war or climate change), the preoccupation with achieving or maintaining success, or the struggle to manage the requirements of daily life all interrupt being and require *reaction*. Reaction, in this context, always implies a paradoxical situation for the self: on the one hand, I am forced to react on my own to the interruption of my being; there is by definition no one who could have prevented the interruption in the first place. On the other hand, reaction involves a shift away from my self and toward the other, to whose requirements I comply in an attempt to have my needs met secondhand, so to speak.

This paradoxical state is starkly evident on both the physical and psychical levels in our current situation. Those who experience food insecurity take second or third jobs to try to alleviate their family's hunger, placing themselves at the whims of multiple employers, each of which has differing expectations of the employee. Those who are driven to self-optimization at the high end of the socio-economic hierarchy might appear to be freer from the requirement to react and the interruption of their being. After all, they can rely on their relative wealth to provide basic economic security, and in a sense, the pressure on them comes from themselves alone. But compliance is rampant in this group, too. The very fact that one has internalized the expectation that one be perfectly successful indicates an undermining of the possibility for actual self-realization. Even if the requirement is that one be one's own best self, compliance is still involved, first because the content of the requirement tends to shift randomly—Work hard! Work less! Become lean and fit! Embrace body positivity!—and second, because regardless of the specific mandates, there is no room for the free exploration of self and world.

What is the alternative to this sorry state of affairs? How do we operate *against* neoliberal self-optimization and *for* a creative, playful self that can meet the world with curiosity instead of apprehension? My answer to these difficult questions involves making explicit and expanding on the healthy, creative self that Winnicott implicitly regards as the default for each human being, a self that—again paradoxically—includes within it what we might normally consider the negative.

Playing, Creativity, Living

Up until now, I have spoken primarily in developmental terms, focusing on one stage after another in the process by which a self takes shape and engages with its world. I have repeatedly pointed out that all of these stages accompany us throughout our lives. Now, I will focus more closely on what it means for creativity to infuse a life and a self in multiple ways. In the process, I will return to the details of the various developmental phases, because in adult life, those (theoretical) temporal steps morph metaphorically into something like planes that now touch each other, now diverge, or into registers of an instrument that allow each pitch to sound in multiple different ways. All states and stages are—at least potentially—aligned with creativity, however. Beginning with the spontaneous gesture emerging willy-nilly from the not-yet self to the playing associated with the transitional object, the self is constituted *as* a creative self; creativity is its core state, its foundational reality that can only be distorted by the wrong conditions.

The unintegration of the originary situation continues to be constitutive of the creative self. Akin to traditional free association, creativity involves what Winnicott alternately calls "relaxation," "formlessness," a "non-purposive state" in which nothing particular is happening—but that is everything. The concentration of a playing child attests to this fact: what is being done is all that exists for the period of time that the playing is taking place. Moving the block to this place or that, the babbling conversation with the stuffed animal, the movements of a self-choreographed dance—from our outside perspective, there is no point to these activities. They do not necessarily have any particular outcome, or even make sense, but the doing of it totally occupies the child's mind, and often body, and in this very process the self is coming into being. In adult life, this experience might be replicated or approximated by being lost in thought; I am fully immersed to the point of not being available to others. But inside that bubble of unavailability, my attention might either be totally focused on one thing or floating freely from one thing to another. Formlessness can, so to speak, take many forms. The key is the experience of unintegration itself.

This experience can be scary; in fact, playing and the attendant creativity is intrinsically precarious.[58] True *un*integration, which characterizes the primary pre-self state can, from the perspective of the already integrated self, look a great deal like terrifying *dis*integration. Paradoxically, if the early self has not been allowed to be unintegrated by the presence of a reliable facilitating environment, its integration is inauthentic, brittle, and in danger of disintegrating. Someone who has, on the other hand, felt what it feels like to be able to reach into the world randomly, but on their own, and whose gestures have met with a solid, but elastic presence surrounding it, can access a reserve of productive unintegration when needed in their adult lives. It is precisely because these people have become whole entities with permeable, but not porous boundaries that they can risk the experience of relaxing—or even losing—their boundedness, thus accessing the creative impulse that dwells within each of us from the start.

Let us take a closer look at unintegration, since it is absolutely crucial for creativity.[59] One of Winnicott's most profound, and complex, insights appears in his late paper "Fear of Breakdown" (1974), written in the last year of his life and published three years after his death. Here, he touches on *emptiness*, relying, as always, on his patients to teach him about its existence, about the fear of it and the value of it. He concludes, "The basis of all learning (as well as of eating) is emptiness. But if emptiness was not experienced as such at the beginning, then it turns up as a state that is feared, yet compulsively sought after."[60] Learning, Winnicott says, presupposes emptiness, and a desire to learn appears to be a fundamental feature of the human being. But what if the state of productive emptiness is avoided, as we tend to do today? It is easy to identify a fear of emptiness in the compulsive taking in of material from the internet. Indeed, the very format of the internet invites such a compulsion: there is always another Google hit to check out, another post to read, another photo to slide my eyes over for a split second. Critiques of the internet as addictive abound, but it is not the internet or social media themselves that cause the compulsive behavior. Instead, in a neoliberal world that tells us that we might cease to exist if we are not constantly seeking—i.e., consuming—ever more information, we cannot tolerate empty time or empty mental space. I have learned from my students, for example, that people now often listen to audio books or recorded lectures at double speed (or faster) in order to fill themselves with the content more quickly. Even the healthy desire to experience the world raw, unmediated by digitalization, can slide into a fear of emptiness. If I am focusing on checking off the things on my bucket list, it is difficult to allow for the disorienting, but ultimately enriching, lack of familiarity that often accompanies a new experience.

Paradoxically, that apparent lust to avoid emptiness through excessive filling up is also a form of longing *for* emptiness: if I "read" more quickly, I can be finished sooner. I am yearning for a kind of void, a state of zero work whose only characteristic is an absence. We see this in interminable internet scrolling, too. There is always a feeling that if I scroll long enough, I will get to a point where I can rest in the absence of any more hits. The fact that this is functionally impossible in the context of digital reality makes the longing sharper and more poignant. There is no end to coerced activity in the digital realm, where every void of information, entertainment, or other stimulus is instantly filled with something new. In the "real" world, the very notion of a bucket list is framed by death: if I finish it, I can die.

The question naturally arises about how to counter this simultaneous fear of and craving for emptiness; shifting the terms slightly, can this fraught relationship to *dis*integration be transformed into an embrace of creative *un*integration? Certainly, acknowledgment of the foundational quality of emptiness is an important first step. Winnicott describes one analysis in which the turning point came when he realized, and said out loud, that the patient experienced himself as not there. The patient's breakthrough came not, as we would expect, when he found himself, but when he realized that he had never existed for himself as a full person. Even more touching is the woman who notes with anguish that she forgets what she has already said to Winnicott—or perhaps, she speculates, she was merely talking with herself. Winnicott replies—in one of his few interventions during the analysis, which needed to be, he recognized, a space for the missing unintegration to take hold—"All sorts of things happen and they wither. This is the myriad deaths you have died."[61] I nearly cried when I read these lines. By making this observation, Winnicott was enacting what is necessary in order for an experience of emptiness to be generative, rather than merely terrifying: by reflecting back the patient's sense of repeatedly being erased, he was negating that very deletion. The effect on the patient was not immediate or dramatic. Instead, she continued to dwell in unintegration while figuratively being held by her analyst, sometimes speaking, sometimes wandering around, sometimes in despair—"I feel I've wasted this session"— sometimes beautifully defiant—"Blast the good girls!"[62]

Winnicott puts his finger on the value of the process when he remarks: "*The negative is now the positive.*"[63]

The "negative" here is an actual *experience* in and across time. In order for the missed unintegration to be able to function retroactively as a breeding space for creativity, the individual must live it, which often means tolerating the exquisite discomfort, even fear, that it engenders. This can only be done in the physical, remembered, or even imagined presence of another in one's life who can in turn tolerate the nothingness surrounding the person going through the process. Admittedly, this is extremely difficult. In one of his most complex passages, Winnicott notes that those who have not been allowed simply to go on being— in effect to be for a while nothing more than unintegrated potential—are in danger of developing too quickly, and too artificially, a self that complies with the expectation that it be something specific: healthy, successful, smart, talented, or whatever (as defined by others). They become bounded, artificially integrated beings without having been allowed first to be unintegrated. In such cases, *dis*integration becomes the greatest fear. I must *keep myself together* at all costs. Falling apart = illness, which is the worst possible catastrophe.

In our rationalist world that privileges a controlled and bounded individual over all else, falling apart is not only scary, it is somehow a moral failure. This is even more the case for mental illness than for physical illness and, of course, the mental has traditionally been starkly separated from the physical. If the doctor can find no organic reason for particular symptoms, it must be "all in your head." Conversely, illnesses such as depression and obsessive-compulsive disorder have only gained legitimacy since they began to be associated with physical changes in the brain. Recently, as I have noted, illness, including mental illness, has to some extent begun to be destigmatized. Mental health problems are increasingly freely recognized as real, as worthy of treatment and insurance coverage. This is an excellent development, both for society and for individuals. Getting a diagnosis and a treatment plan can be a huge relief for those who are suffering, insofar as they discover that there is a name—and often a treatment—for what they thought they were alone in feeling. The destigmatization of mental illness has gone so far in some environments, notably the academic world, that one's diagnosis can become a constitutive part of one's identity, as is evident in the new category of "neurodiverse" as a self-descriptor.

However, here I will elaborate further on the several problems associated with the increasing reliance on and proliferation of diagnosis. It is all too often considered to be the end point, rather than the beginning, of a solution. Actually dealing with a mental illness involves a complex relationship among the person, their illness, and their caregivers, both medical and non, and it takes time. I personally know several people who have been diagnosed by a primary care physician with depression, given antidepressants, and left to recover on their own—or not, more often. Zero attention has been paid to even the immediate context for the depression—which in one case was the death of a spouse, another the loss at age eighteen of friends in a school shooting—much less to any underlying, long-term issues that might contribute to it. Excessive focus on diagnosis brings with it the danger that a person will be reduced to that diagnosis, which blinds us to the idiosyncratic ways in which their illness came into being and the part that it plays in their unique character. This is not to mention the non-ill dimensions of their personality that are obscured in the process. I also worry that the introduction of neurodiversity as an identity marker like race or gender ignores the suffering that mental illness carries, and not just because it is stigmatized. Finally, and returning to

Winnicott, the foregrounding of diagnosis can, if taken too far, be an example of the compulsive filling in of empty spaces that I have identified as a squelching of creative potential. This is not to say that mental illness itself is akin to the productive unintegration necessary for creativity; on the contrary, it is the *dis*integration that Winnicott recognized as the feared flip side of compliance with others' expectations that they give up their contentless going-on-being too abruptly. Recognizing it as such, without judgment, might provide an opportunity to muse about how the early state of nonspecific potentiality can be approximated in later life, perhaps in the process opening up space for a creativity lost to compliance and illness.

PLAYING AND REALITY

I would contend that the need for the negative-as-positive experience that reawakens the possibility for creativity goes far beyond those who identify themselves, or are diagnosed, as mentally ill. After all, the intermediate area that we all inhabit to one degree or another in our childhood remains with us as a potential throughout life. As a reminder, Winnicott says that the phenomena we play with as children are never lost, nor repressed, but rather scatter into our cultural life, because "no human being is free from the strain of relating inner and outer reality."[64] He is thinking primarily of "arts, religion, etc." I will leave it to others to analyze the intermediate-area dimensions of religion, but I can certainly attest to the effect of aesthetic experience, and I would add to it the experience of nature. As I am writing this, I am taking a break to watch the insects whirring around the cherry blossoms outside my window. What strikes me is the combination—or alternation—of direction and indirection they seem to embody. Heavy enough—and equipped with strong enough wings—to move themselves along toward a flower, they are also light enough that they are blown off course by the slightest breeze. They trace little arabesques around the branches— the favorite shape of the German Romantics, by the way—no straight lines here. I am best able to get in touch with my own creativity when I can make such associations freely and shape them into an image that might resonate with others as well.

Indeed, the aesthetic dimension of Winnicott's intermediate area is highlighted by a comparison with the Romantics, who elaborated the creative potential that exists in everyone in the form of a "productive power of imagination" that could effectively create a world—but only, paradoxically, in connection with the really existing world outside the self. If the characteristic activity taking place in the intermediate area involves simultaneously finding and creating a special object, Novalis describes a situation in which "I see outside myself what is inside myself—I believe that what I am just now doing has *happened*, and so forth."[65] Novalis is speaking both spatially and temporally here. Spatially speaking, whatever I am seeing via my productive imagination resides metaphorically both inside of me and in the world outside of me. Temporally, my action in the present coincides with an event that has hypothetically already happened. Similarly—or perhaps conversely: "The true reader must be the amplified author," says Novalis.[66] I take in something from outside myself that in turn activates something creative inside me. I become able to create worlds with my own productive powers of imagination that partake of the essence of both my own reality and that of the work I have read.

Like the intermediate area, then, productive imagination is not merely an expression of what is inside us but more a kind of collaboration between us and the world that plays itself out as activity. The activity might in fact be solitary, such as reading or communing with nature, but it might very well involve others. Playing in a musical ensemble certainly fits the bill, but the experience does not have to be aesthetic in the narrow sense of the word. A conversation in which each participant has the feeling that they are treading on territory that is both safely familiar and excitingly new, or even an afternoon of work together in a lab, can also return us to the exhilarating feeling of dwelling in a third space that does not belong entirely to us but at the same time is not completely the realm of other people. Here, I might differentiate imaginative activity from fantasy. The latter takes place entirely within the mind. It can indeed build worlds inside there, but those worlds do not tend to be as elastically creative and shareable as imaginative activity. That, in contrast, operates on a stage that includes external phenomena, whether they be objects—the moss that becomes a fairy's bed—other people, or an artistic medium—paint, sound, or language.

These media are in turn more than tools to express oneself, more than a direct conduit from inside to outside. Each medium possesses qualities of its own that limit and therefore shape the flow of ideas or feelings from the interior of the self into the external world. In exploring this crucial element of creativity, I will focus primarily on language, for language enacts most vividly the paradox of the me/not-me simultaneity that is associated with intermediate-area activity. Indeed, Winnicott justifies his discussion of transitional phenomena at one point by the need to locate "the root of symbolism in time."[67] For psychoanalysts and other theorists, symbolism, also often called representation, is conditioned on the separation of subject and object; if I am the world, there is no need to communicate myself to the world. Developmentally speaking, even a cry of hunger is "symbolic" in two ways: first, insofar as the cry is not the hunger itself but a representation of it and second, in that it functions to communicate one being's reality to another. On the social level, our world is highly mediated; representation is the ubiquitous social scaffolding of our lives from its beginning. The moment we are named, we are tied into a network of kinship, which in turn links up with societal and historical structures that determine and define us even as we are born as an individual person. It is tempting to regard this fact as a constraint, a constraint that demands resistance if one is to be a creative self. Many of the young people that I work with express an urge to free themselves from the shackles of conformity with societal, familial, and historical structures, and the writers among them wish to free themselves of the constraints of language itself. More broadly, many contemporary thinkers regard the social world as the enemy of individual expression; one frequently encounters the notion that creativity, by definition, works against complacent collective norms. Rebellious artists in this mold abound: the romantic poet pursuing his solitary quest for perfect self-expression alone in his garret; the Dadaist seeking to escape from the tyranny of sense into the non-sense of automatic writing; the Beats countering stifling cliché and euphemism with deliberately provocative self-articulations; and rappers who both reveal the oppressiveness of language and inject it with new meaning.

Far from preventing me from getting in touch with and from expressing who I really am, language and representation in general is—or can be—a crucial part of that process. The poets seek to push through language to something pre- or extralinguistic, but ultimately, they are working with language to create and find something of their own. But Winnicott's approach points out that the fact of language's externality to us is an opportunity for, rather than a hindrance to, creativity. By virtue of the fact that language is not perfectly aligned with experience, it opens up a space for (self)reflection to take place and new connections to be made. In this context, the writer is not so much the source of creativity as a participant in it who engages playfully with the world. Creativity is a complex relationship between self, other, and the space connecting and separating them. In an interview, the remarkable Ocean Vuong put it this way:

> "Poet" in Greek is a maker, but I think a maker at their best is a maker of space rather than a maker of objects. And so I think, for me, it's about: How do I create space? That's the harder work. And I think any architect will tell you that you're sculpting space, you're sculpting light. That's much harder 'cause anyone can fill a page with themselves or their expressions, but how do you collaborate with the material world, with the cultural world?[68]

The creative self does not definitively *precede* that which it creates, but rather comes into being in the space that it simultaneously makes and is made by. The same can be said for the "cultural world," which both constitutes and is constituted by those who make it up.

Vuong's novel *On Earth We're Briefly Gorgeous* performs this creative self-in-process in the context of his own family, liminal on both a spatial and a temporal level. It moves fluidly between Vietnam, where the protagonist Little Dog's grandmother gave birth to his mother during the war, and the area around Hartford, Connecticut, where Little Dog grows up with his mother and grandmother. The nail salon in which Little Dog's mother works, and behind which they live together with the grandmother, forms the center of a kind of nested intermediate area where various notions of home and away, familiar and alien, past and present clash, combine, and play with one another. Here, both past and present trauma permeates the characters' lives. The

grandmother witnessed atrocities perpetrated by American sol-
diers during the war in her homeland and experienced their cav-
alier attitude toward life. The mother was horribly abused by
Little Dog's now absent father, and in turn occasionally hits her
son. Once he begins to work himself, Little Dog encounters the
everyday exploitation of the tobacco pickers that he has joined,
by their bosses and, more broadly, by the postindustrial economic
system. Trauma is notoriously difficult to deal with in art. Indeed,
Theodor Adorno famously proclaimed that "to write poetry after
Auschwitz is barbaric."[69] The twin dangers of reducing trauma
to pathos and missing its essence entirely attend each attempt to
render it literarily. But the language and structure of Vuong's
novel manage both to convey the trauma with its effects intact
and to transform it, as the title implies, into a kind of ephemeral
beauty.

At times, this takes the form of encounters that occur on the
sharp edge between the immigrant family and their American
environment, notably in and as language. In one moment, Little Dog must translate into English something—"oxtail"—that
he has only eaten but never spoken in their native Vietnamese;
in another, he is mocked by bullies for not speaking at all and is
forced to utter words that have little meaning for him, just so he
can be laughed at. Within the family, too, we encounter instances
of talking past one another, as when Little Dog comes out to his
mother, and she worries that he will be killed for wearing dresses.
The two characters both feel great fear, but the nature of their
respective fears differs wildly, based on the personal context of
each. Living in a thoroughly homophobic environment, the son
fears rejection by his mother for his sexual orientation. The
mother, though, translates the notion of homophobia into the
immediate physical danger that she knows from her own life and
that of her mother.

In these scenes, it would seem that language operates—despite its speaker's best intentions—not to facilitate communication, but to point out its impossibility. But that is only the case if one expects *perfect* expression and *perfect* comprehension. It is possible, as the novel demonstrates, that the negative space of noncomprehension can actually facilitate a new kind of communication that transforms the relationship between two selves who are nonidentical. A different kind of translation is activated in which the carrier of meaning is the process itself of translating, rather than either the source language or the target language on their own. In the back-and-forth process that constitutes translation, new nuances are discovered in both languages as they glancingly coincide with and then diverge from one another.

Following Winnicott, a new kind of personal authenticity can also be discovered that differs from our usual notion of a pure, unchanging essence of me-ness. The path to discovery takes us through some confusing word usage, however, as I will show in the next section.

TRUE SELF, FALSE SELF

Winnicott is probably best known for coining the terms *good-enough mother* and *transitional object*. Both have suffered oversimplification, even to some extent within psychoanalytic circles. This is partly a consequence of the way that Winnicott writes: as I have noted, his discussions spiral around and around certain key ideas, gradually opening them up with ever more detail and depth over the course of his entire body of work. In this context, individual terms function like a kind of shorthand, marking the place to which he will return, each time bringing something new to them, and then taking something new away from them. The words themselves have meaning for his theories, to be sure, but it is mostly their functioning *in relation to* that matters. The notion of the good-enough mother functions mostly to differentiate Winnicott's ideas from those surrounding him by focusing attention on the environmental provision that he found neglected in psychoanalytic theory up to that point and by taking the pressure off mothers to be perfect. The transitional object is the concrete center anchoring an entire complex of more abstract ideas: intermediate area – playing – not challenged – illusion/disillusionment – paradox. It is even more tempting to believe that we already understand another of Winnicott's famous contributions—the juxtaposition of "true self" and "false self"—but in fact, the terms are related to one another in complex and nuanced ways.[70]

In the paper that treats the two concepts most directly and thoroughly, Winnicott curiously begins not with the true self, which we might imagine to be the more originary and more central concept, but with the false self. In so doing, he discursively enacts the process of getting at the true self, which is necessarily hidden at the subject's source and its core. My own discussion will follow Winnicott's lead, addressing first the negative and then the positive functioning of the false self, and only later turning toward the issue of how the true self comes into being and remains vibrant. The false self is fascinating in its own right. In order to understand how it emerges and how it can function healthily or pathologically, it is necessary to return once again to the theorized earliest situation, when the repeated interruption of going-on-being can lead to compliance. Over time, such compliance hardens into a false self that is organized along the lines of others' agendas. This can even happen when those agendas are geared toward the well-being of the child, specifically when it comes to feeding.

There is no denying that feeding is a primary component—perhaps *the* primary component—of parenting a child toward thriving. At the very earliest stage of life, we remember, there is awareness neither of hunger as belonging to a self nor of a world that could alleviate the hunger. In a good-enough environment, feeding comes just when it is needed (which in practice, congruent with the notion of "good enough," is a stretch of time, rather than a precise moment). But there comes a time when the infant is just beginning to be able to tolerate a gap between its hunger and eating. In this gap, the infant has the possibility of exercising a kind of proto-agency by crying for food. From now on, if food is provided before the nascent self can ask for it, it becomes a kind of irresistible seduction into compliance. While we can certainly picture this situation literally in the many versions of food as a vector of manipulation by parents and society, it is also a metaphorical reminder about the precarity of the self in the context of relationships structured by power. Especially when a self is new or otherwise vulnerable, it is easily susceptible to taking on contours that are not its own.

I am not talking about coerced obedience to an external standard nor even the kind of conformity with peers that elder generations like to decry in younger generations. Instead, I am thinking of the example of my students for whom the college years can either be an opportunity to experiment with finding and creating a true self or a site of multiple lures toward compliance—or both at once. Even though many of those lures likely emerge in the peer-driven social world of the young people, I worry most about how my colleagues and I might contribute to the fostering of pathologically false selves. It goes with the territory that the student-teacher configuration is an asymmetrical one, and that is, in many ways, appropriate and productive. My students need me to convey knowledge they do not have, to introduce them to ideas they might find compelling, and to live as a role model that they might want to emulate. But I am aware of the immense responsibility that goes with this position. If I jump in too early or too intensely with an idea—if I do not wait for my students to express their hunger for it—I am in danger of drawing them into a passivity resembling the earliest state of absolute dependence. This can happen if we teachers are focused on our own need to be the authority figure or to be in control, or even if we are too focused on our own passion for the material that we are teaching. It is not about us!

On the other hand, though, as I have detailed, an other is necessary for the developing self. It cannot come into and go on being without a protective membrane that gives it a protected space in which to grow. Early on, that membrane was the holding environment itself, which acted as a kind of auxiliary ego before the self's own ego existed. But as the auxiliary ego naturally falls away, a personal psychic skin must take its place. This usually takes the form of another version of the false self, a beneficial false self that is derived from all that the self has taken from the world around it. How is this kind of false self different from the pathological kind? Winnicott sometimes describes the difference in terms of amount—one of the sections in his true self-false self paper is headed "Degrees of False Self"—but a close examination of his discussion reveals that it is a question of *direction*. If the false self emerges defensively, as a *reaction* to demands from outside, it generally functions to push the core self further and further into hiding. If, in contrast, the core self *generates* its own protector-buffer by willingly taking on the language and other attributes of its environment now and then, the false self that emerges tends to be more continuous with the core. In both cases, the false self serves to protect the true self, but the degree, kind, and effect of that protection can vary widely.

Here, finally, we reach the true self, for it is only when the false self arises out of the true self that the false self can foster, rather than hindering "all the sense of real."[71] It is important that Winnicott describes the true self not as an entity, an essence, but in terms of what it *does* and *where it comes from*. In fact, it can only be accessed indirectly: "At the earliest stage the true self is the *theoretical position* from which comes the spontaneous gesture and the personal idea. The spontaneous gesture is the true self in action."[72] It is thoroughly anchored in the body, aligned with the most fundamental physical phenomena—breathing, metabolizing, the working of the organs—and thus a life force that precedes even the Eros of Freud's *Beyond the Pleasure Principle*. In this respect, the true self is more the *urge* to be oneself than it is an identity in the conventional sense of the word. Later—if, of course, the environmental provision of a prosthetic protective membrane has been consistently present for a period of time—this urge takes the form of an illusion of omnipotence: the outside world to which, under unfavorable circumstances, I would feel compelled to comply is understandable as a part of *my* world, so I align myself with it willingly. Put somewhat differently, I begin with the impulse to be, which must be safeguarded by my environment if it is not to be eclipsed in favor of being-for-another. If the shelter in which I mature is adequate, I become able to take in by and as myself that which earlier would have been an impingement on my existence; I have internalized some of the external world and am thus able to function in it smoothly, without losing the spontaneous urge to be myself that led to reaching out into the world in the first place.

In a sense, this beneficial false self that emerges from the inside out, rather than the outside in, functions as the endogenous replacement for the exogenous ego-membrane that the good-enough environment had previously formed. Now I have a shield for my inner reality in the form of some behavior that is compatible with external reality. This false self is structurally, but not functionally, analogous to the pathological false self. The behavior might look the same—in both cases, I act in a way that the outside world approves of—but in the one case, this behavior shields my true self, while in the other case it obscures me. Either kind of false self hides the true self, but differences in the degree and effect of hiding are important. A self-generated false self allows the true self to remain appropriately hidden; a compliance-based false self throws the true self into defensive mode, forcing a kind of hiding that is necessary to ward off the danger of being excessively exposed or further manipulated. There arises in this context the danger that the true self could disappear altogether.

This latter situation is familiar to us: we value authenticity of self over all else and "phoniness"—to quote everyone's required high school anti-hero, Holden Caulfield—is its biggest threat. But Winnicott's contribution is to show how a pure, absolute, and constant authenticity is not only not possible but also not even desirable. For Winnicott, the core of the self is practically sacred, but it can only go on being if it can establish and retain a fundamental inaccessibility. Paradoxically, creative self-expression can only emerge if the self's core can, with the help of a beneficial false self, remain perpetually incommunicado.

"IT IS A JOY TO BE HIDDEN, AND A DISASTER NOT TO BE FOUND"

I think my favorite paper among Winnicott's many publications is his "Communicating and Not Communicating Leading to a Study of Certain Opposites." Embedded casually in its very center is, in turn, my favorite Winnicott quote, one that adorns some of my course descriptions and sits always at the back of my mind as a just-right description of my own personal psychic landscape: "It is a joy to be hidden, and a disaster not to be found." The second part of the quote is straightforwardly comprehensible: the need to be seen, to be recognized as ourselves, is primary, akin to the need for food and shelter. But the first part is a bit more puzzling. How is it a good thing to be hidden? And more fundamentally, how can the two parts of the quotation be reconciled with one another? How can I be found if I cannot be found? This is one of the most fertile of the paradoxes in Winnicott's pantheon, one that most perfectly answers Novalis's question: "Might the highest principle contain within its task the highest paradox? To be a statement that would allow absolutely no peace—that would constantly attract and constantly repels— that would always become incomprehensible again however often one had already comprehended it?"[73] More than containing an intriguing content, it is the form of paradox that does the radical work of undermining toxic binarism. I have discussed this creativity-provoking subversion already in the context of the self's origins as "Schrödinger's baby," and as it relates to its playing in the intermediate area. Now I turn to a close reading of this most profound of Winnicott's paradoxes.

In his characteristic fashion, Winnicott begins the paper with a return to the earliest situation, when the proto-self is absolutely dependent on its facilitating environment to go on being as potential. In this situation, communication is unnecessary; needs are met preemptively. As I have noted, this situation is often regarded as a kind of paradise, standing as the implicit ideal for every subsequent relationship. "She knows what I'm thinking before I do" is a sure sign of love, we tend to think, an ideal that should be striven for, even if we recognize that it will probably never be achieved. Like the primary state of undifferentiation between infant and the caregiving environment in which it is operative, though, this state of supposedly perfect understanding cannot—and must not—last. The *cannot* is clear and constitutes the cause for longing: if only we could (re)achieve this lost paradisiacal understanding of each other! But this state implies a self, or pair of selves, whose contours are uniform, with no difference between the two individuals. The boundary of each person is too porous; in this context, the other's "understanding" of me could just as easily be an injection of the other's reality into me—hardly an ideal situation.

As the self begins to take its own shape, two possibilities arise, according to Winnicott: communication is "either explicit or else dumb [i.e., mute, GMN]." He goes on, "Here then appear two *new* things, the individual's use and enjoyment of modes of communication, and the individual's non-communicating self, or the personal core of a self that is a true isolate."[74] The "two things," in other words, are the two parts of a split self, one that communicates easily and with pleasure with other people—a good false self, in the parlance that I describe above—and one— the true self—that retains its authenticity by remaining hidden and mute. This deceptively simple statement already constitutes to my mind a profound revision of the usual notion of communication and noncommunication. But here, too, as we shall see, what appears to be a clear-cut dichotomy reveals itself, instead, to be a nested set of opposites whose intertwined relationship helps describe and even determine the development of a self, and particularly of a creative self.

Winnicott immediately complicates the opposition communicating/not communicating when he divides "not-communicating" into *simple* not communicating and "a not communicating that is active or reactive." "Simple" not communicating is easy; it is a comfortable silence that seamlessly eases into speaking and returns when the speaking is done. In order to explain the other kind of not communicating, Winnicott needs to carry out another process of splitting, this time between pathology and health. This is a move he makes quite frequently, and it has at least two important implications. First, it demonstrates the great care and respect that Winnicott had for his patients. Indeed, in this and several other papers, he explicitly thanks them for their insights: "Our patients teach us these things, and it is distressing to me that I must give these views as if they were my own."[75] Second, the way in which Winnicott proceeds with his explanation shows us that what might appear to be a clean split between health and illness is actually a continuum.

It quickly becomes clear that the pathology-health spectrum of noncommunication is closely related to the functional distinction between a false self that undermines the true self and a false self that fosters the true self. Everything hinges on the notion of *compliance*: in the most pathological situation, the expectation is that one can only maintain oneself in existence if one complies with the other's demands that it be what the other wants, and communication is more or less entirely oriented toward performing that compliance. The true self has shrunk to the point of near disappearance, and what is left of it can only be in touch with itself via a form of engagement that Winnicott dubs "cul de sac" communication, because it goes nowhere except round and round inside itself. This often manifests as a state of clinical withdrawal, where there appears to be no way for the individual to express what is on the inside and no route for others to access it.

In what Winnicott calls "slighter illness"—which can coexist with normal life to a greater or lesser extent—the person's everyday life is taken up with a kind of communication that does contain an element, and sometimes a significant element, of compliance. The person feels a relatively strong need to with-draw relatively frequently into that hidden true self. Communi-cation with the intact but vulnerable true self is idiosyncratic and private, but has a "feeling of real," as Winnicott says. In other words, such communication can foster the maintenance of an authentic self when its ability to remain hidden is sufficiently reliably ensured; withdrawal into the self and away from the world can be essential to maintain health. It is equally impor-tant to become fluent enough in the language of compliance that one can deploy it as a shield for the necessarily hidden core. Health involves the same juxtaposition of false and true, com-municating and not, but with a lesser degree of compliance and a greater ability to communicate the still necessarily hidden inner core. Intermediate-area-style playing with the boundaries between inner and outer—in art, with particularly trusted inter-locutors, in especially safe environments—is a particularly wel-come refuge for the person with this "slighter illness."

Our newfound appreciation of introverts—to the point of a veritable flood of popular books, articles, and podcasts for and about them—reflects to some extent the relevance of this point of view: we have begun to recognize the value, at least for some people, of withdrawal into the self. If we follow Winnicott's sub-tle, often-paradoxical thinking, we can take this further, locat-ing the ultimate dwelling of the creative self in a profoundly hidden inner core. The creative self's work involves navigating the simultaneous *necessity* of rendering this internal core exter-nal, and the *impossibility* of that same operation. It is the latter horn of that particular dilemma that Winnicott particularly emphasizes, identifying the never-ending process of staying hid-den while nonetheless communicating as that which keeps the artist going.[76] But it is not just those we identify as "creatives" who struggle with and take pleasure in that task. I propose that it is precisely the walking of the line between the disaster of not being found and the joy of being hidden that constitutes the most creative activity of every individual.[77]

The healthy end of the illness-health continuum with regard to communicating does *not* involve a perfect ability to express one's inner world, just as the true self is not an absolutely authentic essence. Instead, the healthy individual navigates the amount and kind of communicating and not communicating in ways that work particularly well for their own singular self. Previously, I have described the way in which cultural experiences, whether aesthetic, religious, or otherwise, manage to extend the benefits of playing in the intermediate area by providing a refuge from the constant demand to resolve paradoxes and be productive. This new paradox has even higher stakes. How do I express my core self without losing the "feeling of real" that attends its communication only within itself?[78] Even more crucially, how do I protect that core from being revealed when it is not ready to be found—or even not actually *there* to be revealed as what is expected to be found? For the exposure of a self can sometimes actually entail its erasure.

In one of the most apocalyptic statements in his entire oeuvre, Winnicott describes "rape, and being eaten by cannibals, as mere bagatelles as compared with the violation of the self's core."[79] Far from minimizing the profound trauma of rape, this declaration points to the underlying reason *why* rape is such a horrific crime; structurally, rape involves the breach of an absolutely inviolable boundary around the very kernel of a person's self. From this structural perspective, radical violation can also take other forms. I think, for example, of the time when I witnessed the effect of being accused of theft by a campus security officer on two young Black boys who were part of a summer program that I directed at my college for a group of students from a high school in the Bronx. The group had found bicycles in the unlocked basement of the dormitory in which they were staying; since the college had given them other sports equipment to use during their stay, they naturally assumed the bicycles were at their disposal as well, and they were simply riding them around in front of the dorm when the custodian called security, without any attempt to discuss the situation with the kids. By the time I got there, the officer had singled out the two most athletic boys and was loudly berating them on the dormitory porch, in plain view of anyone who walked by. Before my eyes, these boys' core selves were being exposed and *remade* into the selves that the officer "knew" them to be. With the confidence of someone who is certain that his view would be reinforced by those around him, he in effect publicly declared the essence of these children to be criminal. Even though I confronted the officer in the strongest possible way, I had to watch the two boys literally shrink, trying to make themselves smaller in a desperate attempt to hide and thus preserve their true selves. From that moment on, no amount of attentiveness, gentle encouragement, or apology on my part could draw the two out of the deep withdrawal that they needed to undertake to save themselves. I felt like I had witnessed the destruction of two souls in that encounter.

As Winnicott says, *"each individual is an isolate, permanently non-communicating, permanently unknown, in fact unfound."*[80] The italics in Winnicott's sentence point to the urgency he felt when he wrote these words, and they are radical words indeed. Not only is Winnicott here reversing John Donne's assertion that "no man is an island";[81] it would seem that he is also contradicting himself. What about the proto-self that cannot exist without an other? What about "primary maternal preoccupation"? In fact, the profound dependence of the self on an other and the self's equally intense isolation are not incompatible concepts. As we are learning in the "self-care" movement, maintaining your boundaries and demanding that others do the same for you is an essential skill that leads to personal satisfaction and an ability to engage more happily with others. But Winnicott is talking about something beyond long baths with a glass of wine. Far from merely emphasizing that we all need some downtime once in a while, Winnicott is focused on a serious danger to the integrity of the self, to its ability to move about freely, and to its potential for creative living. "Finding" someone before they are ready to be found, or in the absence of someone there to be found, forces them to hide what must be hidden even more desperately. The hidden inside, under these conditions, is no longer a space from which I voluntarily emerge in order to share a bit of myself with the world; it is a bunker where I cower in fear of exposure and destruction.

So what does creative communication look like if the self is—must be—an incommunicado isolate? I liken it to our understanding of electrons: we know they exist not because we can see them, hear them, feel them, or register them directly in any way. Instead, they make their presence known to us by their effect—on light, on magnets—and through this effect we can locate them quite well, noting among other things their positioning in one of the three shells around the atom's nucleus. But we can never know precisely where an electron is, or how it moves. It itself remains elusive, even though it is an integral part of the very substance of being, and its movements constitute, in a very real sense, life itself. The core self, too, is—under good-enough conditions—very much there, very much alive, very much creating its own and sometimes other realities, but we will never ever know exactly what it is. Instead, I can best express—and others can best understand—my true self indirectly. The *search* for words via a back-and-forth with another person, with something I am reading, or with language itself is as important for self-expression as the words that I ultimately choose (or that choose me). The gap between my true self and the self another seeks to know is a creative space; in it, I can (and must) constantly play with communicating a core that is enriched or even constituted in the process of communicating. If I have the patience to wait for my interlocutor to do the same with their core self, then both of us get to go through a creative process, and neither of us becomes locked in a cycle of idealization (of self or other) and inevitable disillusionment.

"HULLO OBJECT!" "I DESTROYED YOU." "I LOVE YOU." "YOU HAVE VALUE FOR ME BECAUSE OF YOUR SURVIVAL OF MY DESTRUCTION OF YOU."

With his reassuring reminder that parents need only be "good enough" and his extended detailing of children's play, the popular Winnicott would seem to be a far more sunny and optimistic psychoanalyst than Freud, Klein, or Lacan.[82] But as I have noted, even these positive notions are shot through with the negative. The infant's going-on-being takes place under threat of annihilation; the child's playing is located in the gap between subject and object as much as in their overlap, and it is conditioned by the possibility of an unintegration that can become disintegration under the wrong circumstances. The true self requires a false self; and now we learn that communication is necessarily shadowed by various opposites of it. This is something to embrace, rather than avoid—to welcome, rather than fear. The creativity of the self, its ability to retain its authenticity and move about freely in its own core, has as much to do with recognizing what it cannot, and must not, reveal about itself as with deciding what of itself it will allow into the world.

And that self requires a kind of negative to come into being at all—in fact, a kind of aggression.

Winnicott's understanding of aggression is one of the most important revisions he made to traditional psychoanalytic theory. For Freud, aggression arises out of the frustration experienced by the ego at having to submit to the reality principle; it is fundamentally *reactive* in nature. In his work with children, parents, and patients, Winnicott came to realize that aggression can (also) be *active*, indeed, an active component of the self's essential creativity. In order to understand this phenomenon, it is necessary to return to the complex of ideas that I have discussed above, the intertwining of spontaneous gesture and limit. I noted that in infancy, the ability to be a powerful creator of one's world is paradoxically dependent on the existence of an elastic limit to that power in the form of a parent's reality, which helps shape what would otherwise be blind flailing. In this scenario, the limit has the effect of holding the self, of providing a container within which it can experience the illusion of omnipotence that will gradually give way to a recognition of where one has and does not have the power to determine one's world, with an ample dose of playing with the boundaries between the two mixed in. At a certain point, though—and in certain circumstances in adulthood as well—the self must actively refuse the limit in order to be able to achieve a higher level of authenticity and a better ability to relate to the other as a being with its own separate identity. For in the earlier state (or under some adult conditions), the object is still *perceived* to be primarily part of the self-world set-up. To summarize the series of paradoxes at play here: at first, there is, from the infant's perspective, no limit to itself, but that infant as potential self would not exist without the protective limiting layer of the caregiving environment. Gradually, as the infant matures and the caregiver productively "fails," there is a dawning awareness on the part of the nascent self that its omnipotence is limited by the existence of other selves, although those others are still experienced primarily as extensions of the self. If it is to gain its own contours, the self must refuse this limit. Paradoxically, by refusing a limit, a limit—a boundary—is created between the self and the other that allows them genuinely to relate to one another—another paradox. Paradox on paradox, the ultimate result of the refusal of limit is, then, the recognition of a separation, i.e., a boundary, between self and other. What results is an ability both to be oneself and to relate to others more freely, more creatively.

The earliest discovery of my own creative energy comes as my intrinsic "motility," to use Winnicott's word for the infant's urge to move, meets opposition in the world; this meeting looks for all the world like aggression. Freud regarded the infant's hitting and biting in these situations as evidence of a need to release tension deriving from frustration. Winnicott's mentor, interlocutor, and sometime adversary Melanie Klein brought the object, the mother, into the picture: the infant, she proposes, is driven unconsciously to destroy the mother who is not satisfying it. Winnicott, though, realized something remarkable: the aggression that is associated with motility is not—or not merely—an automatic expelling of tension; it is relationship-seeking. That is, the infant can only experience itself when it meets opposition to itself. More pointedly, I could say that the infant creates itself by feeling itself as limited. In this context, this early aggression is a reaching out into the world more than it is a reaction to the world.

What is more, as Winnicott became increasingly involved in the observation of babies and children with their parents, and in his own analytic practice with adult patients, it became more and more clear to him that aggression arose, not only in relation to objects (the parent, the analyst) who were *not* meeting needs, but also to those who *were*. He began to realize something remarkable: "There is an intermediate stage in healthy development in which the patient's most important experience in relation to the good or potentially satisfying object is the refusal of it. The refusal of it is part of the process of creating it."[83] This statement hints at the exceedingly complex relationship between freedom and limit, and between yes and no. In order to "create" the object—and not incidentally, the subject itself—as a being in its own right, the subject must *destroy* it (in unconscious fantasy), and the object must *survive* the destruction. More precisely, the subject must replace an object that is still perceived as more or less part of the subjective sphere with an object that dwells in a sphere of its own, and this takes place by means of a kind of destruction.

What does this look like in real life? For me, the value of Winnicott's astounding insight has played out in the realms of parenting and teaching. It helped me navigate my daughter's sometimes-aggressive "nos," from toddlerhood through adolescence; I recognize them as a creative gesture more than as defiance. By saying "no" to me, she was bringing me into being as a person she, herself newly a person, could potentially engage with as separate from but still connected to her. My task in these exchanges was to survive. I had to remain present, neither capitulating fully, which would mean disappearing as me, nor "retaliating," as Winnicott says, for example, by hurling her insults back at her or by pouting.[84] This is, I can attest, a difficult task indeed. Depending on the child's age and the specific situation at hand, surviving might involve simple physical not going away or, alternatively, announcing that one has to leave the room because the child's words are so hurtful. It might mean doling out consequences for unacceptable actions or admitting one's own error and acceding to the child's demand. But regardless of the specific actions taken, recasting the child's often-aggressive "no" as a mark of creativity instead of defiance, as an active step forward instead of a regression to babyhood, as joyfully life-, self-, and world-affirming instead of -negating is nothing short of revolutionary. Importantly, Winnicott's theory of aggression is not merely an act of defining as positive what was conventionally defined as negative. Instead, by recognizing the dynamic creativity that can attend an aggressive act, as well as the crucial role of the reaction to that act, he is once again reminding us of the value of a third space, in which things are not only one thing or the other and the stakes are not zero-sum.

The effect of this recasting of aggression reaches beyond child-rearing; for example, it has implications for education as well. The unruly student in a primary or secondary school classroom might need to "destroy" the teacher—and the teacher might need to survive—in order for a productive learning process to be able to begin. In my own work, I have noticed that my college students' initial rejection of the material that I am presenting to them often has the salutary effect of enabling them later to engage with it in a way that demonstrates their own autonomy and simultaneously their recognition that the text in front of them is nuanced, rather than something they need to wholly accept or totally reject.

Interestingly, it is perhaps especially important for the self to refuse something that is good for it from the point of view of the giver, and maybe even from an "objective" point of view. As Winnicott notes, sometimes even the provision of nutrition can become an imposition of the feeder's needs onto the baby.[85] The same phenomenon can often be observed in the giving of advice, which can definitely be used—or at least experienced—as a means of maintaining the receiver's dependence on the giver.

Winnicott's native habitat of psychotherapy can be instructive beyond its own boundaries, too. The more Winnicott worked in this domain, the clearer it became to him that providing an interpretation at all—even if it is brilliantly accurate—could be damaging to the patient's inner life. This gets back to the danger of another person impinging on the core self, that I have already discussed. But the new piece is Winnicott's recognition of the value of the patient's refusal of even the most correct interpretation that the analyst might give. With this refusal, the patient is on the way to experiencing the analyst more as a particular, idiosyncratic individual than as merely a screen on which their own dramas appear.

Indeed, Winnicott's rather confusingly named theory of the use of an object provides quite a radical revision of the traditional psychoanalytic theory of the transference. Freud discovered that his patients were experiencing and sometimes reenacting feelings and conflicts that they had gone through in their lives outside of analysis, usually in early childhood with a parent or other caregiver. He recognized that this phenomenon could be a powerful tool in the analysis: if patients were feeling or acting out with the analyst things that they had repressed, access was gained that would otherwise have been barred. Winnicott, however, realized that as long as the analysand was engaging with the analyst as a here-and-now stand-in for a there-and-then relationship, the analyst remained effectively part of the analysand's inner world. In other words, the subject is engaging with what he called "selfobjects," rather than actual objects, or selves in their own right. Only when the person is able to break through the projection screen by questioning or even rejecting the analyst's contribution are they able to see their analyst as a three-dimensional person, with all their flaws intact. In this way, the analysand is able to create a personal self in the company of an other whom they recognize as a personal self as well. Both are necessarily imperfect, and therefore real. More broadly, saying "no" is often an important step in being able to say "yes" to one's autonomous and singular self.

This operation is certainly not without its difficulties, nor even its dangers, as evidenced by a parenthetical remark following Winnicott's affirmation of refusal: "(This produces a truly formidable problem for the therapist in anorexia nervosa)."[86] He never elaborates on this remark, but we can imagine the implications of saying "no" for a person suffering from anorexia: when that which the patient is refusing is quite literally food, then the psychologically life-affirming effect of refusal can ultimately turn physically deadly. The same could be said of more metaphorical food, of course: necessary help for a suicidal teen or an addict hitting rock bottom, for example. Speaking entirely in the terms of Winnicott's *theory*, it is useful to conceptualize people in situations like these as living in a world in which others function as figures in their purely interior reality—their fantasy. In this theoretical respect, a refusal of that which is offered by those others (food, help, rehabilitation) would be beneficial for the formation of clearer lines between inner and outer, self and other. But Winnicott's parenthesis about anorexia shows that he recognizes that such a refusal would on the practical level be both impossible and potentially fatal. The solution might very well be providing a space that looks like the intermediate area would seem to be key: in a "potential space," safely contained and not challenged by those who surround the self, I can experiment with saying "no" without the dire consequences that attend in the larger environment.

The extreme difficulty—but also the potential beauty—of dwelling together in such a space is evident in Winnicott's discussions of adolescence. Like infancy and toddlerhood, adolescence is a time of tremendous movement, perhaps the most universally dynamic time in the development of a self. This period is quite evidently an extension of the intermediate area, with its experimentation surrounding identity and its probing of boundaries. Interestingly, when describing the fate of intermediate-area playing, Winnicott aligns behaviors that we would normally think of as deviant, or even criminal, with the cultural experiences that constitute an extension of intermediate-area playing. Consider this remarkable statement in the "Transitional Objects" paper: "At this point my subject widens out into that of play, and of artistic creativity and appreciation, and of religious feeling, and of dreaming, and also of fetishism, lying and stealing, the origin and loss of affectionate feeling, drug addiction, the talisman of obsessional rituals, etc."[87] How do these seemingly disparate phenomena line up with one another? On the most basic level, all of these activities involve negotiating self-other boundaries; I am constantly figuring out how to extend myself into the world or take something from the world into myself. Going deeper, we can see that at stake is the construction, protection, and maintenance of a core self, which requires subtle, complex, and ever-varying modes of engagement with the not-self. At times, we feel just barely safe enough, held enough, to venture forth; other times, we are able to trust that we can find in the world what we create in our imagination; eventually, we might even be able to take the risk of destroying the other in fantasy, hoping that it will live to engage with us in its own right.

The boundary around the core is the site of crucially important activity for the care and feeding of the creative self. The crucial protection, sometimes by means of an intentionally deployed false self, against impingement from outside—against "cannibalism"—allows what Winnicott calls, idiosyncratically, the "feeling of real" that characterizes communication within the incommunicado core self, that is, communication purely by the self with the self. This feeling of real is deeply personal: I am me only insofar as I feel real. The core self it is attached to is nonfixed; it is not the same as a kind of essentialist authenticity of the self, which tends to become ossified and—ironically— performative. Instead, the feeling of real acts as a marker: when I feel real, I am not being required to comply with another's notion of who I am. In this respect, the feeling of real is a posi- tive in the form of a negative. Similarly, despite being associated with the true self, it *must* stay hidden within me, as my own per- sonal, secret superpower, and it will inevitably come and go. To the extent that I have the feeling of real, I am able to be con- cerned with and connect to others without losing myself. But in order for that concern and connection to become fully realized and experienced by a full-blown self, I must breach the bound- ary between me and the other and it must be reestablished in a different form. This is the destruction-survival dynamic that I discussed earlier, and it is a delicate dance.

Hence the often-excruciating difficulties associated with ado- lescence, for all parties involved. The teenager's destruction of the parents' selves-as-selfobjects can often feel to the parents like the very kind of penetration of their core that must be protected against at all costs. How can they survive that? Their own feel- ing of real is a crucial bulwark against actual (psychological) destruction, as is an understanding of the pain that their child is in at having to undertake this operation in the first place. For it entails a loss as well as a gain for the teenager: in refusing their parents as the selfobjects that they have remained, to some extent, the adolescent loses a part of the self—quite literally, in the psy- chic sense. But in doing so, they are taking the chance of refind- ing, or redefining their parents as whole other selves with whom they can have a rich, meaningful, albeit ambivalent relationship.

The teenager's job is a difficult one. First, they need to be able to dwell inside a figurative place where they can feel real; this involves the hiding that is, according to Winnicott's statement, a joy. The adolescent is by definition "not quite ready to be found," and it is for this reason that teenagers tend to "form aggregates rather than groups, and by looking alike they emphasize the essential loneliness of each individual."[88] Social media embodies this paradox, even in its vocabulary, especially its verbs. "Liking" or "following" implies a kind of noncommittal commitment to someone or something that assures the retention of my own self while connecting me to a network of others who are ultimately as isolated as I am.

The destruction of the object necessary for establishing a separate but (potentially) connected self and other can be seen as an extension of the need to refuse what the object is offering. If anorexia represents an absolutization of the refusal, criminality might be the logical extreme of the destruction. The establishment of a boundary around the self, together with the forceful violation of others' boundaries, can sometimes become emotionally and even physically violent. As with the example of anorexia, this presents particular difficulties for both the individual who is desperately trying to enact what is imperative for their growth and the individuals or institutions trying to deal with them. It is, however, worth the risk, the effort, and the pain to work through the process, since it can lead to a more robust, empathetic, and creative self. What might such work look like? Here, too, I return to my Winnicottian mantra: Embrace paradox! This is far more difficult than it sounds. As I have detailed, a society oriented nearly totally toward measurable outcomes, achieved by reducing all variables to an absolute minimum, fears ambiguity more than just about anything else. But the alternative is what we are experiencing today: nations unable to accept themselves as flawed and individuals who despair, even to the point of suicide, if they are deemed, or deem themselves to be anything less than perfect.

BY WAY OF CONCLUSION

What does the "optimized" neoliberal self ultimately look like? And what does the Winnicottian self offer as an alternative to it? By way of a conclusion, I here first detail the two models in a general form, then look more closely at the modes of selfhood and engagement with the world that have emerged in the context of the unprecedented challenges we have been experiencing in the form of the COVID-19 pandemic and the recent additions in Ukraine and Gaza to a world full of war. In addition to costing millions of lives worldwide, the pandemic and the wars have thrust individuals and societies into a kind of unwilling experiment, where both the brittleness and the possibility for creativity in both have become starkly evident.

In my concluding remarks, I keep three large contributions of Winnicottian thinking in mind, all of them related to each other:

- First, a new notion of what might be called "thirdness." When dealing with situations in which two things, ideas, or persons are in conflict, we are accustomed to citing the need for some kind of third position. This can take the form of an "objective" arbiter of legitimacy, a kind of Archimedean point of neutrality outside of the self-interested positions of each party. Alternatively, the third position might be a compromise between the two; each must give something up in order to reach the compromise. By contrast, Winnicott's third, the intermediate area—which, as I hope to have shown, extends far beyond a developmental stage—involves a paradoxical kind of experiencing that allows for two things—or multiple things—to be true and real at the same time.

• Second, a new kind of authenticity and creativity in the self, which in turn leads to a new kind of relationship between self and other. Winnicott helps me understand my true self less as an essential me-ness that I can find or lose, and more as a complex dynamic of trueness and falseness, each of whose definition is determined by the relationship to the other. In this context, creativity involves navigating the "dilemma" inherent in every engagement of the true self with its surroundings: "the urgent need to communicate and the still more urgent need not to be found." It is for this reason that, according to Winnicott, "we cannot imagine the artist coming to the end of the task that occupies his whole nature."

• Third, a new tolerance of gaps, which might be gaps of understanding, empty time, or even a sense of who one is. Winnicott shows us a self whose potential originates in a state of undifferentiation and unintegration, a state to which it must periodically return in order not to get swept away by the relentless demand to be *something* and to be *moving forward toward something* at all times.

Linearity and Binarity vs. Spiraling and Betweenness

Our usual notion of development and growth involves a step-wise progression from simple to complex, and from dependent to independent. There has come to be a dualistic moral valuation associated with this linear progression: simple = "primitive," complex = "civilized," dependent = "weak," independent = "strong." The neoliberal worldview tends to ossify the lure of intertwined linearity and binarity by reinforcing the notion that a zero-sum/winner-loser dynamic is as natural and universal in human life as the laws of physics are in the extrahuman world. In this context, attitudes toward both self and other have hardened. We seem compelled by some kind of insidious logic to be constantly vigilant against possible attack from others; it seems that every group or individual sees themselves as vulnerable and the other as all-powerful. To a certain extent, this development represents the welcome exposure of long-standing inequities. That which previously was regarded as simply the way of the world, which members of marginalized groups had to tolerate in order to survive, is now rightly recognized on the personal level as abuse, harassment, and assault, and on the societal level as racism, misogyny, and xenophobia. But at the same time, the very notion of vulnerability has been co-opted by the structurally powerful, losing all meaning in the process. Look, for example, at this headline from the Social Work Today website: "Whites Believe They Are Victims of Racism More Often Than Blacks."[89] This discovery is startling on its face, but is ultimately not surprising in the context of neoliberal thinking, which plays a role in at least two ways. First, we see evidence of the winner-takes-all thinking of neoliberalism. As the article points out, since some progress has unquestionably been made in the arena of lowering discriminatory practices against Black people in the United States since the 1950s (despite recent attempts, some successful, to roll back that progress), in a zero-sum mentality, someone has to lose if others gain. In addition, neoliberalism's reliance on obscuring concrete reality with hyperabstraction is fully evident here. Only an entirely abstract notion of racism could support claims that a white person is being discriminated against because of their race. In fact, racism is contingent on centuries of systemic discrimination and persecution of Black people because they are Black. Lived experience in the present and/or via the transgenerational transmission of historical and structural inequity is necessary for a claim of racism to be authentic. Indeed, when historical reality and lived experience are suppressed, it seems that anyone can take on the status of "victim" at the mercy of a thoroughly evil "perpetrator." Critics of the current situation in turn adopt the same dualistic thinking by trying to debunk the victim status of one or the other side in a dispute, without questioning the underlying terms of the argument. On the intrapersonal or intragroup level, this binarism takes the form of a sometimes-dizzying oscillation between self-hatred and self-glorification.

The Winnicottian alternative to such thinking is, at base, the embrace of paradox—an extraordinarily simple concept that is extraordinarily difficult to put into practice. This goes beyond his intermediate area, a genuinely third space of self-other encounter in which the self learns about its limits but also about a new kind of power that it has to engage creatively with the world. Other paradoxes abound in his work, ranging from the coincidence of being and not-being in the originary state to the fantasized destruction of the other that is associated with the recognition of it as an authentic self. Winnicott's embrace of paradox was not an ideological decision on his part. Rather, he was honestly recording what he was seeing in his patients and in the children and parents he worked with: the intricately woven fabric of often-contradictory thoughts, feelings, and behaviors that makes up a really existing human being. Winnicott's honesty extends to the process of recording his insights. His winding, sometimes-repetitive prose and his sometimes telegraphic, even occasionally misleading nomenclature enacts a process of struggling to understand and convey something that cannot be reduced to binaries, nor streamlined into a simple progression.

Essentialism vs. Relationality

The me/not-me, good/evil, winner/loser, victim/perpetrator dichotomy goes hand in hand with an essentialistic notion of identity. Despite decades of research into the complex interweaving of genetics and environment that makes up an individual's characteristic way of being, the urge to define oneself and others in terms of a kind of crux or marrow that simply *is* remains strong. When it comes to defining others, we could attribute the tendency to laziness, I suppose; it is easier to demonize or idealize than it is to go to the effort of figuring out how someone else actually ticks. But I would suggest that the inclination to essentialize is even more pronounced with regard to ourselves. We expend a good deal of energy searching for and trying to express an authenticity in ourselves, and if we cannot locate it, the only alternative seems to be that we are fake—or hypocritical. Winnicott's intricate discussion of the "true" and "false" selves shows that in fact an "authentic" human self involves layers that are constantly shifting over time, ideally with a core that is—again paradoxically—both crucial to our singularity and fundamentally inaccessible. The performativity that makes up a good portion of our day-to-day behavior has the primary task of protecting this core, but it can all too easily veer into a degree and kind of compliance with others' reality that puts the core in danger of disappearing. In order to prevent that, the self must from time to time—the amount and frequency varies from individual to individual—withdraw into its core, where it can fill up its tank of a "feeling of real" before reemerging into the outside world again. This rhythmicity of being is one of the most tragic victims of the relentless compulsion to be producing, doing, succeeding at all times and in all ways which is the driving force of our neoliberal worldview. And while the "cul-de-sac communication" with our core selves is solitary, the formation of a healthy "false" self involves an elastic relationship with others. Being curious about another without an agenda of our own; waiting for them to reveal their thoughts and feelings; being prepared to wonder about their inevitable contradictoriness without trying to resolve it into simplicity; simply taking the time to be there with another—all of this will foster the going-on-being of a "true" self, and we should seek out those who do it for us as well.

Fear vs. Acceptance of Incomprehension

It has become a cliché to describe ourselves as surrounded by—even drowning in—information, but it is nonetheless important to think about the origins and effects of this state of affairs. Our current addiction to information very likely has its source in the Enlightenment belief that human beings' knowledge of the world is the key to our liberation from its hold over us. If we can understand the biological and physical laws of nature, perhaps we will not be so limited by our bodies and threatened by the exigencies of natural phenomena; by extension, if we can expose the irrational arbitrariness of hereditary rule, then we can construct a system of political power based on individual merit alone. But the Kantian bedrock of European Enlightenment certainty about the possibility and value of increasing knowledge already contained an important fissure: the recognition that we cannot ultimately know the thing-in-itself. Freud went on to detail the extent to which an entire logic exists parallel to the familiar logic of rationalism, a logic that in many ways determines our thoughts, feelings, and behaviors without our being able to understand it in its own terms. In its popularized form the Freudian unconscious has been appropriated to help political and commercial interests measure and manipulate popular opinion and consumer behavior. But the response to the notion of the unconscious that forms the foundation of Freud's thinking has mostly been fear and avoidance. Just as we often feel compelled to fill the emptiness, the undifferentiation on which (paradoxically) our becoming a fully creative self is based, we feel an urgent need to fill the void of our knowledge with more and more information. I am certainly familiar with that restless, uncomfortable feeling: something comes up in discussion during a dinner with friends that no one really knows about, and my fingers are itching for the phone—gotta Google it! What if I simply let myself not know that particular fact? Perhaps sitting with and not knowing could form a brief resting place for my frenetically racing mind.

The COVID-19 pandemic is a highly concentrated laboratory in which to examine our deeply ambivalent relationship to knowledge. During it, we saw a dangerous polarization between those who resist knowing altogether and those who, it could be argued, place an exaggerated emphasis on knowledge as a way to avoid illness and death. It is easier to see that the latter stance is a remnant of Enlightenment optimism about the power of rationality, but its opposite is as well. The reasoning goes like this: "They say that science can provide us with the answers we need, but the fact that the disease still exists proves that it can't—at all—so I reject it completely." COVID-19 has taught us the truth about reason, namely that it will and must always be imperfect, always in a state of nonlinear flux that includes its opposite within; in fact, the way that thinking operates precludes the notion that there is a clean dichotomy of rational and irrational. For one thing, there exists a temporal lapse between question and answer; it takes time for a gap in knowledge to be filled. However, as one colleague described it, we have been conditioned by the information glut to expect answers in a double click. And of course, for many questions no adequate answer even exists. Some things cannot be known.

POSTSCRIPT: A PERSONAL NOTE

The notion of the incommunicado core is probably the Winnicottian idea that most closely resonates with my own life. In my reading, teaching, and writing, I find myself drawn over and over again to texts that seem to center on an irresistible attraction to understanding that simultaneously resists my grasp. Thinking of recent examples, I could cite the catalog description for my Kafka course, where I write: "Jewish in an increasingly anti-Semitic environment, German-speaking surrounded by Czech-speakers, deeply alone in a family that didn't understand him, Kafka produced texts that simultaneously demand and refuse to be interpreted." Or take my lifelong preoccupation with the work of Heinrich von Kleist, the early nineteenth-century German writer who wanted desperately to be able to rely on the scaffolding provided by Enlightenment rationalism but who could not help but see its precarity. A favorite moment among many for me in his work appears in a letter to a friend, where Kleist encounters an old Roman arch; it makes such an impression on him that he even includes a drawing in the letter (figure 2.4).

As I note in an article on what I call the "aesthetics of catastrophe" in his work, Kleist wonders why, when there are no supports, the arch does not collapse. "It stands, I answered myself, because all of the stones want to collapse at once." In other words, the space under the arch is both conditioned by the structure that surrounds it and itself conditions that structure; the laws of physics exist outside the relationship between the dyads formed by adjacent stones, but inhere in them as well.[90]

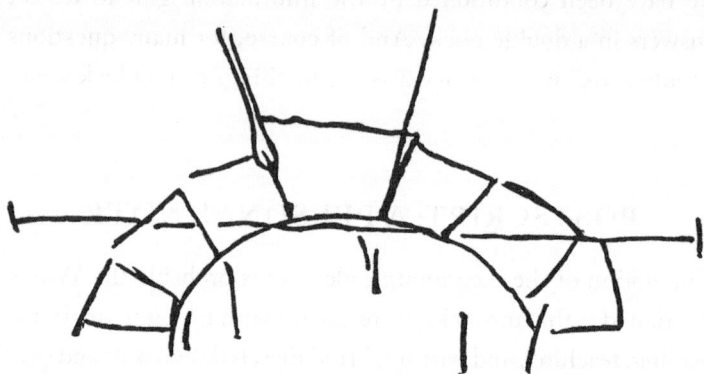

FIGURE 2.4 Heinrich von Kleist, hand-drawn arch in a letter to his friend Rühle von Lilienstern. *Sämtliche Werke und Briefe*, vol. 4 (Munich/Vienna: Hanser, 1982).

This may sound esoteric, but the idea is acutely meaningful to me personally. Without going into details, I can say that the "facilitating environment" in which I grew up was by no means ideal: my true self was effectively absent because of the overwhelming (unconscious) requirement that I comply with others' need for me to be for them. Yet, as I discovered later in life, that absence formed a powerful presence that kept me intact in the face of the tendency to collapse. I was there, it turns out, but so hidden that it seemed—even to me—that I was not. Once an environment was in place in which I could begin to emerge, I became better able to engage in the playing that Winnicott associates with creativity.

Teaching is the mode of creativity that comes most easily to me, perhaps because operating for others is a more familiar mode of being. But unlike the compliant experience from my earlier life, in which a finely honed, pathological false self predominated, my teaching feels real to me precisely because it takes place in a space beyond the dyad. The classroom is the ultimate intermediate area for me; what happens there is not *mine* or *yours* but partakes of *both of us*. Probably because I spent so much of my life desperately trying to read what the other needed from me, nothing makes me more upset than seeing or hearing about "educational" experiences where kids are at the mercy of teachers' moods, insecurities, or power trips. Hence, establishing a learning environment free from the compulsion to comply with power is more than a teaching philosophy for me; it is a personal mission as well.

The more solitary modes of creativity have been, perhaps surprisingly, more difficult for me to engage in. This is likely because the intensity of the demand to be there for the other made solitude feel shameful to me as a child; hence, I craved the joy of being hidden, but in its absence, I had to endure the disaster of not being found. Music was the first space in which I got a little taste of creativity. Feeling how changing the way my breath moved from my lungs through my mouth could shape the sound (I was a clarinetist) was a revelation. Melding my own sound wordlessly with the sounds of my section in the orchestra was a completely novel form of being together. And I even found it exhilarating, albeit terrifying, to perform solos now and again in front of an audience. But in the presence of a private teacher— something I did not have until conservatory—I was unable to reproduce the music that I heard perfectly in my head; the setting was too close to the intimate dyad that was not safe for my inner self. I eventually gave up the instrument in despair, but music still remains a nearly sacred space for me, and the palpable memory of producing it accompanies every bit of creative work that I have done since.

Writing eventually became the primary site of solitary creativity for me, and it has helped me learn how to break out of the rigid inside/outside dichotomy in which I had been trapped. For I find that language itself functions as a third entity between me and my possible readers, and even between me and myself. When I write, the ideas that I plan to convey often become transformed by the process of writing them—it is almost as if a conversation were taking place between my ideas and the language that emerges through my fingers to the page. Like a transitional object, language possesses a reality of its own—its grammar, its phonetics, the conventional meanings of its words—that presents to the writer both a limit and an opening into new realities. To return to the realm of music: for me, writing ideally becomes like a jazz improvisation—something I was actually too inhibited to be able to pull off in my music days!—insofar as it performs a filigree of ideas that are uniquely my own around and through a highly ordered set of existing structures.

Operating in a language that is not native to me has also enhanced my ability to be creative. I am by no means the first to notice that knowing another language changes your relationship to your own language, but I can describe my own experience. Reading in German feels in a way like coming home: the hypotactic nature of German syntax—the frequency of nested constructions—turns out to mirror the way that I tend to think. That is, associations often arise in my mind among various ideas that then seem to arrange themselves like a *matrjoschka*, a Russian doll. This mode of thinking is difficult to reproduce in language, which is intrinsically exclusively linear—unlike music, incidentally, which avails itself of vertically organized harmony and rhythmic combinations in addition to linear melody. But certain grammatical constructions, including subordinate clauses, relative clauses, and prepositional phrases, allow an approximation of simultaneity even in a sequential mode of expression.

These constructions abound in German sentences; add to them the famous German compound nouns and the elaborate extended adjectival forms and you have a language built for a nonlinear thinker like me! Speaking German, I am somehow immersed and detached at the same time. The German words feel lovely in my mouth, but I sometimes cannot believe that these entirely correct and idiomatic sentences are coming out in my voice and being responded to entirely naturally by others. This is similar to writing, where sentences appear on the page that could have come from no one but me, but they strike me as both mine and not mine.

I am realizing as I write this that the condition of creativity for me involves something between solitude and relationality. It is a mental, emotional, and physical state that is not always present and in which I become someone who is both deeply familiar to myself and also fundamentally alien. I am reminded, here, of an essay by Kleist entitled "On the Gradual Fabrication of Thoughts While Speaking." In it, he describes how it is not so much we who know, but rather it is a "certain *condition*, in which we happen to be, that 'knows.'"[91] As Kleist hints, this state feels like it comes over us accidentally and is outside of our control, but in my experience, simply waiting for its random appearance disallows it from happening just as certainly as trying to force it does. Instead—again leaning on Kleist—it seems that in the process of using language, new or more or better language appears in my head and on my page. The relationship that conditions the creative process, then, is primarily to myself and to the language itself, but that language is always connected as well to the people who also use the language and who will read my particular words. None of these relationships is direct and seamless; in all of them, there is an incommunicado core whose silence I respect even while I attempt to approximate its essence. With this and the other concepts I have outlined in my chapter, Winnicott has served as a balancing pole for me as I navigate the tightrope of finding and preserving my singular self while forging a curious, caring connection to others.

CONCLUSION

We have proposed that Milner and Winnicott, each in their distinctive ways, offer an antidote to neoliberal self-optimization—to the instrumentalist ethos of performance, productivity, self-improvement, and positive thinking that characterizes contemporary Western societies and that seems to be gaining ground globally as well. We have specified that this individualistic ethos engenders a steel-cold mentality where zero-sum thinking reigns; where the polarization of political perspectives has reached pathological heights; and where collective forms of social and ethical responsibility have largely been replaced by the notion that it is the obligation of each of us to single-handedly defeat any obstacles that might arise in our lives and to find a means of thriving despite these obstacles. Thriving, in turn, is defined according to strictly pragmatic criteria: it is a matter of making the most of our lives in terms of tangible accomplishments and monetary success.

Milner's poetics of being and Winnicott's ideal of creative living both offer an alternative to this manner of defining the good life. Based on the ideas that we have presented in this book, one could hypothesize that a rewarding life for both is characterized by psychic, even existential, vitality at the same time as it remains nimble in the face of the unexpected. Although the creative self may be less proficient at the practical task of clearing quotidian hurdles than the optimized self, it may ultimately be more resilient in the face of adversity because it regards modifications to its path as an existential given rather than a disaster; because its life is less carefully curated, and because it accepts loss as a necessary component of human life, sudden alterations to its trajectory are less likely to feel like catastrophes than openings toward personal exploration. This is not to say that all life-altering episodes are desirable: some are absolutely shattering. However, some may function like Alain Badiou's truth events: as ruptures in the status quo of the self's everyday situation that generate gateways for growth and new perspectives regarding the directions that this growth should take.[1] In other words, a self that is invested in fashioning its idiosyncratic art of living tends to know how to meet existential detours with grace, agility, and dexterity.

We have seen that Milner's version of creative living revolves around the attempt to neutralize the ego by plunging into the mysterious domain of the drives in order to gain access to items, objects, moments, and experiences that lend her life a special luminosity. Milner seeks to raise mundane objects to the dignity of the Thing so as to obtain what Mari has identified as worldly transcendence: the kind of transcendence that can be experienced within the folds of daily life. One of the central components of such transcendence is selectiveness regarding the objects that one chooses to admit into one's life: quality rather than quantity—and even a deliberate curtailing of the number of objects involved—is what determines the contours of Milner's poetics of being. She descends into the mud of her private sea in order to haul in *only* those treasures that best resonate on the frequency of her desire, engage her imagination, and bring her

the greatest possible satisfaction. The objects in question may
be entirely commonplace but they communicate something about
the Thing's inimitable aura; they contain a glow of sublimity that
sets them apart from the multitude of appealing objects that surround them.

Winnicott's version of creative living, in turn, revolves around
two key ideas: the intricate interplay of hiding and being found
and the activity of playing. The potential for creativity dwells,
he argues, in a core of the self that on the one hand must be protected from demands to mold itself according to the reality of
others, but on the other hand must feel that it can reliably be
seen as it truly is when it chooses to reveal itself. Concretely, this
means that I can hatch my ideas in undisturbed solitude and
experiment with expressing them in the confidence that they will
be taken up and responded to in the spirit in which they origi-
nated. The creative experience then involves, not just the self,
but also a surrounding environment that turns into a space for
play where the self can find and create objects and other phenomena that resonate with it in special ways. Hence, creative living operates across a permeable, but not porous, boundary
between internal and external reality. That is, I can ideally count
on a free flow of play between myself and my surroundings—
which may be other people but may also be a creative medium
such as language, music, or paint—without the danger of being
flooded by the other's reality.

Today's neoliberal society places us in constant danger of being
flooded by the other's—or the symbolic Other's—reality because
it overwhelms us with its seductions, temptations, and provoca-
tions. It incites us to constant productivity and cheerfulness. Our
self is regarded as an infinitely perfectible entity, and the external world presses on us from all sides, urging us to improve ourselves lest we miss out on what life has to offer. Whether we

spend an hour in a crowded subway car or an hour online at home, there is a suffocating too-muchness to our everyday lives that renders us overagitated at the same time as it makes us so psychically and affectively numb that it is difficult to feel genuinely passionate about anything. In this sense, we pay a high price for our attempts to keep up with the fast pace and enervating sociality that typifies life under neoliberalism. Against this backdrop, it is unlikely to be a mere coincidence that both Milner and Winnicott express a great deal of respect for our ability to withdraw to the privacy of our inner worlds, arguably in many ways regarding such withdrawal as a precondition of creative living.

We have learned that both Milner and Winnicott appreciate the parallels between the secluded lives of mystics and the quest for solitude that epitomizes the lives of many artists and other creative individuals. In fact, due to Milner's celebration of the act of diving into the jouissance of her private sea, her model of creative living can sometimes come across as solipsistic. Her pursuit of gleaming beads is usually undertaken alone and can even be impeded by the presence of others. In this context, it is important to reiterate that it is the hegemonic aspects of collective life rather than her interactions with trusted others that Milner finds stifling and life-arresting. Nevertheless, there are times when she appears somewhat skittish about the demands of sociality, even in more intimate settings.

In this manner, Milner counters the mantra of relationality that governs our culture: even though our society is individualistic, it assumes that relationships, especially romantic ones, contribute to the individual's well-being in important ways, going so far as to claim that single people are more likely than their married counterparts to suffer from mental health issues, develop serious illnesses, and die young.[2] In this sense, within the neoliberal mindset, even relationality ultimately feeds the individual's welfare and capacity to stay productive and keep performing. In contrast, Milner is unapologetic in suggesting that her quest for creative living cannot be dissociated from her appreciation of solitude—which in turn should not be confused with loneliness.

Along related lines, creativity for Winnicott is deeply embedded in the incommunicado core of the self and can only unfold if the self can trust that its environment will be curious about it without impeding it—in other words, the self wants the joy of being hidden while it avoids the disaster of not being found. The environment, then, must not merely seek to provide what the self needs but also stay out of the self's way so that it can go on being. Now that we are becoming more aware of the damage associated with neoliberal dictates to be always "on," always available, always producing, perhaps we can take some steps to allow for the kind of solitude that fosters creative play within ourselves and with our world.

As we noted above, neoliberal culture tends to recruit even relationality to serve individualistic aims. As a result, theoretical attempts to criticize this culture often veer toward valorizing sociality as a solution to its ills.[3] This means that solitude is frequently categorically—or at least implicitly—coded as problematic whereas sociality is valorized regardless of the tenor that it takes. In other words, it appears difficult for critiques of neoliberal instrumentalism to distinguish between a selfish individualism and a replenishing solitude, which means that solitude is either not talked about at all or it is devalued as a facet of individualism.

One of the main themes that arises from this book is the possibility that solitude—and the individual's ability to safeguard a noncommunicating core—is a necessary component of human flourishing. In addition, once one accepts this as a possibility, it becomes conceivable to envision forms of political and ethical action that are compatible with solitude, if not directly, then at least in the sense that those who have had a chance to rest in solitary contexts that allow them to drop their socially expected masks, personas, and façades may be able to better engage with collective themes and crises that demand their attention. Even Milner, who leans heavily toward solitude as a crucial element of her poetics of being, admits that the subject's withdrawal from the bustle of collective life may in the long run render it better able to meet the needs of others. That is, even though Milner at times pushes past the model of a replenishing solitude, the ultimate goal of which is to enrich collective life, toward the more radical appreciation of solitude as such, there is no need to underestimate the rewards of a replenishing solitude.

On a basic level, we are talking about the prevention of socially generated exhaustion, which can be a deeply political or ethical issue. For example, a large percentage of doctors, nurses, caregivers, and others in our society who were appropriately defined as "essential workers" in the early days of the COVID-19 pandemic suffer from burnout. This is a collective problem that touches the lives of many, whether they are providers or receivers of professional help. Likewise, as professors, both of us have sometimes felt drained, which means that our students have not received the best education that we can offer. Indeed, feeling worn out is rampant among many people whose jobs entail a constant stream of social interactions. Such people may need ways of resting, of detaching themselves from the unremitting demands of sociality. In short, they need solitude. In this sense, solitude is not merely for artists and other creative individuals. It is something that most of us could at times benefit from. This is a reality that both Milner and Winnicott seem to recognize better than most contemporary theorists and cultural critics.

As we have mentioned, our society is showing a growing awareness of this issue, sometimes perhaps even in ways that veer toward self-indulgence. We do not mean to suggest that replenishing our energies entails a trip to an expensive spa or other costly props. However, there is a great deal to be said for the idea that most of us need time alone, or at least time in the company of intimate others who allow space for, and respect, our singularity rather than expect us to uphold the scaffolding of our socially intelligible selves. In other words, we need a respite from the demands of our crowded work and social lives, from the commotion of everyday demands. As we have just stressed, this does not render us politically or ethically irresponsible but, quite the contrary, can enhance our ability to meet the world in more politically and ethically responsible ways.

It may be possible to argue that the subject's ability to withdraw from the demands of excessive sociality in order to foster its art of living has no intrinsic relationship to collective responsibility—that there is no need to try to think of these two themes together. However, this attitude is hard to adopt not merely because the two of us have been trained to think that more or less anything that human beings do is political but also because, as we put the finishing touches on this book, Russia has been attacking Ukraine for almost a year. Refugees from Ukraine have been streaming into Europe and North America. The price of basic necessities has skyrocketed across the world. And the Global North continues its cynical, even deadly antimigration policies and practices. This is not to speak of the stubborn blindness to the urgency of the impending climate crisis. It is therefore impossible to avoid the question of social responsibility. We obviously believe that it is important to talk about the pursuit of worldly transcendence—even of scintillating treasures—and about our fragile noncommunicating core. Nevertheless, it also seems important to figure out how to discuss such seemingly private considerations in the context of a political situation such as the current one.

Milner's determination to avoid superfluous consumption by privileging the items and objects that genuinely matter to her provides one avenue for thinking about political solidarity in relation to Ukraine and other areas of the world that are suffering from the scarcity of the basic necessities of life. During December 2022 and January 2023, when both of us spent time in Europe, what was striking was the degree to which people in many European countries took it for granted that the sanctions against Russia *had* to hold, regardless of the personal sacrifices that they had to make in the quality of their lives. In order to sever the dependence of their countries on Russian electricity, gas, and oil, many people tried to save energy by lowering the level of heat in their houses and apartments, washing clothes and dishes in the middle of the night, and spending their evenings in candlelight instead of turning on the lights.

We do not remember another time during our lifetime when people were willing, without much grumbling, to undertake such fairly extreme measures of austerity in order to support the population of another country. In addition, due to the considerable increase in the price of food and consumer items, many people gave serious consideration to what it was that they actually needed. The cycle of consumption had, for the time being at least, slowed down considerably, as people weighed the importance of their purchases, often reaching "the conclusion that they did not in fact need certain items. It is unfortunate that Europe needed a war for such awareness about excess consumption to arise. At the same time, the phenomenon indicates that the armor of consumer capitalism *can* be pierced, that there are circumstances where people will stop consuming, and that these circumstances may sometimes even be based more on ethical than practical reasoning. One can only hope that at least some of the discernment that many people have developed during this challenging time remains in place once peace is reestablished and Europe returns to its normal mode of functioning.

Another key feature of our lives, the COVID-19 pandemic, laid bare the flaws at the heart of the neoliberal modes of being that have come to be regarded as natural and eternal. People realized the extent to which they had already given up both the glue that holds societies together and the capacity to be alone with themselves without escaping into boredom or sinking into depression. It is interesting to see how the increasingly evident fragility and amorality inherent in our system has engendered acts of what might be called blind protest: people are groping toward alleviating the deep and abiding pain that they feel in the context of neoliberalism's cold abstractness. This might take the form of demands for flexible work schedules that include the possibility of remote work, which we now know is possible and even beneficial in some cases. Alternatively, some people are considering moving away from traditional work altogether in favor of freelancing, working part-time, or—most radical of all—participating in the "great resignation" that has left many companies and institutions across the employment spectrum scrambling for employees. Outside of the work realm, too, people are turning away from the tyranny of productivity and toward experiences that feed the soul, whether it be reading good books or living off-grid. All of these moves represent a profound and widespread resistance to the requirement that we align ourselves with the abstract laws of the market and the moralistic principles that have come to be attached to that supposed abstraction: stopping = no growth = stagnation; not working = laziness; if you win, I lose.

So far, at least, the potency of this resistance to neoliberal self-optimization is diluted by two factors: first, it tends to emerge out of the desperation of immediately and sharply felt pain and therefore remains relatively inchoate. The relatively unreflected nature of the protest is paired with a primarily self-defensive orientation, the second factor that undercuts its potential for long-term effectiveness. Neoliberal principles are not fundamentally thrown into question if protests against them remain purely reactive and defensive. In Winnicottian terms, the turn inward toward the core self—and the awareness of its shrinkage—is welcome indeed, but as long as the impulse is primarily protective and not creative, compliance remains a key feature. Such a negative false self might even believe that the option to work from home can do the trick of shielding the true self from harm, but ultimately the true self receives no sustenance from such practice. The true self can only emerge creatively when structures are in place that allow for its going-on-being, that is, structures that guarantee food, shelter, healthcare, and aging with dignity.

It may well be that the two of us were drawn to Milner and Winnicott because there is something about their theories that speaks to us personally. Gail is attracted to the processual dimensions of Winnicott's thinking as well as his embrace of paradox. She appreciates the way in which Winnicott works out his ideas over time, returning to them repeatedly and refining them as he gains more insight via his own contemplation and his curiosity about his patients. Gail, too, aspires to go deeper and deeper into the key elements of a good, creative life by trying to understand herself and others in their own authentic terms. This is not easy, especially in the neoliberal environment that tells us that everyone is only out for themselves, and I stand to lose if the other person gains. But Winnicott teaches us that creative engagement with ourselves and others can be learned if we are willing to reconnect with the feeling of simultaneously creating and finding things in the world that are very much ours but that also push us beyond what we thought we were.

This is one of the many paradoxes that attracts Gail to Winnicott. Perhaps the reason that she was immediately captivated by the sentence in the preface to *Playing and Reality*—"your contribution is to ask for a paradox to be accepted and tolerated and respected, and for it not to be resolved"—is because it legitimizes her tendency not to be able to decide among what she sees as various, equally valid possibilities in all kinds of situations. This indecisiveness, as it is conventionally described, is a distinct disadvantage when immediate action must be taken. But taking paradox seriously is a crucial skill when trying to break the deadlock of zero-sum thinking. Again, this is difficult. When the dichotomous terms of a situation seem to be set in stone, coming up with a third term that provides a genuine alternative is very challenging. But working toward such an alternative constitutes a large part of Gail's search for creativity, because she feels so trapped otherwise. When the demand to choose between two equally absolute but also equally impossible "options" is pressing down hard, it is a joyful relief to realize that the dilemma is actually a paradox. When two things can be true at once, a whole new world of possibility is opened up.

This kind of thinking plays an important role in Gail's writing. It is both a challenge and a pleasure to create and rework sentences, paragraphs, and larger structures in such a way that their sometimes contradictory ideas can sit together without canceling each other out. How can language express what is inexpressible? How can I enact what can only be created in solitude as communication to others? Working with Mari has been the most generative possible process in this regard. We share a deep need for time and space alone; hence none of the pressure to be with and for the other has been present in our interactions. Mari has functioned like the ideal play partner for Gail, both solidifying her in her true self and helping her expand its boundaries into exciting new realms.

Mari in turn identifies with Milner's discernment regarding the truth of her desire. She appreciates Milner's discrimination about the kinds of items, objects, moments, and experiences that she allows into her life. There is something about Milner's restraint—which is nevertheless combined with her attempt to render her world magnificent through her sublimatory efforts to raise mundane objects to the dignity of the Thing—that resonates with Mari's relationship to the world's offerings. She has long felt that weighing her priorities carefully—thereby avoiding excess and unnecessary consumption—is an essential component of her particular art of living.

Mari furthermore identifies with Milner's creative practice, which entails a complete surrender of her ego so as to carve out space for the irrational drive energies of the real. As Mari has emphasized, her manner of writing is more or less identical to the creative process that Milner describes: for her to be able to generate a text, she needs to plunge into the shadowy realm beyond her ego, even if doing so is frightening in the sense that the line between creativity and madness tends to blur. Over time, the specter of madness has receded at the same time as creativity— or at least the potential for creativity and creative living—has matured. The trick for safeguarding her potential for creativity against the terror of being completely engulfed by jouissance is retaining enough symbolic points of reference during the times when she allows herself to be lost in her private sea.

This may sound paradoxical: on the one hand, Mari needs to sever herself from the symbolic world in order to descend into the sea of jouissance that makes writing possible; on the other, she needs enough of what Lacan called *quilting points*—symbolic reference points that tether her to the social world—to alleviate her anxiety regarding getting washed out into the open ocean without any anchorage. Fortunately, Gail has shown us that paradoxes do not need to be resolved. For Mari, Gail has also been an ideal partner in the dance of ideas that has produced this book. Gail has been reliably present and responsive, when necessary, at the same time as she has known when to allow silence to serve its essential function of forging space for writing. She, in short, has provided the perfect Winnicottian holding environment—which offers a sense of stability at the same time as it allows for an independent exploration of ideas—and thereby made this collaborative project possible; she has, with a great deal of tact, recognized that sometimes the gift of solitude is just as important as the gift of companionship. An ideal friendship, for both of us, is one that retains its vitality despite periods of noncommunication. The synergy that has resulted in *The Creative Self* has given us precisely this type of friendship, which is a blessing of enormous magnitude.

NOTES

PREFACE

1. Mari Ruti, *The Singularity of Being: Lacan and the Immortal Within* (New York: Fordham University Press, 2012), 26.
2. Marion Milner, *Eternity's Sunshine: A Way of Keeping a Diary* (New York: Routledge, 2011), 153.

1. MARION MILNER'S POETICS OF BEING

1. Admittedly, the version of Lacanian theory that circulates among American academics who do not specialize in Lacanian theory—who may have read a few of his essays but not his seminars—can make it sound like Lacan posits a primordial unity between mother and infant during the preoedipal stage. However, this is a misreading of Lacanian theory in that Lacan emphasizes that the subject's sense that such a unity once existed is a retroactive fantasy that does not reflect the realities of jouissance, which are more chaotic than comforting.
2. Jacques Lacan, *The Seminar of Jacques Lacan, Book VII (1959–1960): The Ethics of Psychoanalysis*, trans. Dennis Porter (New York: Norton, 1992), 141. I discuss this example—and a few others—in detail in *The Singularity of Being: Lacan and the Immortal Within* (New York: Fordham University Press, 2012), and *Distillations: Theory, Ethics, Affect* (New York: Bloomsbury, 2018).
3. Lacan, *The Ethics of Psychoanalysis*, 112.

4. I first used this concept in *The Call of Character: Living a Life Worth Living* (New York: Columbia University Press, 2013).

5. Jacques Lacan, *The Seminar of Jacques Lacan, Book VIII (1960–1961): Transference*, trans. Bruce Fink (Cambridge: Polity Press, 2015), 170–71.

6. Todd McGowan argues along similar lines in *Capitalism and Desire* (New York: Columbia University Press, 2016).

7. Again, for a brilliant analysis of this line of reasoning, see McGowan, *Capitalism and Desire*.

8. See, for instance, Rhonda Byrne's immensely popular *The Secret* (New York: Atria Books, 2006).

9. The Frankfurt School, which became active between the two world wars, was initially associated with the Institute for Social Research in Frankfurt. It consisted of thinkers who were critical of both capitalism and communism and who leaned heavily on Hegel, Marx, and Freud to launch their critiques of inegalitarian social structures. After Hitler's rise to power, the Frankfurt School was moved to New York City, where scholars such as Theodor Adorno, Max Horkheimer, and Herbert Marcuse kept researching and writing. By the 1950s, some of the school's members had moved back to Germany while others remained in the United States. In 1953, the school was officially reestablished in Frankfurt. Jürgen Habermas's theories of "communicative action"—the idea that rational communication could resolve social tensions—began to dominate the Frankfurt School during the 1960s. More contemporary Frankfurt School thinkers include Axel Honneth and (to some extent) Amy Allen.

A broader definition of critical theory emerged from a mixture of continental philosophy, psychoanalysis (especially Lacanian theory), and poststructuralism (including deconstruction) in the Paris of the 1960s. During the 1970s and 1980s, while Habermas became a major figure in the Anglo-American social sciences, this broader version of critical theory began to dominate the Anglo-American humanities. By the 1990s, Anglo-American thinkers had developed their distinctive version of critical theory, which drew heavily not only on its French roots but also on feminist theory, queer theory, critical race theory, and postcolonial theory. One could argue that French—and other continental European—theorists have never fully caught up with these later developments, paying much less attention to gender, race, and ethnicity than their Anglo-American counterparts. In its current version, Anglo-American critical theory sometimes favors affect theory—which, among other things, explores the traumatizing impact of structural inequalities on human emotional life—over psychoanalysis because of the assumption that psychoanalysis is incapable of addressing the kinds of social, collective socioeconomic, and political concerns that preoccupy contemporary theorists. Key thinkers in affect theory include Sara Ahmed, Lauren Berlant, Ann Cvetkovich, Sienna Ngai, and Kathleen Stewart. Many of these thinkers are also fluent in psychoanalytic theory.

Although it may be true that there are versions of psychoanalysis that focus exclusively on the individual psyche, there are nevertheless also plenty of psychoanalytic thinkers who have explored the interconnectedness of the social and the psychic. The list of psychoanalytic thinkers who combine social considerations—including the impact of structural traumatization on human emotional life—with the investigation of human psychic and affective life is too long to include in its entirely, but here are some major scholars from various genres of psychoanalysis that jump to mind: Amy Allen, Jessica Benjamin, Richard Boothby, Alfie Bown, Judith Butler, Teresa Brennan, Jill Gentile, Sheldon George, Anne Anlin Cheng, Mladen Dolar, David Eng, Jennifer Friedlander, Alice Jardine, Julia Kristeva, Teresa de Lauretis, Jonathan Lear, Lynne Layton, Noëlle McAfee, Todd McGowan, Hilary Neroni, Adam Phillips, Eric Santner, Kaja Silverman, Gautam Basu Thakur, Jamieson Webster, Slavoj Žižek, and Alenka Zupančič. I participate in this version of critical theory as well.

10. Habermas himself was invested in psychoanalysis in his early work but lost interest in it in his later, most influential work such as *The Theory of Communicative Action: Reason and the Rationalization of Society*, trans. Thomas McCarthy (Boston: Beacon Press, 1985).

11. Amy Allen has published an impressive array of books at the intersection of critical theory—both the Frankfurt School version and the broader version that I refer to at the end of note #9—and psychoanalysis. Here, it suffices to name her two latest books: *The End of Progress:*

Decolonizing the Normative Foundations of Critical Theory (New York: Columbia University Press, 2017) and *Critique on the Couch: Why Critical Theory Needs Psychoanalysis* (New York: Columbia University Press, 2020). Allen and I have also collaborated on a book called *Critical Theory Between Klein and Lacan: A Dialogue* (New York: Bloomsbury, 2019). Allen defines herself more as a Foucauldian than as a Frankfurt School scholar. Yet her knowledge of the latter, including its recent developments, is remarkable. Noëlle McAfee also uses a mixture of critical theory, including Frankfurt School critical theory, and psychoanalysis in *Fear of Breakdown: Politics and Psychoanalysis* (New York: Columbia University Press, 2019). The title of her book refers to an article by Winnicott, "Fear of Breakdown," *International Review of Psychoanalysis* I (1974): 103–7.

12. See, for instance, Axel Honneth and Joel Whitebook, "Fusion or Omnipotence? A Dialogue," in *Transitional Subjects: Critical Theory and Object Relations*, ed. Amy Allen and Brian O'Connor (New York: Columbia University Press, 2019). Whereas Allen and McAfee have engaged with the broad version of critical theory, including feminist theory, that I refer to at the end of note 9, Honneth advances a bafflingly conservative, gendered version of Winnicott. Winnicott can be read in a variety of ways, and Honneth has chosen a retrograde route by returning to the kind of idealization of the mother-child relationship that is largely incompatible with progressive critical theoretical, especially feminist sensibilities. Both Allen and McAfee are critical of Honneth's interpretation of Winnicott. Gail Newman also develops an argument against that interpretation in her chapter of the present book.

13. See, for instance, Theodor Adorno and Max Horkheimer, *Dialectic of Enlightenment: Philosophical Fragments*, trans. Edmund Jephcott (Stanford, CA: Stanford University Press, 2002); and Theodor Adorno, *Minima Moralia: Reflections from a Damaged Life*, trans. Edmund Jephcott (New York: Verso, 2005). *Dialectic of Enlightenment* was first published in 1947 (before this, it was circulated among colleagues in 1944), and *Minima Moralia* was first published in 1951.

14. See, for example, Homi Bhabha, *The Location of Culture* (New York: Routledge, 1994); Paul Gilroy, *The Black Atlantic: Modernity and Double-Consciousness* (Cambridge, MA: Harvard University Press,

1993); and Edward Said, *Culture and Imperialism* (New York: Vintage, 1994). Seyla Benhabib also argues along these lines in *The Claims of Culture: Equality and Diversity in the Global Era* (Princeton. NJ: Princeton University Press, 2002). Unfortunately, the critiques of entrenched nationalism and conservative identity politics staged by these thinkers seem to have been largely lost in contemporary theory and politics alike. An exception to this trend is Madhavi Menon's *Indifference to Difference: On Queer Universalism* (Minneapolis: University of Minnesota Press, 2015).

15. As Amy Allen has shown, the same argument could be applied to Michel Foucault, whom Habermas also accused of destroying reason. See Amy Allen, "Feminism, Foucault, and the Critique of Reason: Rereading the *History of Madness*," *Foucault Studies* 16 (2013): 15–31.

16. For a compelling interpretation of these themes, see Gary Mullen, *Adorno on Politics After Auschwitz* (Lanham, MD: Lexington Books, 2016).

17. See Herbert Marcuse, *Eros and Civilization: A Philosophical Inquiry into Freud* (Boston: Beacon Press, 1974), and *One-Dimensional Man* (Boston: Beacon Press, 1964).

18. Foucault's antipathy toward psychoanalysis was partly due to his unfortunate personal experiences with it: as a gay man in the 1950s, he fell victim to a highly normalizing form of psychoanalytic clinical practice that pathologized his sexuality. His incisive critiques of psychoanalysis are therefore understandable. Yet his theories have a great deal in common with nonnormalizing genres of psychoanalysis, such as Lacanian theory. He himself admits as much in his 1981–1982 *The Hermeneutics of the Subject: Lectures at the Collège de France*, trans. Graham Burchell (New York: Palgrave Macmillan, 2005), 29–30.

19. See Michel Foucault, *The Birth of Biopolitics: Lectures at the Collège de France, 1978–1979*, trans. Graham Burchell (New York: Picador, 2008).

20. Foucault, *The Birth of Biopolitics*.

21. Foucault, *The Birth of Biopolitics*, 69.

22. See, for instance, Julia Kristeva, *New Maladies of the Soul*, trans. Ross Guberman (New York: Columbia University Press, 1997), and *Intimate Revolt: The Powers and Limits of Psychoanalysis*, trans. Jeanine Herman (New York: Columbia University Press, 2003).

23. Kristeva, *Intimate Revolt*.

24. Authors within the field of Afropessimism tend to argue along these lines. See, for example, Jared Sexton, *Amalgamation Schemes: Antiblackness and the Critique of Multiracialism* (Minneapolis: University of Minnesota Press, 2008); and Frank B. Wilderson III, *Afropessimism* (New York: Liveright, 2021). For a directly related argument, see Jackie Wang, *Carceral Capitalism* (Los Angeles: Semiotext(e), 2018).

25. See Lauren Berlant, *Cruel Optimism* (Durham, NC: Duke University Press, 2011).

26. See José Muñoz, *Cruising Utopia: The Then and There of Queer Futurity* (New York: NYU Press, 2009).

27. Friedrich Nietzsche, *The Gay Science*, trans. Walter Kaufmann (New York: Vintage Books, 1974), 240.

28. Nietzsche, *The Gay Science*.

29. Alexander Nehamas, *Life as Literature* (Cambridge, MA: Harvard University Press, 1987), 191.

30. Among the most accessible of Badiou's texts are: Alain Badiou, *Ethics: An Essay on the Understanding of Evil*, trans. Peter Hallward (New York: Verso, 2013), and *In Praise of Love*, trans. Peter Bush (New York: New Press, 2012).

31. I discuss the sadder frequencies of the event in greater detail in the final chapter of *Distillations: Theory, Ethics, Affect*.

32. Nietzsche, *The Gay Science*, 232.

33. Nietzsche, *The Gay Science*.

34. Although Nietzsche was certainly cognizant of an entity akin to the unconscious, his theories predate Freud's work, which brought the unconscious to the forefront of our conception of subjectivity, thereby introducing the notion of a split subject, a subject that contains elements of being that it itself has no knowledge of but that, to a large extent, determine its behavior. After the discovery of the unconscious, it has been impossible for even those who resist psychoanalytic theory to conceive of the subject as a fully self-identical, let alone a fully self-mastering, entity.

35. Jonathan Lear, *Therapeutic Action: An Earnest Plea for Irony* (New York: Other Press, 2004), 81.

36. I have discussed the convergences between Nietzsche and psychoanalysis in greater detail in *A World of Fragile Things: Psychoanalysis and the Art of Living* (Albany: SUNY Press, 2009).

37. The emergence of autotheory as a theoretical genre is often associated with Paul Preciado's *Testo Junkie: Sex, Drugs, and Biopolitics in the Pharmacopornographic Era*, trans. Bruce Benderson (New York: The Feminist Press, 2013); and Maggie Nelson's *The Argonauts* (New York: Graywolf Press, 2015). Preciado coins the term *autotheory* in *Testo Junkie*. An important reference point for many contemporary autotheoretical writers is the later work of Roland Barthes, including *A Lover's Discourse*, trans. Richard Howard (New York: Hill and Wang, 1978), and *Roland Barthes by Roland Barthes* (New York: Farrar, Straus & Giroux, 1977).

38. See, for example, Lauren Fournier, *Autotheory as Feminist Practice in Art, Writing, and Criticism* (Cambridge, MA: MIT Press, 2021); and Sharon Holland, *The Erotic Life of Racism* (Durham, NC: Duke University Press, 2012).

39. I have had a chance to examine Milner's diaries at the Milner Archives in London, and it is true—as she states in *A Life of One's Own*—that she does not keep a diary consistently and that sometimes her entries consist of lists of items, almost like shopping lists.

40. See Martin Heidegger, "The Thing," in *Poetry, Language, Thought*, trans. Albert Hofstadter (New York: Harper Perennial, 2013).

41. Roland Barthes, *Camera Lucida: Reflections on Photography*, trans. Richard Howard (New York: Hill and Wang, 2010).

42. Marion Milner, *Eternity's Sunshine: A Way of Keeping a Diary* (New York: Routledge, 2011), 172.

43. Milner, *Eternity's Sunshine*, 171.

44. Milner, *Eternity's Sunshine*.

45. Milner, *Eternity's Sunshine*, 171–72.

46. Marion Milner, *An Experiment in Leisure* (New York: Routledge, 2011), 151–52.

47. Marion Milner, *A Life of One's Own* (New York: Routledge, 2011), 5.

48. Of Slavoj Žižek's many books, let me merely mention one: *Interrogating with the Real* (New York: Bloomsbury, 2013). Lee Edelman's courting of pure negativity is evident in both *No Future: Queer Theory and the Death Drive* (Durham, NC: Duke University Press, 2004), and *Bad Education: Why Queer Theory Teaches Us Nothing* (Durham, NC: Duke University Press, 2023).

49. On literary creativity, see Lacan's reading of James Joyce in Jacques Lacan, *The Seminar of Jacques Lacan, Book XXIII (1975–1976): The Sinthome*, trans. Luke Thurston (New York: Polity Press, 2016).

50. See for instance, Judith Butler's critique of the ahistoricity of Lacanian theory in Judith Butler, Ernesto Laclau, and Slavoj Žižek, *Contingency, Hegemony, Universality: Contemporary Dialogues on the Left* (London: Verso, 2000). See also Lynne Huffer, *Mad for Foucault: Rethinking the Foundations of Queer Theory* (New York: Columbia University Press, 2010).

51. Milner, *Eternity's Sunshine*, 113.

52. Milner, *Eternity's Sunshine*.

53. Milner, *Eternity's Sunshine*, 186.

54. Milner, *Eternity's Sunshine*, 112.

55. Milner, *An Experiment in Leisure*, 138, 134.

56. Milner, *An Experiment in Leisure*, 134.

57. Milner, *An Experiment in Leisure*, 147.

58. Milner, *An Experiment in Leisure*, 153.

59. Milner, *Eternity's Sunshine*, 82.

60. Milner, *An Experiment in Leisure*, 56.

61. Milner, *An Experiment in Leisure*.

62. Milner, *An Experiment in Leisure*.

63. Milner, *An Experiment in Leisure*, 118–19.

64. Milner, *An Experiment in Leisure*, 31.

65. Milner, *An Experiment in Leisure*, 138.

66. Milner, *An Experiment in Leisure*.

67. Milner, *An Experiment in Leisure*.

68. Milner, *An Experiment in Leisure*, 145.

69. Milner, *An Experiment in Leisure*, 172.

70. Milner, *An Experiment in Leisure*.

71. Milner, *An Experiment in Leisure*.

72. Milner, *An Experiment in Leisure*.

73. D. W. Winnicott, "Creativity and Its Origins," in *Playing and Reality* (New York: Routledge, 2005): 87–115; 87.

74. D. W. Winnicott, "Playing: Creative Activity and the Search for the Self," in *Playing and Reality*, 71–86; 73.

75. Winnicott, "Playing: Creative Activity and the Search for the Self."

76. Winnicott, "Creativity and Its Origins," 91.

77. Winnicott, "Creativity and Its Origins."

78. Winnicott, "Creativity and Its Origins," 93.

79. Winnicott, "Creativity and Its Origins," 87.

80. Winnicott, "Creativity and Its Origins." 87.

81. See Sigmund Freud, "Mourning and Melancholia," in *The Standard Edition of the Complete Psychological Works of Sigmund Freud*, trans. James Strachey (London: Hogarth Press, 1957): 239–60.

82. Winnicott, "Creativity and Its Origins," 92.

83. See D. W. Winnicott, "Mind and Its Relation to the Pscyhe-Soma," in *Through Paediatrics to Psycho-Analysis: Collected Papers* (New York: Routledge, 1975), 243–54; 243.

84. D. W. Winnicott, "Ego Distortion in Terms of True and False Self," in *The Maturation Processes and the Facilitating Environment: Studies in the Theory of Emotional Development* (London: Karnac Books, 1960), 140–52; 148.

85. I owe this articulation to Gail (personal communication).

86. Winnicott, "Ego Distortion in Terms of True and False Self," 148.

87. Winnicott, "Ego Distortion in Terms of True and False Self."

88. Winnicott, "Ego Distortion in Terms of True and False Self," 149.

89. Winnicott, "Ego Distortion in Terms of True and False Self," 150.

90. D. W. Winnicott, "Communicating and Not Communicating Leading to a Study of Certain Opposites," in *The Maturation Processes and the Facilitating Environment*, 179.

91. Winnicott, "Communicating and Not Communicating," 187.

92. Winnicott, "Communicating and Not Communicating."

93. Winnicott, "Communicating and Not Communicating," 184.

94. Winnicott, "Communicating and Not Communicating."

95. Winnicott, "Communicating and Not Communicating," 186.

96. Winnicott, "Communicating and Not Communicating," 185.

97. Winnicott, "Communicating and Not Communicating," 190.

98. Winnicott, "Communicating and Not Communicating," 187.

99. Winnicott, "Communicating and Not Communicating," 190.

100. Winnicott, "Communicating and Not Communicating," 186; emphasis in the original.

101. Winnicott, "Communicating and Not Communicating," 189.

102. D. W. Winnicott, "The Use of an Object and Relating through Iden-
     tifications," in *Playing and Reality*, 116.

103. At the heart of Winnicott's conception of the holding environment
     resides the so-called "good-enough mother": a mother who knows
     when to give the child space even when she is physically present. In
     order to avoid demonizing the mother for the subject's developmental
     failures, it might be productive to envision the holding environment
     as being composed of several individuals, including—depending on the
     situation—the father, members of the extended family, siblings, day
     care staff, and hired help. That is, in the contemporary world, it is less
     common than it was during Winnicott's time for the mother to be the
     sole caretaker. Moreover, Winnicott himself already admitted that
     the caretaker could be someone other than the mother. In this sense,
     the "good-enough mother" is more a caretaking function than a
     person.

104. Winnicott, "The Use of an Object and Relating through Identifica-
     tions," 150, 152.

105. Winnicott, "Creativity and Its Origins," 94–95.

106. Milner, *Eternity's Sunshine*, 113.

107. Milner, *Eternity's Sunshine*.

108. Milner, *Eternity's Sunshine*, 61.

109. Milner, *Eternity's Sunshine*, 62.

110. See Marion Milner, *On Not Being Able to Paint* (New York: Routledge,
     2010).

111. Milner, *Eternity's Sunshine*, 63.

112. Milner, *Eternity's Sunshine*.

113. Milner, *Eternity's Sunshine*, 101.

114. Milner, *Eternity's Sunshine*, 181–82.

115. Milner, *Eternity's Sunshine*, 53.

116. Milner, *Eternity's Sunshine*, 61.

117. See Julia Kristeva, *Revolution in Poetic Language*, trans. Margaret
     Waller (New York: Columbia University Press, 1984).

118. Kathryn Kuitenbrouwer and I talk about this difference in our coau-
     thored book, *The Unquiet Ocean: Freeing Your Inner Writer* (forthcom-
     ing), which gives a detailed personal account of our writing practices.
     For Kathryn, the drafting process is erotic rather than agonizing. For
     me, unfortunately, it is mostly agonizing.

119. For a more detailed version of this argument, see *The Unquiet Ocean* (forthcoming).
120. Milner, *Eternity's Sunshine*, 110.
121. Milner, *Eternity's Sunshine*.
122. Milner, *Eternity's Sunshine*, 65.
123. Milner, *Eternity's Sunshine*.
124. Julia Kristeva, *Black Sun: Depression and Melancholia*, trans. Leon S. Roudiez (New York: Columbia University Press, 1989), 99.
125. Kristeva, *Black Sun*.
126. Milner, *Eternity's Sunshine*, 56.
127. Milner, *Eternity's Sunshine*.
128. Milner, *Eternity's Sunshine*, 56–57.
129. Milner, *Eternity's Sunshine*, 196.
130. Milner, *Eternity's Sunshine*.
131. Milner, *Eternity's Sunshine*.
132. Milner, *Eternity's Sunshine*.
133. Milner, *Eternity's Sunshine*.
134. Winnicott, "Fear of Breakdown," 104.
135. Winnicott, "Fear of Breakdown," 105.
136. Winnicott, "Fear of Breakdown."
137. Winnicott, "Fear of Breakdown," 107; emphasis in the original.
138. Winnicott, "Playing: Creative Activity and the Search for the Self," 86.
139. Winnicott, "Playing: Creative Activity and the Search for the Self," 75.
140. This has long been one of my main disagreements with Judith Butler, whose work I otherwise appreciate. Butler's relentless valorization of relationality at times feels depleting. It sounds noble, but some of us are incapable of rising to the required level of sociality. This does not mean that we are unethical. It merely means that we are introverted. One reason I am drawn to Lacanian theory is that Lacan does not have a whole lot of regard for the virtues of sociality, viewing it primarily as a source of anxiety or collective conformity. I am obviously not talking about our relationships with close friends, but about the expectation that the healthy thing to do is invariably to maintain an extensive "social life." I also believe that relationality is just as often a site of violence as it is a site of ethical responsibility.
141. See Barthes, *Roland Barthes by Roland Barthes*.

142. See Friedrich Nietzsche, *Untimely Meditations*, trans. R. J. Hollingdale (Cambridge: Cambridge University Press, 1984).

143. Milner, *Eternity's Sunshine*, 61.

2. "ASKING FOR PARADOX TO BE RESPECTED"

1. D. W. Winnicott, "Preface," in *Playing and Reality* (New York: Routledge, 2005), xvi.

2. My discussion of neoliberalism owes a great deal to a clear, concise outline of its history by George Monbiot in *The Guardian* that appeared—presciently—six months before the election of Donald Trump in 2016. https://www.theguardian.com/books/2016/apr/15/neoliberalism-ideology-problem-george-monbiot.

3. The term was coined by Michel Foucault, as Mari outlines in chapter 1 of this book.

4. This famous quotation from a letter that Freud wrote to his friend, analysand, and ultimate rescuer from the Nazis, Marie Bonaparte, forms the title of a key text on psychoanalysis and gender, Shoshana Felman's *What Does a Woman Want: Reading and Sexual Difference* (Baltimore, MD: Johns Hopkins University Press, 1993).

5. D. W. Winnicott, "The Theory of the Parent-Infant Relationship," *International Journal of Psycho-Analysis* 41 (1960): 585–95; 586.

6. Winnicott, "The Theory of the Parent-Infant Relationship," 586.

7. Winnicott, "The Theory of the Parent-Infant Relationship," 586.

8. This term appears in multiple places throughout Winnicott's works, notably in the title of the compilation of his papers originally published in 1965, *The Maturational Processes and the Facilitating Environment* (New York: Routledge, 2018).

9. For a compelling history and interpretation of this controversy, see Karin Ahbel-Rappe, " 'I No Longer Believe': Did Freud Abandon the Seduction Theory?," *Journal of the American Psychoanalytic Association* 54, no. 1 (2006): 171–99.

10. D. W. Winnicott, *The Spontaneous Gesture. Selected Letters by D. W. Winnicott*, ed. Robert Rodman (Cambridge, MA: Harvard University Press, 1987), 158, quoted in Joona Taipale, "The Illusion of Contact:

Insights from Winnicott's 1952 Letter to Klein," *International Journal of Psychoanalysis* 102, no. 1 (2021): 31–50, 36–37.

11. Winnicott, "The Theory of the Parent-Infant Relationship," 590.

12. D. W. Winnicott, "Primitive Emotional Development," in *Through Paediatrics to Psycho-Analysis: Collected Papers* (New York: Routledge, 2014), 145–56; 149.

13. D. W. Winnicott, "Communicating and Not Communicating Leading to a Study of Certain Opposites," in *The Maturational Processes and the Facilitating Environment*, 179–92; 192.

14. D. W. Winnicott, "Psychoses and Child Care," in *Through Paediatrics to Psycho-Analysis*, 219–28; 222.

15. Axel Honneth, *The Struggle for Recognition: The Moral Grammar of Social Conflicts*, trans. Joel Anderson (Cambridge, MA: MIT Press, 1995), 98.

16. Honneth, *The Struggle for Recognition*, 98–99.

17. Both Noëlle McAfee in her *Fear of Breakdown* and Joel Whitebook address problems in Honneth's engagement with Winnicott. In a recent article, Whitebook goes so far as to critique Honneth's "misuse" of Winnicott, "requiring [Winnicottian] psychoanalysis to subordinate itself to—*to be seamlessly translatable into*—the demands of Critical Theory, which, in his case, means his theory of recognition." Joel Whitebook, "Misuse of Winnicott: On Axel Honneth's Appropriation of Psychoanalysis," *Constellations* 28 (2021): 306–21; 307; emphasis in the original.

18. Whitebook, "Misuse of Winnicott," 105.

19. See Mari's discussion of Lacanian lack in her chapter in the present book.

20. D. W. Winnicott, "Pediatrics and Psychiatry," in *Through Paediatrics to Psycho-Analysis*, 157–73; 163.

21. D. W. Winnicott, "Anxiety Associated with Insecurity," in *Through Paediatrics to Psycho-Analysis*, 97–100; 99.

22. Honneth, *The Struggle for Recognition*, 99.

23. Whitebook, "Misuse of Winnicott," 312.

24. Clare Winnicott, "Introduction," in *Deprivation and Delinquency* (New York: Routledge, 2015), 1. For a description of the program, see "The Evacuation of Children During the Second World War," The

History Press, August 30, 2016, https://www.thehistorypress.co.uk
/articles/the-evacuation-of-children-during-the-second-world-war
/#:~:text=The%20Government%20Evacuation%20Scheme%20
had,prolonged%2C%20destructive%2C%20aerial%20bombardment.

25. D. W. Winnicott, "Hate in the Counter-Transference," in *Through Pae-diatrics to Psycho-Analysis*, 194–203.

26. This is the title of a radio talk given by Winnicott in 1949. See D. W. Winnicott, *Collected Works*, Vol. 3 (Oxford: Oxford University Press, 2016).

27. D. W. Winnicott, "Primary Maternal Preoccupation," in *Through Pae-diatrics to Psycho-Analysis*, 300–305; 301.

28. Winnicott, "Primary Maternal Preoccupation," 302.

29. Bracha Ettinger, "From Protoethical Compassion to Responsibility," *Athena* 2 (2006): 100–35; 104, quoted in Wendy Holloway, "Rereading Winnicott's 'Primary Maternal Preoccupation,'" *Feminism & Psychol-ogy* 22, no. 1 (2011): 20–40; 21.

30. Winnicott, "Primary Maternal Preoccupation," 304.

31. Winnicott, "Primary Maternal Preoccupation," 301.

32. Honneth, *The Struggle for Recognition*, 99.

33. Honneth, *The Struggle for Recognition*, 98–99.

34. Holloway, "Rereading Winnicott's 'Primary Maternal Preoccupation,'" 20–21; Honneth, *The Struggle for Recognition*, 98–99.

35. Winnicott, "Theory of the Parent-Infant Relationship," 592.

36. The value of spontaneity is emphasized throughout Winnicott's work, for example in his "Aggression in Relation to Emotional Develop-ment," in *Through Paediatrics to Psycho-Analysis*, 204–18.

37. Winnicott, "Aggression in Relation to Emotional Development," 211.

38. Winnicott, "Aggression in Relation to Emotional Development," 212.

39. Novalis, "Letter to Friedrich Schlegel," in Novalis (Friedrich von Hardenberg), *Schriften*, Vol. IV, 333, ed. Richard Samuel (Stuttgart: Kohlhammer, 1981-83); translation mine.

40. Novalis, *Schriften*, Vol. III, 429, Fragment 820. Henceforth cited in the following format: III, 429–30, 820. All translations are my own.

41. Novalis, *Schriften*, II, 535, 46.

42. Novalis, *Schriften*, II, 535, 41.

43. Novalis, *Schriften*, II, 523, 9.

44. Novalis, *Schriften*, II, 266, 555.

45. F. Robert Rodman, *Winnicott: His Life and Work* (Boston: Da Capo, 2004), 375.

46. See D. W. Winnicott, "Transitional Objects and Transitional Phenomena," in *Playing and Reality*, 1–34.

47. Winnicott, "Transitional Objects and Transitional Phenomena," 5.

48. In this respect, in the same way that in Lacanian theory an object comes to contain a sliver of the *objet a*, the transitional object is imbued with unique significance. See Mari's discussion of the *objet a* in her chapter in this book.

49. Winnicott, "Transitional Objects and Transitional Phenomena," 7.

50. Winnicott, "Transitional Objects and Transitional Phenomena," 3; emphasis in the original.

51. Winnicott, "Transitional Objects and Transitional Phenomena," 7.

52. Both Winnicott and, as Mari notes, José Muñoz focus on the idea of the "good-enough" as a crucial antidote to existing realities. But whereas, for Muñoz, it represents a step up from an otherwise inadequate provision by the world for the self, for Winnicott, the idea of the good-enough mother countered unrealistic and unnecessary expectations of maternal perfection.

53. Winnicott, "Transitional Objects and Transitional Phenomena," 6.

54. D. W. Winnicott, "Preface," in *Playing and Reality*, xvi.

55. Winnicott, "Preface," 2; emphasis mine.

56. Winnicott, "Preface," 18.

57. Winnicott, "The Theory of the Parent-Infant Relationship," 591.

58. See, for instance, D. W. Winnicott, "Playing: A Theoretical Statement," in *Playing and Reality*, 51–70.

59. It is interesting to note that Winnicott shares Milner's fascination with a state of nonboundedness. For Milner, as Mari details in her chapter in the present book, freeing "the imagination from the shackles of the ego" requires that the self be able to tolerate emptiness. For Winnicott, a similarly fecund emptiness is the precondition for the very coming into being of the ego.

60. D. W. Winnicott, "Fear of Breakdown," in *The British School of Psychoanalysis: The Independent Tradition*," ed. Gregorio Kohon (New Haven, CT: Yale University Press, 1986), 173–82; 181.

61. D. W. Winnicott, "Playing: Creative Activity and the Search for the Self," in *Playing and Reality*, 71–86; 81.

62. Winnicott, "Playing: Creative Activity and the Search for the Self," 82, 84.

63. Winnicott, "Playing: Creative Activity and the Search for the Self," 84; emphasis in the original.

64. Winnicott, "Transitional Objects and Transitional Phenomena," 18.

65. Novalis, *Schriften*, III, 372, 601.

66. Novalis, *Schriften*, II, 470, 125.

67. Winnicott, "Transitional Objects and Transitional Phenomena," 8.

68. Hua Hsu, "Ocean Vuong is Still Learning," interview, *New Yorker*, April 10, 2022, https://www.newyorker.com/culture/the-new-yorker -interview/ocean-vuong-is-still-learning.

69. Theodor Adorno, *Prisms*, trans. Shierry Weber Nicholsen and Samuel Weber (Cambridge, MA: MIT Press, 1983), 34.

70. In the interest of avoiding distraction, and in the spirit of Winnicott's usage, I will from now on write true self and false self without quotation marks.

71. Winnicott, "Communicating and Not Communicating," 184.

72. D. W. Winnicott, "Ego Distortion in Terms of True and False Self," in *The Maturational Processes and the Facilitating Environment*, 140–52; 148; emphasis mine.

73. Novalis, *Schriften*, II, 523, 9.

74. Winnicott, "Communicating and Not Communicating," 182.

75. Winnicott, "Communicating and Not Communicating."

76. Winnicott, "Communicating and Not Communicating," 185.

77. It occurs to me that the bit of true self that we allow others to glimpse fleetingly in the process of holding the balance between hiding and being found is akin to the bits of the Lacanian Thing that Mari discusses in her chapter in the present book. In both cases, contact with the whole thing would be both impossible and disastrous. In the Lacanian model, the hotly desired *jouissance* associated with the supposedly lost Thing would, in its unadulterated form, overwhelm the self; hence the value of the phenomena and experiences that provide a sliver of the Thing by arresting the flow from unsatisfying *objet a* to *objet a*. Winnicott characteristically presents the perfect mixture of

communicating and not communicating as a dilemma, a process of seeking without the goal of ever finding (or allowing to be found) completely.

78. Winnicott, "Communicating and Not Communicating," 184.
79. Winnicott, "Communicating and Not Communicating," 187.
80. Winnicott, "Communicating and Not Communicating."
81. John Donne, "No Man Is an Island," http://www.poemswithoutfrontiers.com/No_Man_Is_an_Island.html.

> No man is an island,
> Entire of itself.
> Each is a piece of the continent,
> A part of the main.
> If a clod be washed away by the sea,
> Europe is the less.
> As well as if a promontory were.
> As well as if a manner of thine own
> Or of thine friend's were.
> Each man's death diminishes me,
> For I am involved in mankind.
> Therefore, send not to know
> For whom the bell tolls,
> It tolls for thee.

82. D. W. Winnicott, "The Use of an Object," in *Playing and Reality*, 86–94; 90.
83. Winnicott, "Communicating and Not Communicating," 182.
84. Winnicott, "Communicating and Not Communicating," 91.
85. Winnicott, "The Theory of the Parent-Infant Relationship," 592.
86. Winnicott, "Communicating and Not Communicating," 182.
87. Winnicott, "Transitional Objects and Transitional Phenomena," 7.
88. Winnicott, "Communicating and Not Communicating," 190.
89. "Whites Believe They are Victims of Racism More Often Than Blacks," https://www.socialworktoday.com/news/dn_060311.shtml.
90. Heinrich von Kleist, *Sämtliche Werke und Briefe* [Collected Works and Letters], ed. H. Sembdner (Munich: Deutscher Taschenbuch Verlag,

2001), 593; translation mine. My article is, "Pregnancy, Thirdness, and the Aesthetics of Catastrophe in Heinrich von Kleist," *Psychoanalytic Quarterly* 81, no. 1 (2012): 127–56.

91. Heinrich von Kleist, *An Abyss Deep Enough: Letters of Heinrich von Kleist, with a Selection of Essays and Anecdotes*, ed. and trans. P. B. Miller (New York: Dutton, 1982), 222.

CONCLUSION

1. See Alain Badiou, *Being and Event*, trans. Oliver Feltham (New York: Bloomsbury, 2013), and—for those looking for a more accessible text—Badiou, *Ethics: An Essay on the Understanding of Evil*, trans. Peter Hallward (New York: Verso, 2013).

2. See Bella DePaulo, *Singled Out: How Singles Are Stereotyped, Stigmatized, and Ignored, and Still Live Happily Ever After* (New York: St. Martin's Griffin, 2007).

3. Judith Butler's influential work is an excellent example of the valorization of primordial sociality and the ethical virtues of relationality. Among her many books, one could single out *Giving an Account of Oneself* (New York: Fordham University Press, 2005), and *Dispossession: The Performative in the Political* (New York: Polity Press, 2013). The same tendency can also be seen in the work of Marxist critics such as Hardt and Negri. See Michael Hardt and Antonio Negri, *Multitude: War and Democracy in the Age of Empire* (New York: Penguin, 2005), and *Commonwealth* (Cambridge, MA: Harvard University Press, 2009). Relational forms of psychoanalytic theory obviously also transport us in a relational direction. Even some thinkers who draw their inspiration primarily from Winnicott, such as Axel Honneth, recruit Winnicott into justifying their relational models of subjectivity and politics alike. See, for instance, Axel Honneth and Joel Whitebook, "Fusion or Omnipotence? A Dialogue," in *Transitional Subjects: Critical Theory and Object Relations*, ed. Amy Allen and Brian O'Connor (New York: Columbia University Press, 2019). Notable exceptions to these trends are some versions of queer theory, which pursue the opposite attitude of advocating the act of opting out of

sociality and political action altogether. For a detailed account of queer theory's antisocial tendencies, see Mari Ruti, *The Ethics of Opting Out: Queer Theory's Defiant Subjects* (New York: Columbia University Press, 2016).

INDEX

Thing's power to guide desire (artwork, scientific theories, material culture, etc.), 18–19; and psychoanalysis, 3, 118; replaced by productivity in neoliberal narrative of the good life, 25–26; Ruti and, 105–7, 252; as secondary to survival but indispensable to thriving, 5; and self-fashioning, 19 (*see also* self-fashioning, self-reinvention); and surrendering the ego, 77–79, 104–12, 117 (*see also under* Milner, Marion); teaching as, 236–37; and true and false selves, 229 (*see also* true and false selves); and the true self as hidden, 98, 210, 214–15; Winnicott and, 81, 193–94, 229; and writing, 203–5. *See also* arts and humanities; creative living; creative self
criminality, 225, 227
critical theory, 30–31, 122, 256–57n9, 257–58n11, 258n12, 267n17
cruel optimism (Berlant's term), 48–49, 56, 63
cultural world (arts, religion, etc.), 59, 169, 199, 203, 215

Davis, Angela, 57
death, 134, 182, 196
democracy, 46
depression, 27–29, 47–48, 77–78, 83, 149, 197
desire: arrested by specific special objects, 17–18, 63, 68; and being selective in sublimatory practices, 127–28; and consumer capitalism, 17, 43, 130; and creativity, 14; and direction of life, 43; and jouissance, 71–72; Lacan and the truth of the subject's desire, 71–72, 126; and Lacanian lack-in-being, 12–21; and lures of neoliberal consumer culture, 22–24, 126; Milner and, 68; and *objets a*, 17; Other's desire vs. our own authentic desire, 17, 63, 69–71; Ruti and, 63–64; and sense of entitlement, 128–29. *See also* Thing, the
disillusionment, and child development, 178, 179, 180, 189, 206
disintegration of the self, 85, 87, 109, 116, 194, 197–98
Donne, John, 216

economics: and binary thinking, 150–53; distractions of neoliberal consumer culture, 21–23; *homo economicus*, 34–35, 145; innovation valued mainly as a means to wealth, 25; and Reagan and Thatcher era of the 1980s, 30; rise of neoliberal ideologies, 29–30, 144–45; and rise of the individual, 142–47; self-perpetuating dynamic of consumer culture, 23–24, 130; and structural forms of suffering, 22. *See also* consumer capitalism; neoliberalism; poverty; wealth

distinction between singularity
and ego-centered individuality,
119–123; and intolerance of
empty time or empty mental
space, 195; and Kantian
rationalism, 171 (*see also* Kant,
Immanuel); and linearity,
229–231; lures of neoliberal
consumer culture, 21–24, 126;
meaning of term in
contemporary progressive
theory, 1; neoliberal approaches
to mental health, 149–150; rise
of neoliberal ideologies, 29–30,
144–45; and rise of the
individual, 144–47, 163; and
zero-sum mentality, 4, 151, 189,
230, 241, 251. *See also* consumer
capitalism
neoliberal self-optimization, 11, 241;
contradiction of hyper-
individualism combined with
hyperstandardization, 148;
creative living as antidote to, 1,
12, 119 (*see also* creative living);
defined/described, 2; as
dominant ideology in the West,
24, 147–48; and education,
147–48; and fast pace of life,
40–44; and fear of stagnation/
passivity, 161–62; as impediment
to creativity and authenticity,
148–49; and individuals viewed
as responsible for their destinies
regardless of circumstances, 26,
46 (*see also* responsibility); and

interruption of being, 192; and
"intimate revolt," 44; and
Kristeva's critique of society of
spectacle, 43–44; lures of, 21–31,
243; and Milner's poetics of
being, 8, 12, 58, 123, 132 (*see also*
Milner, Marion); negative
impacts of, 40–49, 146–150,
243–45; and Nietzsche's model
of self-fashioning, 51; and
positive thinking, 26–27; and
primacy of wealth as route to
self-fulfillment, 24–26; and
prioritizing individualistic
self-help, 26; and Reagan and
Thatcher era of the 1980s, 30;
and relationality, 245; resisting
self-optimization ethos by living
a creative, playful life, 192,
241–45; resisting self-
optimization ethos in response
to crises, 249–250; resisting
self-optimization ethos through
small acts and by choosing what
is important, 123–131; and sense
of entitlement, 128–29; and
surrendering the ego, 124; and
transforming impediments into
advantages, 51, 52, 55; and
Winnicott's false self, 80; and
Winnicott's ideal of creative
living, 241 (*see also* Winnicott,
D. W.); yearning for alternatives
to, 12. *See also* consumer
capitalism; instrumentalism;
performance principle

self (*continued*)
 unintegration of the self (*see* unintegration of the self); violation of the self's core, 215–16. *See also* creative self; ego; individuals and individualism; subject
self, development of, 9; and adolescence, 224–28; and aggression/aggressive refusal, 218–228; and communication, 211–18; and compliance with other's agendas, 206–7; and creativity, 170–74; dangers of "finding" someone before they are ready to be found, 93, 99–100, 217; and disillusionment, 178, 179, 181, 189, 206; and emptiness, 269n59; and the external world, 159–160; and facilitating environment/holding environment, 100–101, 115, 116, 157–58, 164, 169, 194, 207, 211, 264n103; and feeding, 206–7; Fichte and, 172–73; Freud and, 154–57; and "going-on-being," 161–62, 165, 171, 206; and the "good enough" mother, 164, 178, 180, 205–6, 264n103, 269n52; Honneth and, 162–64, 168; and infant–caregiver relationship, 13–14, 100–101, 156–174, 189, 206–7, 219–222; and infant's maturation toward the ability to wait for its needs to be met, 207; and

intermediate area between internal and external reality, 169, 174–183; Klein and, 156–57, 173; Kristeva and, 110–11; Lacan and, 110–11, 255n1; and language acquisition, 110–11; and melancholia, 111; Novalis and, 172–74, 176; and Oedipus complex, 154–56; paradoxes of, 161, 166–67, 171, 173–74, 211–12; path from unintegration to ego-integration, 86–87; preoedipal situation (Klein's ideas), 156–57; problems during development, 101, 170, 171, 194; proto-self, 153, 157–162, 169, 175, 211–12; and rivalry over a contested object or narrative, 154–56; and role of an other person in the self's coming into being, 154, 157–164, 166–68, 189, 208, 219–222; and "selfobjects," 223–24, 226; and social media, 227; and spontaneous gestures of the infant, 170–71; and "symbiosis," 162–63, 168; three stages of, 169, 175–76; and too-immediately satisfying objects, 170, 171; and transitional objects, 175–183 (*see also* transitional objects); and "unit status," 161; Winnicott and, 153–54, 157–183, 211–12
self-fashioning, self-reinvention, 4; and agency, 136; and creativity, 19, 74–75; and creativity replaced

by productivity in neoliberal
narrative of the good life, 25–26;
as distinct from self-
improvement, 134; and handling
the unexpected, 135–36; Milner
and, 76, 132–37; Nietzsche and,
50–52; and psychoanalysis,
53–54, 133–37; self as always a
work in progress, 133; and
surrendering the ego (Milner's
ideas), 75–77. *See also* creative self
"selfobjects," 223–24, 226
self-optimization. *See* neoliberal
self-optimization
self-reliance, 146–47, 190
Seurat, Georges, 62–63
sexism, 9, 20, 27, 45, 54
singularity, 135; distinction between
singularity and ego-centered
individuality, 119–123
slavery, 45
social compliance, 69, 70, 82, 84, 91,
92, 97, 192, 199, 206–8, 210,
213–14, 232, 236, 250
social inequalities, 20, 22;
complicated role of capitalism
in history of social hierarchies,
45–46; and lack-in-being
distinguished from structural
forms of lack, 20; and limited
agency, 52; and neoliberal
worldview, 230–31; and
overconsumption, 131; structural
inequalities and positive
thinking, 27; structural trauma
and psychoanalysis, 257n9.

See also homophobia; racism;
sexism
sociality: Butler and, 265n140,
272n3; and introversion,
265n140; and need for solitude,
122, 244–47; social world as
enemy of creative expression,
202; valorization of, 244–46,
265n140. *See also* extroversion
social media, 227
social responsibility, 33, 247–48
social support systems, collapse of, 30
society, modern: and ambivalent
relation to knowledge, 233–35;
and binary thinking, 150–53,
183–86; and collective
responsibility, 247–48; and
COVID-19 pandemic, 6–7,
190–91, 228, 234–35, 246, 249;
creativity as the antithesis of
social compliance, 82; cultural
world, 59, 169, 199, 203, 215;
discontents of neoliberal
self-optimization, 40–49, 243–45;
and fear of stagnation/passivity,
161–62; feeling of futility
generated by social compliance,
82; and government as ideally a
benign facilitating presence,
189–190; and intimate revolt,
71–72; and intolerance of empty
time or empty mental space, 195;
and lack of third space, 190–91;
and longing for emptiness,
195–96; and patriarchy and
rivalry over contested objects or

the self's core, 215–16; and
yearning for a creative life,
84–85, 89
Trump, Donald, 32–33, 46
two-dimensionality of everyday
life, 187–88

Ukraine, Russian invasion of, 155,
191, 228, 247, 248
unconscious, 52, 233–34, 260n34
unintegration of the self, 114;
capacity to move between states
of unintegration and
integration, 118; and creativity,
117, 194–97; and infancy, 161,
194; Milner's fears of madness/
unintegration, 109, 113; and
psychoanalysis, 116–18; Ruti's
fears of madness/unintegration,
108–9; as sometimes healthy,
117–18; Winnicott and fears of
breakdown, 113–19, 194–95.
See also ego
"unit status" (Winnicott's term), 161

victimhood, 231
violence, and high price of human
inventiveness, 19–20
Vuong, Ocean, 203

warfare, 155, 159–160, 247
Watterson, Bill, 178–183
wealth, 24–26, 38–40, 47, 192
West, the: and creativity, 32;
economic motivations as central
to Western world, 1; and

instrumentalist reason, 31–32;
and paradoxes of capitalism,
46–47; and patriarchy and
rivalry over contested objects or
narratives, 154–56; rise of
neoliberal ideologies, 29–30,
144–45; rise of the individual
beginning with the
Enlightenment, 141–154;
self-optimization as dominant
ideology, 24 (*see also* neoliberal
self-optimization)
Whitebook, Joel, 164, 267n17
"wide perception" (Milner's
concept), 60–62, 73, 76, 91, 103
Winnicott, D. W., 8–9; and
adolescence, 224–28; and
aggression, 218–228; and
annihilation as alternative to
being, 191; and anorexia, 224;
career, 153, 165; and children's
transitional objects, 86–87, 94,
175–183, 201, 206 (*see also*
transitional objects); and
communication, 93–102, 211–18
(*see also* communication); and
the creative self, 169–171, 243
(*see also specific topics under this
heading*); and creativity, 4, 81,
82, 193–94, 229; and
development of the self, 157–183,
211–12 (*see also* self, development
of; *specific topics under this
heading*); and embrace of
paradoxes, 141, 169, 231, 250–52;
and emptiness, 194–96, 269n59;

writing: and intermediate area between internal and external reality, 203–5; and interpreting literature, 185–86; Milner and, 77–79, 112; and need for solitude, 96; Newman and, 185–86, 237–38; Ruti and, 96–97, 105–8, 252–53, 264n118; Winnicott and, 205–6; writer's block, 106–7

young people: and compliance with others' agendas, 207–8; and discontents of neoliberal self-optimization, 147–150; and mental health problems, 7, 47–48, 147–150; and refusal of beneficial objects, advice, etc., 221–23; shifts in life goals, 7; uncertainty faced by, in modern world, 47–48; Winnicott's insights on adolescence, 224–28. *See also* children; education

zero-sum mentality, 4, 151, 189, 230, 241, 249, 251

Žižek, Slavoj, 71

Printed and bound by CPI Group (UK) Ltd, Croydon, CR0 4YY

10/07/2025

14701729-0003